STEPHEN SPENDER

Also by Hugh David

The Fitzrovians
Heroes, Mavericks and Bounders

STEPHEN SPENDER

A Portrait with Background

Hugh David

HEINEMANN : LONDON

First published in Great Britain 1992
by William Heinemann Ltd
an imprint of Reed Consumer Books Ltd
Michelin House, 81 Fulham Road, London SW3 6RB
and Auckland, Melbourne, Singapore and Toronto

Copyright © 1992 by Hugh David

The author has asserted his moral rights

A CIP catalogue record for this book
is available at the British Library

ISBN 0 434 17506 4

Typeset by Deltatype Ltd, Ellesmere Port
Printed in Great Britain
by Mackays of Chatham Plc

CONTENTS

━━━

THE DYNASTY

Simplified family tree illustrating the relationship of the Spender, Schuster and Weber families.

Names printed in CAPITALS indicate individuals specifically referred to in this book.

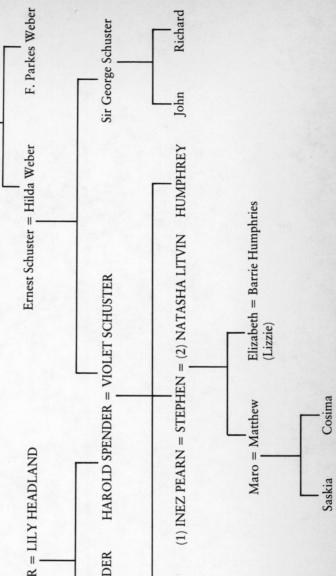

PREFACE

At an early stage, Sir Stephen and Lady Spender decided that they would prefer to have nothing to do with this book. It cannot therefore be called an authorised biography; that, if it comes at all, will come later. Rather, this is, I hope, a portrait of one man and the extraordinary events which shaped the course of his life.

Far from giving an author greater freedom, writing an unauthorised biography, particularly of a living subject, imposes its own disciplines. Denied access to the *fons et origo*, the freelance biographer is on his own. He must seek his quarry where he may, through all manner of published and unpublished records, while all the time striving to maintain a proper, professional relationship with that subject.

On the other hand he is spared the awkward obligations of the authorised, 'in house' biographer: skate over this, keep mum about that. Within the parameters of British (and US) libel laws, he can say what he likes and paint the picture he sees. Inevitably, the view will be different from that of his subject who is — to pursue the metaphor — on the other side of the frame. Thus, although there might be fewer real felicities in what follows than in an aided biography — 'I've just found this; might be useful' — at the same time I hope there are none of the fudges and compromises.

I have been fortunate in two respects. Sir Stephen is a writer whose published work has always contained personal and autobiographical references. In addition, a great number of his private papers and letters are now lodged with libraries and universities in Britain and America. Leafing through these — the fragile holographs, the sheaths of photocopies and the intimidating spools of microfiche — gives a different, sometimes tantalisingly variant, account of the life he has semi-publicly documented. Mutual friends and acquaintances have also fleshed out the documentary record with their own personal recollections and assessments.

In the cases where Life and Art diverge I have generally chosen to follow the Life path. All significant deviations from the received story are, however, explained in the Notes at the end of this book.

I hope the account which follows of the private and public sides of the formative years of a writer will go some way towards establishing his place in the Auden-dominated world of mid-century British poetry and letters. I have tried to give A Portrait with Background (a phrase first used by Tom Driberg to describe his biography of Guy Burgess) of the first forty years of Sir Stephen's life. It was these years (roughly 1910–1950) which set the tone for the forty-and-more which were to follow. The First World War shattered his childhood. The Spanish Civil War and then the Second World War were seminal influences in his emergence, first as a young poet in the 'Auden group' and then as an internationally respected writer and academic. More than anything else, his reaction to the conflict in the Europe of 1929–1945 set the tone for the rest of his life.

I make no apology for not having mentioned every poem Sir Stephen has published — and while researching this book I have discovered more than a dozen unpublished ones — or even some of the books he has written. Nor am I repentant about resorting to 'second-hand' material. Quite as much as Sir Stephen's, the writings of friends and contemporaries such as Virginia Woolf, John Lehmann and Cuthbert Worsley were often of immense assistance in the search for that mystical grail — How It Seemed At The Time.

━━━━━━

I am grateful to many people for their continued encouragement, their patience in answering my sometimes impertinent questions and their kindness, which not infrequently went far beyond what I could reasonably expect. Given the parameters of the book, many talked on the understanding that their views would be unattributed, or for 'background use only'. I have respected their wishes.

I would, however, particularly like to thank Michael Church; Lady Coldstream (Monica Hoyer); the late C. H. Corbett-Palmer (Hugh Corbett); Ed Hall R. P. Heazell (The Hall School, Hampstead); Michael Hull (UCS Old Boys (Old Gowers) Club); Philippa Ingram; Michael Mara; Charles Osborne the Oxford and Cambridge University Club; Lt. Col. Derek Scott Lowe; David Self; Michael Shelden; G. D. Slaughter (University College School, Hampstead), and Nan A. Talese (Doubleday, New York). Thanks, too, on a more personal level, to the staff at St Thomas's Hospital, London, without whom, etc, etc.

Peter Ellis sacrificed most of a holiday and spent much of his first visit to America in the reference rooms of the New York Public Library on my behalf. My agent, Bill Hamilton, and my editor, Tom Weldon, quite properly nagged and kept me up to the mark; while my mother and, until his death, my father were diplomatically supportive – aware that a good meal was frequently of more use than a pointed enquiry about how far I had got.

I am grateful to Lady Coldstream (Monica Hoyer) for allowing me to reproduce extracts from the unpublished diary of the late Sir William Coldstream; to Faber and Faber for permission to quote from *The Strings Are False* by Louis MacNeice; to Charles Osborne for allowing me to quote from his book *W.H. Auden*, and to Alan Ross and the *London Magazine* for permission to quote extracts from T.C. Worsley's novel *Fellow Travellers*, first published by London Magazine Editions.

The extracts from Christopher Isherwood's *Lions and Shadows* and *Christopher and His Kind* are reprinted by permission of Methuen London. The extracts from *Goodbye to Berlin* are reprinted by permission of the Estate of Christopher Isherwood and The Hogarth Press. The extracts from *The Diary* of Virginia Woolf (Volumes Four and Five) and *The Letters of Virginia Woolf* (Volume Five) are reprinted by permission of the Estate of Virginia Woolf and The Hogarth Press.

Every effort has been made to trace the copyright-holders of material quoted, but in a few cases this has proved impossible. The publishers will be happy to rectify any omission in any subsequent edition of this book.

Research facilities were generously extended to me by the governors, headmaster and staff of University College School, Hampstead; by the curators of the Alfred Berg Collection at the New York Public Library; by the Bodleian Library, Oxford; and by the Tate Gallery Archive, London. The London Library (and not least its photocopier) was also invaluable.

In accordance with the wishes of Sir Stephen Spender, I have not quoted from his published work nor reproduced any of his unpublished writings or correspondence to which I have been given access by third parties.

Hugh David
Luxor – London
December 1991

PROLOGUE

'Degree, Priority and Place'

Within the family, it was a proud if rather hollow boast that only George Eliot was a better novelist than Lily. The elder children used to brag about it, and cherished memories of the exciting moment that day in 1873 when they were first shown the two-column review in the *Spectator* which proclaimed their mother's *Parted Lives* 'the best novel of the year, bar only *Middlemarch*'.[1] Lily, by all accounts, took it in her stride. In more ways than one, the grandmother whom Stephen Spender never knew (she died in 1895) was an immensely professional writer.

She had begun modestly enough, contributing occasional reviews and essays to a range of mid-century magazines and periodicals including the *London Quarterly Review*, the *Englishwoman's Journal*, the *Dublin University Review* and the *British Quarterly*. Then, in 1869 she began writing fiction, publishing a hefty 'three-decker' novel or at the very least a collection of short stories virtually every year until her death in 1895. *Parted Lives* was her third novel, its title like those of many of her other books – *Jocelyn's Mistake* (1875), *Mark Eylmer's Revenge* (1876), *Lady Hazleton's Confession* (1890), *No Humdrum Life for Me* (1892) or *The Wooing of Doris* (1895) – hinting at its ardour-and-aspidistra theme of blighted love and parlour passion among the upper-middle classes of Victorian England.

Of blighted love, Lily knew next to nothing; her own marriage was close and happy. But when she came to write about characters with names such as Jocelyn, Mark Eylmer or Lady Hazleton, Lily was on far firmer ground, for she was very much a part of the privileged world she described.

Born Lily Headland on 22 February 1835, she had grown up in one of the grand and gracious Adam town-houses which then lined Portland Place in the West End of London. Her father, Dr Edward Headland, was among the most eminent London physicians of the period; and with its proper complement of servants – housemaids, cooks, a butler, a governess for the children – his tall, stucco-fronted house emphasised the family's prominent place in the early Victorian scheme of things.

But if the façade was pure Forsyte, behind the front door Dr Headland's household was not in the least 'Victorian'. For from what little we know of him, Edward Headland resembles an early twentieth-century free-thinker – a Webb, a Shaw or a Raverat perhaps – far more closely than he does the crusty, Trollopean image of a Victorian doctor. Not only had he defied convention by marrying a Spanish girl (the daughter of one Ferdinand de Medina), he went on to take a wholly modern view of his children's upbringing, and saw to it that his daughters as well as his sons were as thoroughly prepared as possible for the world beyond Portland Place.

Thus in the early 1850s Lily emerged from Queen's College, a private girls' school set among the doctors' consulting rooms of Harley Street, with far more than the normal social accomplishments of a girl of her class. She had mastered water-colour painting, embroidery and the piano; but, according to one of her sons, she was also 'a fair scholar and a good modern linguist'. She was proficient in French, in German and (because she had decided to 'rise in the early dawn' and teach herself) also in Greek. Given her mother's background, she doubtless too had some knowledge of Spanish.

It was like something out of Jane Austen rather than George Eliot then, when this cultivated, metropolitan and independent-minded young woman met John Kent Spender, the 'physician to the Mineral Water Hospital' at the spa town of Bath in Somerset.

For all that he was 'a provincial', John Kent Spender too came from a good (or good-ish) family. His father was yet another doctor – and indeed a previous holder of the post at the Mineral Water Hospital. His grandfather was the splendidly named

Onesiphorus Spender of Bradford-on-Avon, a small town ten miles or so south-east of Bath where the Spender family had lived since the sixteenth century. He didn't yet have 'money', not as Dr Headland would have understood the term. But his 'prospects' seemed reasonable.

At any rate Headland was evidently satisfied. Soon, Lily and John Kent Spender announced their engagement. After a decent interval they were married, and in 1858 they set up home in rooms above Dr Spender's practice in Gay Street, Bath.

In the late 1850s the town to which John Kent Spender brought his twenty-three-year-old wife was a stylish, if essentially eighteenth-century place which continued to remind visitors of Richard Brinsley Sheridan's play *The Rivals* (1775): 'Sir Anthony Absolute still strides along the Bath Parade: and Sir Lucius O'Trigger still ambles down Milsom Street.'[2] But socially and geographically it was hardly London; and both materially and intellectually the new Mrs Spender soon began to miss the stimulation of the capital. She was determined to be more than a provincial physician's wife and unhappy, too, about being wholly dependant on the income of a notably liberal provincial physician. As one of his sons remembered, John Kent

> had a free as well as a paying consulting-room, and he was always transferring his patients from the paying to the free room. Add to this that he was perpetually telling his richer patients that there was nothing whatever the matter with them, and that he held most ailments to be imaginary, and nearly all drugs useless, and it is scarcely surprising that he did not make a fortune out of medicine.[3]

Fiercely loyal to her husband, despite his strange other-worldly ways, and subsequently to her children – ultimately there were eight, four boys and four girls – by the early 1860s Lily had realised that, if the Spenders were going to have 'the

good things which she thought [they] ought to enjoy', she was
going to have to provide them herself.

She dutifully plunged into the round of charitable work then
deemed suitable for a woman in her position. She joined all the
committees founded to ameliorate the educational and social
problems which even then confronted the town. But she also
began writing, ignoring the obloquy which, two decades later,
was still attached to 'that singular anomaly, the lady novelist'.[4]

And, despite her husband's growing reputation and success,
'the good things' were soon being paid for out of the tidy
proceeds of Mrs J. K. Spender's burgeoning literary career – with
the utmost propriety, Lily published all her work under her
married name. She banked her royalties and amassed what she
called her 'funds'. Her eldest son Alfred (born in December
1862) later recalled that

> There was first the fund for the university education of the
> four sons, £400 each (the rest to be found by scholarships), a
> total of £1,600; then the fund to provide holidays for the
> family; and finally the fund to add to my father's savings to
> enable him to retire before he was worn out, and to provide
> for daughters hereafter.[5]

As Alfred went on to acknowledge, 'all this was accomp-
lished'. He and his younger brother Harold (born on 22 June
1864) duly went up to Oxford. So too, unexpectedly perhaps,
did one of their sisters. There were family holidays in the Lake
District, the Channel Islands, Northern Ireland, Switzerland and
even Italy. There was money left over, too. Alfred noted in the
opening pages of his two-volume autobiography, *Life, Jour-
nalism and Politics*, first published in 1927, that he was still
'administering a Trust which is distributing the income of the
residue [of his parents' estate] to various members of the family'.

More than thirty years after her death, then, Lily was still
providing 'the good things' for her family. There was another,
less tangible but equally enduring legacy, too. For, through her
industry and determination, Lily had put the Spenders on the
map. At the time of her death in 1895 the family was small beer

in comparison with intellectual dynasties such as the Stracheys, the Huxleys or the Beerbohms, but 'Lily's boys' were already beginning to make their mark.

———

Twenty years earlier, in the mid-1870s, Lily had seen to that, and laid the foundations of the literate liberalism (with a small if not always a capital 'L') which would characterise the life and work of her sons Alfred and Harold Spender and reach its apogee in the career of Harold's son, Stephen.

'A born hostess and social magnet: steady writer of novels: a devoted public worker: and, above all, a splendid parent', in 1875 she was forty years of age and in her prime.[6] Her career as the second George Eliot was going well and 'funds' were accumulating. In addition, her husband's reputation in Bath was at last approaching that of his father-in-law in London.

John Kent had already made his name as the author of medical books and articles, and as a contributor to the *Cambridge Dictionary of Medicine*. Now, he was becoming nationally known as an authority on the treatment of rheumatic pain: until late in his life his son Alfred was occasionally asked whether he 'was any relation of "Spender on the Pigmentations of Rheumatism"'.

In 1870 John Kent had been able to move his family and their attendant servants and pets from the cramped rooms in Gay Street to a larger and much more prestigious property, No. 17 The Circus. The Circus was only a stone's throw from Bath's more famous Royal Crescent and at the centre of the most fashionable part of the town. William Pitt the Younger and Robert Clive ('Clive of India') had both lived there. The portrait painter Thomas Gainsborough had once lived at No. 17, while the explorer David Livingstone was a near (but presumably absent) neighbour until his death at Old Chitambo in what was then Northern Rhodesia in 1873.

Though he still often prescribed no more than a few glasses of Bath's spa water (which in *The Pickwick Papers* Charles

Dickens had described as tasting like 'warm flat irons') John
Kent was being visited in his new consulting rooms by some of
the most eminent figures of the day. One such, Samuel Carter
Hall, a retired publisher who in his youth had known
Wordsworth, Leigh Hunt and even Byron and Shelley, soon
became a friend of the family.

All seemed set fair, and the opening pages of both Alfred
Spender's *Life, Journalism and Politics* and his brother Harold's
shorter but very similar autobiography *The Fire of Life* (1926)
provide a few snap-shots of the family's life at this period. There
was Lily whose 'pen flew over the paper; she went on with a
circle of noisy children romping about her; she would write on
the beach at the seaside, and, when all the rooms were flooded
out at home, she put a table on the landing between dining-room
and drawing-room and continued to write.'[7] There was John
Kent, too, who 'all through his busy life [. . .] laboured hard to
keep up his Latin and Greek, and really lived up to his own
maxim to spend at least an hour a day on "some good
author." '[8]

Harold noted the reaction this had on him, Alfred and their
younger brother Hugh (subsequently a popular novelist with a
fecundity which rivalled his mother's). 'Seeing both our parents
writing books, we concluded that it was the universal occupa-
tion of men – and women too, and we were surprised to meet
anyone who did not think so.'[9] Too young themselves to engage
in the universal occupation of writing, the children were
nevertheless as dutiful in their reading as their father. According
to Alfred, by the time they were in their mid-teens they had been
'put to' or had discovered for themselves a formidable list of
authors:

We pounced on the new Tennyson or the new Browning, the
latest essay of Matthew Arnold, the latest volume of Froude,
the new instalment of *Fors* or *Præterita*, laboured faithfully at
Daniel Deronda, or Darwin's *Earthworms*, or the *Data of
Ethics*. At the same time we devoted evenings to reading
Shakespeare out loud, and passed through our Keats phase

and our Shelley phase and our Byron phase. I was brought up to believe Wordsworth the greatest of modern poets [. . .]

Between the ages of twelve and sixteen I read the whole of Scott's novels, conscientiously doing the grind at the introductions as the price of the joy to follow. I felt a void when they were finished, but never much disposition to return to them. Harrison Ainsworth and Wilkie Collins satisfied an appetite for shockers, and the *Moonstone* and the *Woman in White* still seem to me among the very best. There followed George Eliot and Thackeray, who were read through from end to end with the same thoroughness, and hard on these the early Hardy's and Meredith's, which my mother got at once when they appeared, and passed on to us.[10]

As if that was not enough, there were also the 'reigning Americans': Emerson, Thoreau, Edgar Allan Poe, Nathaniel Hawthorne, Russell Lowell and, a little later, Walt Whitman.

Occasionally, however, there were respites. Once, the children were taken to a private concert given by the elderly Jenny Lind, the 'Swedish Nightingale' who had delighted a previous generation of concert-goers. There were fairly frequent visits to London too: one of Alfred's earliest memories was of seeing Benjamin Disraeli addressing the House of Commons. Lily also saw to it that each of her children learnt a musical instrument and was taught to ride and swim.

Alfred owned a bicycle, a fifty-inch 'penny-farthing' on which he would ride as far as Oxford. He and Harold were also sent off on annual walking tours, surely the most thoroughly Rousseauean part of the 'free growth' programme by which John and Lily Spender chose to bring up their children. Alfred recalled:

From the time that I was fifteen and my brother Harold fourteen we were given five pounds each at the beginning of the Easter holidays and told to go; and if we returned within a fortnight we felt disgraced. We planned our routes with maps and time-tables, roamed all over Devonshire and Cornwall – down the north coast and back by the south coast – or explored the Isle of Purbeck and the New Forest, coming back over Salisbury Plain. Hotels were barred as beyond our means;

and we bargained every night for bed and breakfast in farmhouses and labourers' cottages, and were more than once reduced to a fourpenny bed in a common doss-house. As the money ran out we tightened our belts and prolonged our marches, which were sometimes as much as thirty miles in the day.[11]

These tours and treats, Alfred explained, took place only during the school holidays for, as might be expected, Lily and John Kent Spender were 'zealots for education', and took a keen interest in their children's schooling. Both the elder boys were sent to the Bath Classical and Mathematical Preparatory School ('For the Sons of Gentlemen Exclusively') and then allowed to choose between going as boarders to Winchester or remaining at home in Bath as day boys at the local Bath College. Perhaps realising which side their bread was buttered, both opted for the latter course.

The College had only recently been founded when Alfred arrived there in the mid-1870s. It was one of a new generation of 'reformed' public schools which had been established in the years immediately after 1864 when a Parliamentary Commission had denounced the slack, complacent irrelevancy of much of the teaching at Eton, Westminster and the other traditional public schools. In consequence, academic standards at Bath were high; almost formidably so:

On four days in the week we learnt sixty lines of Greek and Latin by heart, and at the end of the term we were expected to be able to recite a Greek play or a book of Virgil from end to end. On Saturday night there was the School Debating Society, and between Saturday and Monday an English essay to be wedged in between Chapels and ordinary preparation.[12]

Maybe it was all necessary, for the headmaster, T. W. Dunn, made it a rule that 'he would have no boy in the sixth-form who could not reasonably be expected to win a scholarship at Oxford or Cambridge'. Whatever, both Alfred and a little later Harold (they were known as 'Spender I' and 'Spender II' respectively) thrived under the tough but benign regime. Alfred was head boy for three successive years. With no undue modesty, in *Life, Journalism and Politics* he recalled too that he was 'in the top flight of scholars' when he completed his year in the sixth form and, much to Dunn's (and no doubt Lily's) satisfaction, matriculated to Balliol College, Oxford with an Exhibition in Classics in 1882.

There he quickly, if rather self-consciously, became a member of the 'Balliol set', hob-nobbing with such 'smugs' as 'the unparalleled' George Nathaniel Curzon (later to be Viceroy of India), 'the delightful and copious talker' Cosmo Lang (a future Archbishop of Canterbury) and A. H. Hawkins who subsequently became better known as the novelist Anthony Hope.

Of Harold's academic career rather less is known. However, the fact that he was head boy at Bath College in the academic year 1882–83 and followed his brother to Oxford in 1884 suggests that he too was in or very near the top flight of scholars.

———

It was at Oxford that, briefly and for the only time in his life, Harold Spender outshone his elder brother. Like Alfred, he had fitted into Lily's scheme of things and gone up to the university as an Exhibitioner – but to the markedly less fashionable University College. A few years previously 'Univ' had (in Harold's phrase) 'fallen to a very low place on the river' after its then Master had sent the entire College down, having failed to find the undergraduate responsible for what was then termed the 'screwing up' of a Proctor. Numbers were still well down in 1884, and Harold found Lang ('many-gifted, silver in speech'), Hawkins and the other members of his brother's 'brilliant' Balliol set more conducive than the Univ 'hearties' he roomed with on 'the High'.

Like Alfred, he took a First in Mods (1884). But in 1887 he bettered his brother's second-class degree by gaining a First in his *Literae Humaniores* (classics and philosophy) Finals. Ultimately, however, it was a Pyrrhic victory. In later life, both literally and metaphorically Harold was always to remain the younger son; 'Spender II' to Alfred's starry eminence.

Given the bookishness of their parents, it was inevitable that both he and Alfred should have gravitated to literature or at least to journalism when they came down from Oxford in the mid 1880s. Ink flowed in their veins. Quite apart from Lily, two of their uncles, William Saunders and Edward Spender, were involved with 'the prints'. They 'had been the first to show the power of the telegraph for the purpose of news; for it was William Saunders who brought the actual wire into St Paul's Cathedral on the day of the Thanksgiving Service for the recovery of the then Prince of Wales (afterwards Edward VII) from typhoid fever' [13] in 1872. Their scoops had shown Harold the 'full glamour of Fleet Street' and, like Thackeray's Arthur Pendennis, at an early age he decided on a career amidst 'the daily, crowded varied existence of that "Street of Adventure". I wanted the full phosphorescent glitter of its restless eddies and currents.'[14]

He got it – but it was Alfred who really found the glitter. After an apprenticeship on the Hull-based *Eastern Morning News* (1886–90) he jettisoned his Christian name in favour of the more authoritative 'J. A. Spender', and came to London. He was briefly on the staff of the ailing *Pall Mall Gazette*, then jumped ship and began a long association with the *Westminster Gazette*, first as assistant editor and then (from 1896 until 1922) as editor. In 1937 he was even created a Companion of Honour. Harold did not fare so well. His obituary entry in *Who Was Who, 1921–1930* gives the bare bones of a career precariously split between the 'Street of Adventure' and Grub Street. He too was on the staff of the *Pall Mall Gazette* (1891–93) and the *Westminster Gazette* (1893–95), but impatience or – as he would probably have preferred to see it – the maintenance of the principles he had absorbed from Lily and John Kent Spender at The Circus prohibited his ever settling down. Without J. A.'s *gravitas*, he contented himself with a rootless but comfortable life, writing biographies, novels and other books on an enormous variety of subjects, and contributing successively to the

Daily Chronicle (1895–99), the *Manchester Guardian* (1899–1900) and the *Daily News* (1900–14). But no C.H. crowned his career: by the end of his life Harold Spender was merely 'Commander Greek Order of the Redeemer; LL.D. (Athens)' and a Fellow of the Royal Geographical Society.

The years leading up to the outbreak of war in 1914 saw the effective demise of the 'man of letters', that essentially Victorian polymath epitomised by figures such as Lord Macaulay, Thomas Carlyle and Virginia Woolf's father, Sir Leslie Stephen, the founder-editor of the *Dictionary of National Biography*. In their different ways both J.A. — thundering mightily from the editor's chair at the *Westminster Gazette* offices in Tudor Street, London — and more particularly Harold were each to personify his last incarnation. It would, however, be quite wrong to see them as failures, existing on the same level of abject penury as the wretched Edwin Reardon, the struggling writer-hero of George Gissing's novel *New Grub Street* (1891). Even Harold was well able both to maintain his principles — an early chapter in *The Fire of Life* is entitled 'Sold But Not Bought' — and, from 1904, to keep a wife, servants and young family on the proceeds of his work.

————

His wife, Stephen Spender's mother, was born Violet Hilda Schuster, and was what John Kent Spender might, in the fashion of the day, have called a 'good catch'. Despite the fact that by blood she was 'entirely German', given the Spender's medical bent she was *suitable* since she too came from a family of doctors — and they were every bit as eminent as the Spenders and the Headlands.

Violet's grandfather on her mother's side was Sir Herman (originally Hermann) Weber, a well-known physician of the mid-Victorian period who lived in Grosvenor Street, Mayfair and specialised in the treatment of consumption (tuberculosis). Knighted in 1899, he was a renowned collector of Greek coins (which were later bequeathed to the British Museum) and a friend of William Gladstone. Symbolically sealing his intimate connection with the Old Order, he died on Armistice Day, 11 November 1918, at the age of ninety-five. One of his two sons F. Parkes Weber (Violet's uncle) followed him into medicine and became a specialist in rare diseases, publishing a series of books and monographs with such titles as *Medical Teleology and Miscellaneous Subjects*. Extraordinarily, when this was published in 1958 Parkes Weber was ninety-seven years of age.

Among the few non-medical men in the family was Violet's father, Ernest Joseph Schuster (1850–1924), a successful barrister who was called to the bar in 1890 and eventually 'took silk' and became a King's Counsel in 1922. He too was technically German. Although he was born in London, he was educated in Frankfurt-on-Main, the city from which the Schusters originated. He read law at the universities of Geneva and Munich, and graduated as a Doctor of Laws from the latter. At some time in the early 1870s, however, Ernest returned to Britain and by 1873 was working with his father as a partner in Schuster, Son & Co., a successful firm of civil and commercial lawyers which had chambers in Cannon Street in the City of London.[15]

Historically, the Schusters had been merchant bankers and, more problematically, 'of Jewish race'. But they 'had adopted the Christian religious faith under the influence of [Ernest's] mother who, herself Jewish, had become one of the most devout believers of Christianity'.[16] Not even the oblique shadow of Judaism, however, could hinder Ernest's inexorable rise. Within three years he was in a position to propose to – and be accepted by – Hilda, Herman Weber's intelligent, plain-speaking, liberal daughter. They were married in 1876.

Ernest's continuing success at the bar also ensured that, from birth, his three children were at least superficially regarded as members of the English liberal upper-middle class. Violet, George – later Sir George Schuster, KCSI, KCMG, CBE, MC – and their much-loved younger brother Alfred (who was killed in the Great War) grew up in a world of servants, silver-service dinner parties in the evenings and starched linen on the dining-table. There was a house in Hampstead (later to be sold in favour of a smaller flat in Albert Court, Kensington, right behind the Royal Albert Hall) and a foreign holiday every year, usually in Switzerland. Courtesy of Sir Herman, there was even a carriage and pair to take them on drives through what was then the open countryside around Harrow.

But at a deeper level things were not quite so simple. By descent, Violet, George and Alfred remained members of the high German-Jewish bourgeoisie, and were not allowed to forget it. Born in 1877, at a time when anti-German, and specifically anti-Bismarckian feelings were running particularly high in Britain, Violet never did. She was always very 'sensitive', and the dislocating effect of being to all intents and purposes the child of two warring cultures – together with the eccentric, 'artistic' leanings of her mother, Hilda Schuster – profoundly marked her life.

Four years her junior, her brother George too was deeply scarred by his schizophrenic pedigree. Three-quarters of a century later he was to write:

> My family background had therefore a distinctive German colouring – not a very good setting for my early years since the prevailing feeling in England at the time was very definitely hostile to Germans. This background had two effects on me. On the one hand I embarked upon my schooldays with a sort of inferiority complex. On the other hand it helped to give me a special appreciation of English character and English ways of life backed by a deep love for the English countryside. These feelings have, throughout my life, had a dominant influence on my outlook.[17]

A strain of this anomic rootlessness entered the family blood when Violet married Harold Spender in 1904. And tempered by something of Lily's practical energy, it can be seen, not too fancifully, in the character of her third child – her son, Stephen.

PART ONE

——

The Making
of a Poet

ONE

A Little Liberal

Half-German, at least a quarter Jewish and one-eighth Italian, he was the second son of a second son, and a Sunday child. But the London posts were regular and more frequent in the early years of this century than they are today, and *The Times* was able to announce his safe delivery the following Monday morning:

> **Spender.** – On Sunday, the 28 Feb., 1909, at 47 Campden House Court, W., **Violet**, the wife of **Harold Spender**, of a son.[1]

The boy, who was soon christened Stephen Harold, was his parents' third child. He was born in the last months of the reign of King Edward VII, in the Indian summer of Edwardian England, but he arrived into what was still an essentially upper-middle-class Victorian household.

With his reddish walrus moustaches and, on all but the rarest of occasions, a stiff formality of manner, his father Harold Spender seemed to embody the discipline and decorum of the old century rather than the amoral hedonism of King Edward and the surviving members of his Marlborough House Set. On that Sunday at the end of February 1909 he was forty-four years of age. He had already written four books (another fourteen were to follow) which ranged from political history to somewhat undistinguished fiction. He was well-known as a traveller and mountaineer. In Liberal circles at least, he was also seen as a 'crusading journalist' – we would now say essayist or political commentator – nominally on the staff of the London *Daily News.*

Thirteen years his junior, his wife Violet also contributed to the *fin de siècle* milieu of the house in Campden House Court. Something of a Jane Welsh to his very willing Carlyle, she had little in common with the monstrous regiment of suffragists, suffragettes and 'New Women' whom George Bernard Shaw had already begun depicting in plays such as *Major Barbara* (1905). Rather, she was mysteriously 'delicate' – that ineffably Victorian state of womanhood, and a condition which in itself cannot have been improved by four years of almost continual pregnancy.

There were, it was true, periods in which she radiated an infectious, vibrant gaiety. Then, perfumed, bejewelled, dressed in the finest satins and as beautiful as a Titian *vénitienne*, she would kiss the children goodnight before accompanying her husband to a dinner party or the theatre. But such moments alternated with recurring bouts of illness.

More and more frequently she retreated to a darkened room or, wrapped in a plaid rug, lay prostrate on the drawing-room chaise-longue – that other recourse of the nineteenth-century *femme en dérangement* – in the very best Elizabeth Barrett Browning tradition. 'Sssh, you've given Mummy a headache,' the servants would whisper on these occasions, and corral the children – Michael, Christine, Stephen and Humphrey – into the safety of the upstairs nursery.

It was of course money which supported this tottering, anachronistic edifice of upper-middle-class domesticity. It paid for the small battalion of doctors, nurses, cooks, governesses, secretaries, companions and general servants who made it possible. It greased the wheels of everyday life and allowed the ménage to function with almost military efficiency until long after the First World War. As late as the summer of 1921, for instance, Harold took the family for a holiday in Oxford, and had to hire a lorry to get the children, the servants, the dog, the cat and all the luggage up there.[2]

Money, however, there was. Even after the catastrophic fall in the value of the pound caused by the war, the Spenders remained 'comfortably off'. Then as now there were frequent references to the good old pre-war days. Then, Violet used to tell the children, 'we were rich'; then, she had honeymooned beside the pyramids in Egypt. Now she was five pounds overdrawn at the bank.[3] Harold too would gloomily fulminate that there was just enough money to keep the family out of the workhouse.[4] But even as a child Spender was aware that Harold's 'just' was a relative term – there would continue to be *just* enough, he somehow intuitively knew, for him to be able to do whatever he wanted with his life. After the better part of a century exact figures are difficult to arrive at, but there is no reason to dispute Spender's later estimate that throughout his childhood and schooldays his father's income from literary and journalistic work (augmented by periodic disbursements from the family trust which had taken over Lily Spender's 'funds') amounted to a respectable £2,000 a year.[5]

For all its totemic importance as a 'good address' in *The Times*'s announcement of his birth, the now demolished house in Campden House Court where Harold and Violet had lived since their marriage in 1904 played no further part in Spender's life. Indeed, he seemingly retained no recollection at all of the four years he spent there.

Rather, his earliest memories were of a country childhood, for in the summer of 1913 the family was, in Harold's phrase, 'compelled' to move out of London. In his autobiography Harold merely cites 'domestic reasons'[6] for this seismic upheaval, but in all likelihood they were connected with a weakening in Violet's already chronic condition. There certainly seems no other explanation for the sudden decision to lease The Bluff, a large country house high on the cliffs above the seaside town of Sheringham in Norfolk. It could only have been an inconvenience as far as Harold's own career was concerned. Not only was he still on the staff of the *Daily News*, in 1913 he was also beginning work on a biography of the Prime Minister, H. H. Asquith.

The Bluff was to be the family's home for the next six years. For the first few months Harold had frequently to commute back to London, working in the *News* offices at 67 Fleet Street and staying, often for weeks at time, at one or other of his clubs (the National Liberal, the Alpine or the Whitefriars). But, perhaps because of its sheer isolation, the new house soon became his 'home'. There, with Captain Devoto, his secretary, and his family around him, he could at last live the life of 'a man of letters', the kind of life which his elder and more famous brother J. A. Spender had been enjoying in Kent since he became editor of the *Westminster Gazette* in January 1896. He certainly made the best of things: 'at the end of the six years I found that during my stay in Norfolk I had written no less than five books – two novels and three biographies, which seems to prove, in spite of Anatole France, man can write in the provinces.'[7]

His four young children also quickly adapted to the move. Indeed, for them in the carefree months before the outbreak of the First World War life at The Bluff was little short of magical. From the livid, sooty, clanging, crowded metropolis they had been transported to a house by the sea. They were free to roam the fields, lanes, dykes, ditches and woods around Sheringham and the nearby village of East Runton. They suddenly became aware of the cold sleeting power of the rain and felt the force of winds which could buckle and humble a hedge. The pools and eddies on the deserted beach were only a few hundred yards away, the caves and climbable crags of the soft cliffs almost literally on their doorstep. And all the while the wide milling clouds came scudding in from the North Sea, keeping up their own pantomime, as it seemed for the exclusive entertainment of the children: Sometimes, they thought, a cloud would look just like a milk-jug. Then only seconds later, it would be more like a cat.

When Harold was at home he would sometimes take Spender, Michael and Humphrey off for long walks on the common or out on rabbit-shooting and beach-combing expeditions. These were secret times – 'Away from the women at last!' – when the lines would vanish from his face. He would tell the boys adventure stories and tales about his mountaineering exploits in the Alps, acting out every last step of a climb – '*Hold on to your ice axe! Keep the rope well round you! Follow close behind me*' ...[8] – and momentarily becoming more like an older brother than a 'furious papa'.

In his early autobiography *World Within World* Spender recalled this prelapsarian idyll with almost photographic clarity.[9] But it was the teeming Norfolk wildlife which most delighted him. In the bushes there were hairy yellow caterpillars which he collected up and kept in match-boxes. There were butterflies fumbling the hollyhocks in the garden, or waiting in a concupiscent torpor, their wings so tightly folded that a razor blade would not prise them apart. Beneath the surface of secret, favourite ponds, newts wriggled; actors in a private theatre at which he was the only spectator. Farther afield, primroses took over the woods every spring. In summer the lush bracken grew as high as his shoulders, while out on the wind-swept scrubland along the cliff-top rabbits played among the heather and gorse and brambles.

Soon it occurred to Spender that he might become a naturalist, chronicling, ordering and submerging himself in this lush, fecund new world. The notion was to remain with him for several years, until the family took a summer holiday in the Lake District.

Quite when this was, however, remains uncertain. In *World Within World*[10] Spender wrote that he was eight or nine at the time (i.e. that it was in the summer of 1917 or 1918). But in an edition of BBC Radio's *Desert Island Discs*,[11] and his later *Journals*[12] he more realistically suggested that it was earlier, in 1915 or 1916. (In the *Journals* he plumped for 1915; but, given the fact that the family had apparently gone to the Lakes principally to escape the occasional bombs being dropped on Sheringham by German Zeppelins, there is concrete evidence to suggest that 1916 is probably the correct date.)

Whichever, the holiday was of crucial importance in his life.[13] Like the trip to Oxford it was planned with military precision and undertaken in stages. There were overnight stops *en route* –

the last at an hotel in Leeds where Spender disgraced himself by allowing his caterpillars to escape in the lift – but finally the family (and doubtless its attendant servants, dog and cat) arrived at Skelgill Farm, near Derwent Water in Cumbria.

It was all so different from Norfolk! The steely expanse of Derwent Water and the other lakes, the grandeur of Helvellyn, Skiddaw and the surrounding mountains – even the giant black slugs which crawled over the paths after it had rained – were unlike anything Spender had previously seen. So was the low, white-fronted farm-house in which Harold had arranged for the family to stay. It all made a vivid, lasting impression. (Indeed, Spender was able to recognise Skelgill Farm again when he returned to the Lake District more than sixty years later, in 1979.) But it was not a direct, *en plein* connection with the glacial screes and corries of this new natural world which was to enthral and influence him (as childhood stomps across the 'rounded slopes' of a 'limestone landscape' had already influenced the young W. H. Auden). Rather, Spender's plans to become a naturalist with a long white beard like Charles Darwin's[14] were abruptly abandoned when he encountered that other Lake District phenomenon – the poetry of William Wordsworth.

In both *World Within World* and the *Journals* he described his most abiding memory of that holiday. It was not the slugs, caterpillars or boat trips on Derwent Water, but of how he had lain in bed in the evenings listening while his father quietly read appropriate Wordsworthian lyrics to Violet as they sat on the lawn outside his room.

As befitted a son of John Kent and Lily Spender – and a man who in *his* childhood had known Wordsworth's friend Samuel Carter Hall – Harold also made it his business to introduce the children to Wordsworth's simpler ballads during bracing day-time walks around Derwent Water and over a 'little mountain' called Catbells. Spender in particular was entranced. The erstwhile naturalist could not after all have failed to be delighted by the opening lines of 'To a Small Celandine':

> Pansies, lilies, kingcups, daisies,
> Let them live upon their praises;
> Long as there's a sun that sets,
> Primroses will have their glory;
> Long as there are violets,
> They will have a place in story . . .

But it went deeper than that. For him, the clouds, the lakes, the plants, the mountains and even the creepy-crawlies all came together at the sound of those words. The words seemed to give them a reality that was if anything *more* real, *more* magical than the pulsating biology which was revealed by his magnifying-glass. At the sound of them, Darwin and his beard lost their appeal and, metaphorically at least, the caterpillars were abandoned. Always emotionally closer to his fragile, volatile mother than to his repressed and dutiful rather than doting father, by the time he was six or seven Spender had become something of a *Romantischer*, a toddling Werther. What's more (if we are to believe his own account) he had already decided that he was going to be a poet – like William Wordsworth. He wrote his first poem when he was about eight or nine years old (in other words at about the time of the holiday in the Lake District) and could still remember it more than seventy years later.[15] A short, sub-Wordsworthian apostrophe inevitably aimed in the general direction of that wild, Romantic 'Nature' which he had encountered in the Lake District, it successfully rhymed 'powers' with 'hours', but within an archaic, archly 'poetic' structure which would continue to circumscribe his work – like many another adolescent's – until his late teens.

━━━━━

Back in Sheringham in 1916, however, poetry was at a discount. Spender and his elder sister Christine's pantomimic, *jug–cat* interpretation of the sky had been invested with a new seriousness as the thick, lowering clouds showed themselves to be the harbourers of nightmares as well as daydreams:

> I remember spending a whole afternoon in 1916 watching the
> assemblage of the armada of Zeppelins which afterwards
> sailed across England, smashing up buildings and killing
> people in the well-lighted towns of the Midlands [Harold
> wrote]. No effort was made to stop them. They calmly and
> quietly assembled off the coast and then sailed away inland.
> We heard the throbbing of their engines quietening down as
> they passed away to attack the heart of England.[16]

The outbreak of the Great War in 1914 had fundamentally
changed the character of life at The Bluff. 'The first bomb of the
war fell in a garden just behind my house,' Harold recalled.[17]
(Later he characteristically noted that he had 'managed to
persuade [his] friends in the Press to raise a real hullabaloo over
the undefended state of our coast'.)[18] 'A shadow seemed to pass
across the sun,' he wrote.

Spender could not but notice it. Albeit subconsciously, the
five-year-old realised that in the sudden metaphorical gloom
both his father and the world had changed abruptly and
irrevocably. Far from the hill-walking, story-telling,
Wordsworth-reading man of letters who had shared those secret
men-only outings in a land of lost content, Harold was now a
frightening representative of a new, strange and very adult
dispensation.

Naturally somewhat bellicose but, at the age of fifty-one, too
old to enlist, he had given up his position on the *Daily News*
shortly after the outbreak of hostilities – 'in order,' he said, 'to
place myself as far as possible at the disposal of the Govern-
ment.' Soon he was busying himself in a basically self-appointed
role as recruiting officer for the Norfolk Volunteers. He
doggedly patrolled the cliffs and lanes around Sheringham,
familiarised himself with 'the complex machinery of the Maxim
and Lewis Guns' and even taught Michael to shoot. One evening
a week he also 'did his bit' as an equally self-appointed lord of
the manor by entertaining the real troops who were in training
camps in his part of Norfolk to what he called 'sing-songs' at The
Bluff.

To Spender it was all frankly bewildering and awful. Once he had lain in bed listening to Harold reading the poetry of Wordsworth. Now up in the nursery all he could hear were the echoes of the beer-fuelled ribaldry of the soldiers downstairs – '*I don't want to be a soldier, I don't want my bollocks shot away . . .*'; '*Mademoiselle from Armenteers, Parley-vous! . . .*' It was shocking confirmation that things were changing, and for the worse. He was growing up; and in a complex, symbolic way 'The War' and all it represented marked the end of his childhood.

At the age of five or six, Spender was probably too young to appreciate the fact that, as the war dragged on, journalists and commentators such as G.K. Chesterton and Hilaire Belloc and newspapers including the *Daily Mail* and the *Daily Mirror* were beginning to cite the Schusters and – to a lesser extent – the Spenders as representatives of the 'enemy within'. To him things were far more simple: at least in spirit, the frightful Germans had already invaded the land of lost content. *But he was half German! . . .* His mother was pure German, *echt Deutsch*. Nevertheless, his father was out hunting 'Jerry', 'the Boche' and 'the Hun' with English soldiers . . . He still loved his father. But he loved his mother too. Surely *she* wasn't a Hun or a Jerry . . . Or was she? Why did she shout at him? And why was she now so often ill, in bed at home or away in hospitals and nursing homes? *It hadn't always been like this.* Once, once . . .

It is tempting to imagine that, tearful and confused, it was the seven-year-old Spender and not Michael (born in 1907) or Humphrey (the baby of the family, born in 1910) who took his worries to Harold at this period. One or other of them certainly did:

> . . . one of my small boys one day asked a very pertinent question:
> 'Father,' he said, 'what would happen if the Germans landed in the rain?'
> 'Sonny,' I replied. 'Whatever the frightfulness of the Germans, they will never be quite so frightful as that!'[19]

It is tempting too to make the worst of Harold's answer and the effect it must have had on the boy. That patronising, full-stopped *Sonny* and the glib, adult, exclamation-marked cleverness of his response seem vividly illustrative of a cold, self-centred arrogance. But, for all his earlier – and even then only occasional – bouts of *bonhomie*, this seems to have been the real measure of the man whom Spender was now encountering for the first time in what from all the evidence appear to have been his true colours.

Harold's 320-page autobiography *The Fire of Life* is, for instance, only more memorable for its wearying hortatory addresses ('On, and Always On!' is the title of its final chapter) than it is for sheer egocentric dullness; although the latter takes some beating. It is difficult to think of another man who has written a full account of his life which contains just one reference to his wife – Harold merely reveals that Violet 'possessed great literary gifts' – and none at all to his children. Harold Spender did. The passage quoted above is about the closest he comes to mentioning Michael, Christine, Stephen or Humphrey. None is listed in his index – although, by contrast, there are thirty-two separate references to David Lloyd George, some many pages long.

Cold and emotionally costive, then, Harold rapidly began to personify 'real life' in the young Spender's mind. Beach-combing and rabbit-shooting were now things of the past, and the sensitive boy came to dread his father's mock-heroic military metaphors, lofty lectures and oratorical conversational style. (And not unreasonably, perhaps: while Queen Victoria once noted that that other Liberal, William Ewart Gladstone 'speaks to Me as if I was a public meeting', one of Spender's school-friends was later to dub Harold 'The Man of Wrath'.) Memories of Harold's characteristic interpretation of Spender's request for a couple of pennies to pay a bus fare as an attempt to 'get round my flank', and of his heavy-handed insistence that even a casual game of football involved notions of Duty, Discipline, Manliness and Fair Play continued to rankle with him for more than half a century. In 1940 he was still able to assemble a litany of the buzz-words which littered even Harold's meal-time 'banter' – *Concentrate; games; caning; fellows; manners; discipline; self-control; cleanliness; examination; scholarships; dunce; backward; healthy . . .*[20]

Spender was himself older than Harold had been in 1914 before he began to mourn his father and form some assessment of his personality.[21] Hence, what he was to call an 'uncharitable' attitude towards Harold colours the selective account of his own childhood which he gave in *World Within World*, first published in 1951, and much of his earlier work, including the novel *The Backward Son* (1940). In 'Day Boy', a memoir of his schooldays which was written in 1934, for example, he seems to go out of his way to stress his father's remoteness and adds three years to his age in his dogmatic assertion that Harold was forty-five years older than his eldest child.[22]

———

But it was not just Harold, his cliff-top 'manoeuvres' and The War. Other Zeppelins were also massing over the cosy insularity of a life in which a succession of nannies, governesses and five or six servants[23] had hitherto effectively shielded 'young Master Stephen' from the slings and arrows of outrageous fortune. Chief amongst these was the rapid and alarming decline in his mother's physical and mental health.

Whatever was the true nature of her condition – from the scant evidence available it seems more than likely that by this time she had undergone at least one bout of abdominal surgery – Violet was certainly spending longer and longer resting alone in her darkened room. More worryingly, her moods were becoming increasingly volatile. Depending upon which was prevalent, she would variously nag, fuss over or shout at the children, at once bewildering them and leaving them emotionally adrift somewhere between her unpredictable, whirling affections and Harold's increasingly monstrous Blimpishness. One Christmas Day she threw open the door of the nursery in which Spender and his brothers and sister were squabbling. White-faced and haggard like some matinée Medea, she then berated them for their ingratitude and adumbrated the miseries of mother-hood.[24]

All at once, Spender was being forced to confront a rude, crude real world of Forsterian 'telegrams and anger'. It was something of which he knew – and wanted to know – nothing, and for which he was almost ludicrously ill-equipped.

Always his father's favourite, his elder brother Michael was 'shaping up' well under the uncertain and increasingly alarming wartime dispensation at The Bluff. He was clever and quick. Naturally perhaps, as an eldest child he also identified with his parents rather than his younger brothers and sister. Now he was always out with Harold – as often as not pointing his shot-gun at more than rabbits – while Spender remained, in all senses of the term, his mother's boy. Shy and diffident, the young Werther even had a slight speech defect which led to his confusing similar sounding words such as 'exhibition' and 'expedition', 'shoulder' and 'soldier'. As he saw it he was limp, round-shouldered (quite unlike a soldier!) and, in his own words, flabby.

In his frequently anthologised (and possibly his most famous) poem 'Rough' Spender was later to look back at this seminal period in his life. He described how the local village boys – with whom he had for too long been forbidden to associate – took their revenge on him the moment he emerged from the comfort-able cocoon that was The Bluff. Their slings and arrows were real enough: they threw mud at him, mercilessly mimicked his *shoulder-soldier* lisp and, on at least one occasion, even wrestled him to the ground.

But the fact that when he came to include 'Rough' in his *Collected Poems* he retitled it 'My Parents'[25] adds another dimension to the issue. For by that gesture he seems to be retrospectively holding Harold and Violet responsible for all the misery he undoubtedly felt at this time – and, indeed, for all his later guilt and uncertainty. It was all the fault of his cold, uncommunicative father and his nervy, over-protective mother!

It was a convenient, convincing story, and in large measure it was true. His parents *were* keeping him from children who were rough, and cosseting him with his sister as part of their reactionary domestic regime. They *were* prohibiting his forming the socially necessary friendships through which even an infant gains a knowledge of the scheme of things . . .

'Rough'/'My Parents' was written fifteen (or more) years after the time which it describes. By then both Harold and Violet were dead, and the *faux-naïf* thrust of the poem was Spender's own. By that time he had more than atoned for what was no more than his parents' class-based snobbishness. Like so many of his class and generation, he had consummated but not conquered a prurient infatuation with the forbidden fruit of 'roughness' which suffuses the poem. Working-class lads – 'rough trade' – the pliable, priapic, wanton, *willing* proletariat were to pre-occupy him for the next twenty-five years.[26]

In the immediate present, however, he was having to get used to dealing with other children on a pre-sexual daily basis. No less a 'zealot for education' than his parents, Harold had fixed and very definite ideas about his children's education. On at least one occasion he actually strode into a classroom and barked at the teacher: 'You must make my son Stephen work harder!'

Michael had already set out along the well-worn, inevitable trail: the rudiments of the Three Rs at home, prep school, a suitable public school and then – God and funds willing – Oxbridge. Now, inexorably it was Spender's turn to square up to what Harold called the 'rigorous no-treat regime' that was going to make him a Man.

To begin with, every day Harold himself drove Spender and Christine in a pony-and-trap the three miles to East Runton where Miss Harcourt ran a 'suitable' kindergarten. There, inevitably, despite Miss Harcourt's well-meaning gentility, there were more fights.[27] But occasionally there was time for more orthodox pleasures. Briefly, at the age of seven, he even found himself in love with one of his classmates, a girl called Penelope.

Other than academically, however, the two years which he spent at Miss Harcourt's did little to temper the pampered specialness of his early childhood – nor to prepare him for the brutal realities of life at preparatory school. Given his upbringing, little or nothing could. Nevertheless, it was into this which he now, suddenly and apparently voluntarily, plunged himself.

Ostensibly, it was the last thing he should have done. To have cold-bloodedly decided to go to boarding-school,[28] just as he had earlier decided to be a poet, was asking for trouble. But as we have seen, things were not quite as simple as that; pressures were mounting. Inevitably cast in the role of younger brother, Spender was beginning to experience the feelings of gauche inadequacy which were to recur throughout his life; and quite naturally, he wanted to do no more than redeem himself by emulating Michael's success.

Just before Christmas in 1918 this paragon had come home from his preparatory school wearing long grey flannel trousers and a blazer with a badge on the pocket. He would have been twelve at the time, but his hair was cropped, he talked knowledgeably about everything he had learnt, and he held his shoulders back.[29] In short, he was all that Spender wasn't.

Spender opted to follow him to the Old School House, then the preparatory wing of Gresham's School at Holt in Norfolk. It was a rash decision, and inevitably he regretted it almost immediately. The results of an early across-the-board general knowledge test of the whole school were only the start of his troubles. Michael effortlessly scored a creditable ninety per cent, but Spender came bottom with just half of one per cent;[30] and the boy who had arrived at Gresham's with what amounted to a sick-note from his mother saying that he was 'nervous' was now further humiliated by being dubbed 'the backward son'.[31]

The root of the problem was that, suddenly separated from The Bluff and his mother for the first time, Spender was desperately homesick. Holt was actually only seven or eight miles from Sheringham, but it might just as well have been on the other side of the world. He contemplated running away, but dismissed the idea because he could not face the 'shockedness' this would have caused his parents. Instead, he retreated into an introverted loneliness in which once again the caterpillars he had brought from the garden at home were his only real 'friends'.

Even Michael – 'Spender Major' – refused to speak to him. As in most boarding-schools, at 'The O.S.H' senior boys did not consort with juniors, even if they happened to be their brothers. Nor was the headmaster, G.W.S. Howson, a sympathetic father-substitute. He blustered and shouted, berating even nine-year-olds for their massacring of the English language and the inadequacies of their fathers, particularly if those fathers were –like Spender's – not men enough to beat them.

The hugger-mugger of the dormitories, too, was so unlike the literate, liberal peace of the bedroom at home which he shared with his brother Humphrey. That had satin wallpaper, wine-red curtains, and a green carpet. There were Holbein reproductions on the walls, rugs, books and toys.[32]

Quiet and introverted the new 'Spender Minor' was magnificently unprepared for the day-to-day reality of which Michael's pressed trousers and smart blazer were only the public manifestation. He was appalled by the very idea of the school's communal cold showers and completely broken by a bastardised version of the 'Honour System' which Howson had introduced at Gresham's. Intended as a liberal measure in which the boys would be largely self-regulating, confessing their own short-comings, and, *pro bono publico*, denouncing those of their classmates, this had made Gresham's and the O.S.H. into what W.H. Auden (who entered the main school in 1920, the year after Spender left the prep) described as 'a Fascist state'. He went on:

> It meant that the whole of our moral life was based on fear, on fear of the community, not to mention the temptation it offered to the natural informer, and fear is not a healthy basis.[33]

Spender was an early victim of this tactical Terror, and it left a deep scar. A later story makes him seem like a latter-day cross between Oliver Twist and Tom Brown and suggests that the O.S.H. resembled a latter-day Dotheboys Hall. In it, Spender described how, after he and a few others had taken too much bread one day in his first term, their housemaster branded them 'Food Hogs' but then left their punishment to their peers. Spender had ropes tied to his hands and feet which the prepubescent *Gauleiters* proceeded to pull in different directions.[34] Then — and on many another occasion — he was also locked under the assembly-hall stage in a hole into which fish-heads and/or scraps of food were apparently dropped. (In 'Day Boy' Spender called this dungeon the Bloater Hole; when he wrote *World Within World* fifteen years later it had become the Kipper Hole.[35] Neither account, however, explains why anyone would want to keep rotting fish-heads below the platform in the main hall of a boys' preparatory school.)

Lest he broke down in front of them, he dared not confide any of this to the two members of the O.S.H. staff whom he sensed would have been sympathetic to his plight, his English teacher Miss Bristowe and the matron Miss Newcombe (who was inevitably known as 'the Newt'). Indeed, it is conceivable that no one would have known of his discomfiture at all if Spender had not gone straight from his first ordeal in the Bloater Hole for a piano lesson with Gresham's music master Walter Greatorex, who later also taught Auden both piano and organ.

'He was what the ideal schoolmaster should be,' Auden later recalled of Greatorex, 'ready to be a friend and not a beak, to give the adolescent all the comfort and stimulus of a personal relation, without at the same time making any demands for himself in return.'[36]

As Auden's fond reminiscence implies. Greatorex was — almost inevitably — homosexual. He had come to Gresham's under something of a cloud; but his treatment of Spender was above reproach. Wiping away the boy's tears, he spoke some of the wisest words Spender had ever heard. They brought consolation, and were also to prove strikingly accurate. He might continue to be unhappy until he was twenty, Greatorex warned him. But then everything would change; he would travel abroad, go up to university and enjoy the happiest period of his life.[37]

In 1919 this seemed a distant prospect, and indeed Spender was to remain a boarder at the O.S.H. for another three terms, silently enduring the indignities of the Bloater Hole and drawing only scant comfort from a friend's assurance that terms were just ninety-one days long.

It was a period of deep unhappiness for him – he later wrote of schools as prisons and compared his own childhood to a spell in a concentration camp[38] – and well into adulthood the memory of it would remain a bench-mark of wretchedness. Eventually, however, even Harold noticed that something was amiss. At the beginning of 1920 – just as Michael was triumphantly preparing to move up from the Old School House into the main school –Spender was withdrawn from Gresham's and transferred to another prep school. His 'backwardness', a complete failure to emulate the starry eminence of Michael, and his round shoulders may have had something to do with the decision.[39]

Neither the true name nor the precise location of this new school can now be established. Other than one suggestion that it was in Worthing,[40] Spender never made any precise reference to it in his published autobiographies and diaries. But his almost embarrassingly autobiographical novel *The Backward Son* gives a detailed evocation of his time there, and offers many clues.

The book follows some eighteen months in the life of Geoffrey Brand who has been withdrawn from 'Wickham's' and sent to another private school, 'Tisselthorp House', this time on the outskirts of 'Limpet', a Sussex seaside town. The almost exact correlation between episodes in it and passages in *World Within World* suggests that *The Backward Son* was certainly drawn from life. And the fact that Geoffrey's family background corresponds so closely to Spender's own only lends further corroboration to the 'fictional' parts of the story. Tangential detail is changed, but in all essentials they are the same. Geoffrey is one of four children (three boys and one girl), the second son of a politician and man of letters called Hubert Brand.[41] His mother's maiden name is Schroeder. He himself is round-shouldered, graceless, thin and clumsy.[42]

He does not fit in at Tisselthorp where, among the ninety boys, only he and a doctor's son come from what he calls the upper-middle classes. In the hope of winning popularity he feigns an interest in the Arsenal football team and stamp collecting. Apart from English – his text-book English Grammar and Exercises contained enticing quotations from works such as *Julius Caesar, The Ancient Mariner, The Village Blacksmith* and *We Are Seven* – the lessons bore him. And he hates and fears games, beatings and the dormitory bullies who even steal his diary.[43] Soon he is literally praying to get back to his 'lovely, lovely, lovely home'.[44]

There can be only little doubt that Spender's life at the real-life Tisselthorp House (which he later compared to a 'brothel for flagellants')[45] was even worse than it had been at the Old School House in Holt. Nor did it improve when, after a year, he briefly and vaingloriously became 'Spender Major' following Humphrey's arrival. Indeed, in the light of the frequent beatings and occasional slaps round the face he received from the bullies, even the 'liberal' ways of Howson and the O.S.H. (where, for all its other faults, corporal punishment was virtually unknown) came to seem homely and civilised.

The brothers' biggest problem arose when it was somehow discovered by the other boys that their mother's maiden name was Schuster. Dubbed 'Huns' by their tormentors, in those days only months after the end of the Great War they literally held hands for mutual support. And on the one occasion when Spender did actually fight their corner and wrestle with another boy – knocking his head through a window in the process – he was banned from school prayers and caned by the headmaster.[46]

Walter Greatorex's words cannot then have been any particular consolation; but unexpectedly everything was soon to change.

At about the time that Spender was removed from the Old School House, Harold had finally given up his tenancy of The Bluff. Again it is difficult to know precisely why. But the war was now over; he was working on another biography (this time of that other Liberal giant, David Lloyd George) and Violet was growing progressively weaker. It was probably a combination of all three factors which led to his decision to move back to London and install his servants, pets and growing family in a suitably large house in Hampstead, a 'beautiful and suburban village' (as it had been described in 1897) on the northern fringe of the city proper. It was hilly, affluent – and perhaps more importantly, then as now, it was vaguely 'artistic'. No. 10 Frognal was less than a mile away from Hampstead Heath and even closer to the cottage in which John Keats had lived one hundred years previously, a fact which was not without significance during the adolescence of the *soi-disant* poet. For he soon discovered that the best of the *Letters* of this spiritual neighbour were all about what he secretly continued to think of as the highest of vocations, poetry.[47] The literary milieu suited the rest of the family too. By September 1919, in what seems like an echo of John Kent and Lily's educational zealotry, Harold had his children producing a family newspaper, *The Frognal Gazette*.

The imposing three-floored, double-fronted house with a florid Edwardian red-brick facing (Geoffrey Brand lived in a 'great red-brick, ugly Hampstead house')[48] was to be Spender's home – or, as time went on, his London base – for the next ten years. It squatted at the bottom of the hill but was still satisfactorily larger than most of the other houses in Frognal. A panelled front door (now bricked up) opened into an entrance hall, from which doors led into the dining-room and, at the back, Harold's clubby, cluttered, grey-painted study. Up on the first floor were the spacious drawing-room and Harold and Violet's bedroom. Upstairs again were the still not-ungenerous bedrooms of Michael, Christine, Spender and Humphrey (who shared) and the servants.

One of the upstairs rooms quickly became a sick-room, however, for Violet was now in visible and inevitable decline. Dr MacFadden, the family physician, was a frequent visitor to the house in the autumn of 1921. But his attentions were of no avail. Worn out by pregnancy and recurring abdominal problems in addition to her always delicate state (now diagnosed as cardiac syncope) his patient was just fading away. MacFadden carried out an emergency operation at the house on 4 December 1921, but even that was too late. Violet died the same day.[49] She was forty-four years old.

The effect on Harold was predictable. His wife's early death plunged him still farther into the cold and moody remoteness which had been triggered by the outbreak of war seven years before. Another shadow had passed across the sun; now more than ever to Spender he became that Audenesque spectre of the 'furious papa' and 'The Man of Wrath' who so terrified his friends.

In the immediate aftermath of Violet's death, however, crucial decisions had to be taken. Telegrams were sent summoning Michael home from Gresham's, Christine back from her school and Spender and Humphrey back from their hateful prep school. 'My little ones! You are all your old father has left,' Harold told them melodramatically as they assembled for the funeral.[50] And, as such, he did not intend letting them go again – not all of them at any rate. Michael should (of course) continue at public school. But Christine, Spender and Humphrey were for the moment to remain at home as companions for their father in his hour of need.

That moment, however – that awkward, awful hour – was soon indefinitely prolonged. And to Spender, as Christmas 1921 came and went, the return to Frognal must have seemed only the lesser of two evils. He had escaped the barbarities of his prep school only to be almost literally imprisoned in his own home. For, since his wife's death, Harold had become more posses-sively protective of his 'little ones' than even Violet at her obsessive, neurotic worst. He hated it if they were out of his sight and forbade them to leave the house unless they were accompanied by him or one of the servants.

There was just one exception. Rather than relying on the dubious talents of home tutors – to whom in the same situation the education of any other upper-middle-class boy of Spender's less than robust constitution might well have been entrusted – Harold had quickly decided that he should go back to school, although not as a boarder. And, happily, an entirely suitable day preparatory school for boys was very conveniently situated, less than a mile away down the Finchley Road.

Although Spender does not mention the fact in 'Day Boy' or even *World Within World*,[51] he spent the last two terms of the 1921–22 educational year (the period between January and July 1922 when he was still too young to begin at public school) at The Hall, the most prestigious of Hampstead's many prep schools.

Established in 1889, then as now The Hall specialised in providing essential bedrock education for the sons of what has been dubbed the 'Hampstead mafia', the district's long-established community of 'politicians, lawyers, artists, polemicists, musicians [and] media stars'.[52] Harold (an early polemicist?) must have doubly blessed his good fortune; firstly for the sheer convenience of the place, and secondly for the alacrity with which his 'backward son' took to it only weeks after Violet's death. It was indeed remarkable that in his brief two-term stay at The Hall, Spender was promoted into a higher class and even 'featured in the Swimming sports'.[53]

––––––

For this reason, and because he still insisted on his younger sons' company in the evenings, in the summer of 1922 Harold decided that Spender would not follow Michael to Gresham's, nor indeed would he attend any public boarding school. Rather, he would once again remain a day boy and get his secondary education locally. It was the obvious solution to all the domestic problems at No. 10 – not least because to Harold's and even Spender's eyes another uniquely suitable school crowned the hill at the top of Frognal. Indeed, its steeply pitched roof and ornate Edwardian cupola were clearly visible from the upstairs windows. It was, literally, only a brisk two-minute walk away.

As its name implies, University College School had originally been part of University College London, and it had never quite shed the College's 'radical' ethos. Like U.C.L., in 1922 it still embodied something of the sceptical views of the eighteenth-century English Enlightenment, most notably those of the philosopher Jeremy Bentham. It too strove to provide 'adequate opportunities for obtaining literary and scientific education at a moderate expense'. Founded in 1830, it also preserved Bentham's 'Place-capturing, or Extempore degradation and promotion principle' and was run on comparatively democratic lines, with a board of Monitors and sub-Monitors and a headmaster who at least consulted an 'Electoral College' on all matters affecting the boys' welfare.

It eschewed all forms of corporal punishment; it had no chapel and offered resolutely non-denominational education to some 400 boys from middle- and working-class homes. Its fees were a comparatively modest £13 a term (although at least a quarter of the boys received London County Council scholarships). Its many sports teams and lively debating, art, musical and scientific societies attested to the vibrancy of its social and cultural life.

Harold had taken Spender there for an interview with the headmaster shortly after Violet's death[54] and all sides had announced themselves happy with the outcome. Thus, in 1922, at the age of thirteen, Spender became a day boy in the less-than-successful ρ (Rho) House (one of eight, democratically designated by a mixture of Greek and English letters – β, Δ, λ, M, η, Q, ρ and U) at University College School (U.C.S.), Hampstead.

The headmaster, Guy Kendall, was impressed by his initial interview and slotted him into the fourth form. There, Spender soon found his feet in what, after the agony of his early prep school days, was comparative freedom. Despite the moods and mists of adolescence, he later recalled, he was happy and treated with gentleness and friendship.[55] It seemed just possible that Walter Greatorex's words might actually be coming true. The erstwhile backward son was even proving to be a competent, promising scholar. Surprising everyone, he coped well with a timetable which, with its stress on English, Latin, Greek and, to a lesser extent, mathematics, had changed little since the latter half of the nineteenth century.

On the games field, however, he was less successful. Despite wanting to join in as much as he had with the rough boys of Norfolk, a morbid adolescent preoccupation with all manner of largely imaginary physical shortcomings together with his innate shyness prohibited any real success on the cricket pitch or rugby field. Merely walking down the street was sometimes an ordeal, while turning out in shorts was nothing less than torture.[56] (Unhappy memories of the O.S.H. communal showers also meant that he could never bring himself to use the lavatories at U.C.S. during morning break.) Unsurprisingly, therefore, Spender's name never once featured in the sports reports which filled half of each termly issue of the school magazine, *The Gower* (named after the Bloomsbury street in which U.C.S. had once shared premises with U.C.L.).

But contrast, references to 'S.H. Spender' very quickly began to figure in the detailed accounts of the House and social life of the school which occupied the back pages of the magazine. 'Two promising oil sketches' of his were specially commended in the inter-house art competition for the Arnholz Vase in the summer of 1924.[57] Soon too, the once cowering and timorous Spender was receiving regular mentions in the ρ House Notes: 'Spender has been elected to fill the vacancy on the Electoral College,' it was reported in July 1925. Six months later he had won a stripe in the school's Officer Training Corps (O.T.C.) and been co-opted to the committees of the League of Nations Union (Junior Branch), the Library and the Debating Society.[58]

Suddenly, in the unexpectedly convivial surroundings of U.C.S. Spender had begun to discover himself. In retrospect it seems inevitable that he should have been drawn to the school's Library – in the autumn of 1926 he impulsively presented it with a copy of Samuel Butler's *The Way of All Flesh*[59] – the Debating Society and even the League of Nations Union. But, even though this was still less than a decade after the end of the Great War, his membership of the school's Officer Training Corps, and still more his achieving the rank of lance-corporal, seems unexpected and out of character.

It was; and it still remains so. At fifteen he was 'tall, languid, rather good-looking, an arty-crafty type', according to Derek Scott-Lowe, a friend and near-contemporary at U.C.S. (who subsequently joined the regular Army and retired with the rank of Lieutenant-Colonel).[60] Drill surely would have presented problems every bit as acute as those he faced on the rugby field or in the boys' lavatory. Command and authority must also have come as less than second nature to the would-be Wordsworth.

It is likely, then, that this flirtation with the communal life was short-lived and unsatisfactory. There are no further references to L/Cpl. Spender in *The Gower*; and Scott-Lowe has no recollections of him in the O.T.C. beyond a vague memory of him occasionally turning up at school in khaki uniform. Nevertheless, Spender was certainly among the large contingent of U.C.S. boys who attended the annual O.T.C. camp at Tidworth Park on Salisbury Plain during the late summer of 1925. 'In spite of the rain, most people enjoyed themselves,' *The Gower* commented laconically.[61] Spender did too, in a way; for, rather like the Lake District holiday, the experience indirectly catalysed his literary career.

The March 1926 edition of *The Gower* contained what seems to be his first published poem.[62] 'Camp', ascribed to 'S.H.S.', is a Miltonic (or just possibly Wordsworthian) effusion in fourteen lines, rhymed like a sonnet but technically uncertain, in which he attempted to externalise some of his thoughts about what had gone on at Tidworth Park. It bristles with archaisms ('Can'st, 'O'er', 'maketh', 'Dost thou . . .') and emphatic capital letters, and comes to a bathetic, unsatisfactory conclusion with a final couplet in which the poet asks rhetorically whether anyone else has realised that war is 'a slut'.

It is a definite improvement on his Lakeland ode to Nature, and no better and certainly no worse than any of the other occasional verse published by *The Gower* at this period. (A sonnet, 'The Rowing Rhythm', by one 'G.K.' in the March 1927 edition begins with the words 'Good is it when with muscles tight, the knees/Flung wide, hands gripping, the tense body straight . . .')

———

By the early spring of 1926 Harold had become an infuriating and embarrassing parent. He still insisted on kissing his teenage son goodbye as he left for school in the morning – and on doing so at the front gate, in full view of all the other boys making their way up the hill to U.C.S.[63] When, on one awful occasion, he presented the prizes at the U.C.S. speech-day Spender was mortified to see that the other boys were laughing at his windy rhetoric.[64] Wholly typically too, when Spender once announced that he had finished reading a book by Bernard Shaw, he exploded: 'I have heard of other people having children like that, but I have always prayed God I might be spared!'[65]

In the General Election campaign back in 1923 he had stood (hopelessly and unsuccessfully) as the Liberal candidate for Bath, where of course he had grown up, and dragged the hapless Humphrey and Spender down to help with the canvassing. Harold's slogan was 'Vote for a Wise and Careful Spender', but they rode around the town in a donkey-cart festooned with placards saying 'Vote for Daddy' and were produced at public meetings at the drop of another of Harold's military metaphors. 'I have brought up my reserves!' he announced.[66] Spender winced. Even then he had no desire to be his father's reserve; later he wrote of his contempt for Harold's speeches and public platform voice.[67]

It seems distinctly possible that Harold's disappointment at his son's indifference to politics – symbolically prefigured one night in 1918 when, left in a cab outside No. 10 Downing Street, the nine-year-old boy had relieved himself through the window

and virtually splashed the emerging Prime Minister's shoes[68] –
was at the root of their antipathy. Harold certainly had political
ambitions for his second son and in all seriousness suggested that
he should stop wasting his time writing poetry and reading
books. He should aim to be the Prime Minister – like Asquith
and Lloyd George. (The man who always called himself 'H.S.'
inevitably referred to them as 'H.H.A.' and 'L.G.' respectively.)
Spender considered the notion, lying in bed at night at the age of
eleven or twelve and imagining himself a Boy Wonder, a reborn
William Pitt the Younger holding the House of Commons in
thrall.[69] But eventually he dismissed it out of hand.

For all that he could only take him in small doses, however,
after his mother's death Spender slowly came to love his father
–albeit on his own terms, his increasing maturity allowing him
to recognise and accept Harold's relative failure as a writer, a
father and a man.[70] In the evenings at Frognal he would draw
him obsessively, even though each sketch he made seemed to
give further confirmation that there was a worrying limit to the
Spenders' imagination and sensibility. He could see it in
Harold's face.

By by 1926 he and everyone else at Frognal had also seen – or
been forced to recognise – something else. Harold was seriously
ill. 'These are the words of a dying man,' he had taken to saying
at the end of his homilies,[71] and this time there did seem to be
something behind the rhetoric. Symptoms showed themselves
with worrying rapidity. First it was his teeth; then his feet. A
little later it was his eyes, and he bravely underwent a 'treatment'
during which leeches were placed over them. Nothing, however,
did any good, for in the first weeks of 1926 he was diagnosed as
suffering from Banti's disease, a degenerative condition charac-
terised by anaemia, internal bleeding and the enlargement of the
spleen, which is often associated with an excessive consumption
of alcohol (although there is no direct evidence of this in his
case). Within another few weeks he had been admitted to a
nursing home at Child's Hill, barely two miles away from
Frognal.

Curiously, Spender too was often ill at this time, and indeed he worried that in some dim, psychological way the vague, unidentifiable fevers from which he suffered were related to his feelings about Harold. Was he confined to a room in the isolation ward at the London Fever Hospital[72] as a punishment for disloyalty, treachery even? Or was he somehow empathising with the alternately adored and derided man who was nevertheless his father?

One further index of the precarious, love-hate relationship between ailing father and self-absorbed younger son is worthy of note. Early in April 1926 Harold took Spender for a walk in Kew Gardens, gave him ten pounds (more money than Spender had ever possessed before) and insisted that he and a school-friend went ahead with a walking holiday on Dartmoor. Each intuitively knew – and knew the other knew – that Harold was dying; but Spender went, realising that he would not see his father again, and that somewhere down in Devon a telegram would be waiting for him.[73]

It was. Back at the Mountfield Nursing Home it had quickly been decided to remove Harold's already distended spleen. The operation was carried out on 14 April, but it proved too much of a shock to the patient's sixty-one-year-old constitution. He died of heart failure the following morning, and Spender abandoned his holiday and took the train back to Paddington.

The abrupt removal from his life of his cold, demanding but suddenly loveable father evoked ambivalent feelings; all the more so since he had lost him little more than four years after the expected, but none the less unsettling, death of his mother. Suddenly, at the age of just seventeen, Spender was to all intents and purposes his own man and, except when Michael was home from Gresham's, at least the titular master of the house at No. 10 Frognal.

O welche Lust . . . Suddenly, he no longer had to play up to Harold's Victorian notions of Manliness, Discipline and Duty. No one could cane him or even threaten to do so. He could write, paint, drop his shoulders and generally enjoy himself without being more than normally concerned with Examinations, Scholarships, Firsts and all of Harold's other upper-case shibboleths. Merely being at U.C.S. had cured him of 'un-neccesary unhappiness';[74] now (as he rather unkindly put it in *World Within World*) he was flourishing.[75] After one final bout of what was diagnosed as rheumatic fever which paralysed his legs and confined him to bed for several weeks – he chose to see it as an expiation or necessary 'epilogue' to his relationship with his father[76] – he made a complete recovery and began a new, free life.

On his way back from the funeral, he wrote in a later poem, 'The Public Son of a Public Man', the tears ran down his face. But he had already turned that face against Harold. His father was a failure. He was contemptible. Now he, Stephen, the backward son, was confirming his appointment with fame.[77]

———

He returned to school; and *The Gower* bears spectacular witness to the way in which, in the months immediately following his father's death, Spender began courting that fame. Column after column records how he plunged into everything in which he had previously merely dabbled. He wrote, he painted and – publicly at least – suddenly 'came out of himself'.

His poem 'Camp' had obviously been well-received for, from now on, *The Gower* included increasingly large quantities of his poetry and prose – although this may have had something to do with the fact that, tellingly in itself, the newly orphaned Spender became one of the magazine's four co-editors in the autumn of 1926. His involvement with other out-of-school activities, which brought him into contact with further members of the U.C.S.'s 'arty-crafty' clique, also increased dramatically at this period.

He was happier at school than in what he still thought of as the 'cloistered monastery' at the bottom of the hill; and he threw himself into extra-curricular activity in an attempt to legitimise the time he spent out of the house. He continued to pitch for the elusive Arnholtz Vase, but it always remained just beyond his reach: 'It was interesting to see Spender honouring Victorianism with an oil portrait of its god, but the boldness of its Guevaran perspective clashed badly with his tentative and worried brush strokes.'[78] (Who was that god – Matthew Arnold, Thomas Carlyle, *his father*? Neither the arch prose of *The Gower* nor the school record yields any clues.) It is reasonable to assume too that it was Spender, by now a full committee member, who invited his father's friend H. Wilson Harris, the editor of *Headway* (and twenty years later the author of a biography of J. A. Spender) to address a meeting of the school's League of Nations Union in November 1926.

It was, though, at the fortnightly after-school meetings of the Debating Society that Spender really made his mark. It was as if he was using the platform to conduct a posthumous argument with his father, to prove him wrong. Harold had had his public meetings; Spender had the school hall. As a committee member of the Debating Society he also had a say in its choice of subjects – which ranged from the weighty to the trivial and downright quixotic – and enjoyed something approaching 'front-bench' access to the floor whenever he decided to speak. But, although he assiduously prepared his own contributions and had frequent recourse to notes, he remained a nervous speaker and was not often singled out for special mention in the minutes – he seems to have been as 'tentative and worried' an orator as he was an artist.

There are tantalisingly few accounts of his performance on the floor, but of those which survive none is more vivid than the record of a debate in February 1927. The motion was that 'This House would welcome a Victorian Revival':

> The speeches from the House were chiefly notable for the total inappropriateness of those for the Opposition, and the persistence of *S.H. Spender* in raising imaginary points of order and personal explanation.[79]

It would, for instance, be interesting to know how he voted when, on 20 October 1925, the society debated fascism. General R.B.D. Blakeney, then president of the embryonic, pre-Mosley British fascist movement, proposed the motion that 'This House welcomes the growth of the Fascist Movement in Great Britain' before a packed audience. (Despite his presence, it was still lost by a margin of thirty votes.) What, too, were Spender's thoughts nearly a year later when a motion that 'This House considers Britons to be slaves' was lost by nineteen votes to thirty-three? How did he jump in March 1927 when, at the last meeting he could attend before leaving U.C.S., the Debating Society turned its mind to the idea that 'This House believes in unconditional Pacifism'?

We do know that Spender was keenly interested in the League of Nations and Free Trade at this period.[80] He was also in favour of Chiang Kai-shek and the Chinese Nationalists, and spoke in support of their advance during a poorly attended meeting of the Debating Society at the beginning of February 1927. The motion was carried by thirty votes to eleven. We know too that, a fortnight later, Spender found himself on the losing side when, rather surprisingly perhaps, he chose to second a light-hearted motion which suggested that 'This House believes that bull-fighting is a Sport for Britons':

> Spender told the House that bull-fighting existed in various forms already, such as the lions feeding at the Zoo, the Sub-Monitors in Junior lockers, and principal speakers at debates, and that another form would not make any difference.[81]

Despite this rather flippant advocacy — we can imagine Spender's nervous over-scripting killing the impact of his jokes — the motion was lost by sixteen votes to forty-one.

One further, wholly typical glimpse of the seventeen-year-old Spender also exists. *The Gower* published an extended account of proceedings at the Debating Society on the evening of Tuesday, 19 October 1926. This time it was considering the ostensibly unpromising idea that 'This House tenders its support to Vegetarianism':

> The Proposer, Mr Thorp, cited the classic example of Mr Bernard Shaw, a vegetarian, who is over seventy years of age and is still able to swim two miles at a time. He asked the

House not to be led away by the picture of certain vegetarians who ran about with hair flying, and clothed in djibbahs; and he stated that the quantity of food required by a vegetarian could be grown in two-fifths of the space required to pasture sufficient meat for a meat-eater.

Spender opposing, startled the House by declaring that he had been converted by the proposer's speech. Later he quoted an eminent scientist to prove that plants suffer as much pain as animals. Clark pointed out that vegetarianism was more hygienic; while Wellington, who deplored the action of the opposer, complained that if no animals were killed the animal species would become more powerful than the human.

[The motion] was eventually carried by 28 votes to 18.[82]

This is the authentic voice of the young Spender; diffident and deferential – while simultaneously demanding to be heard. Its unique characteristic note of innocence, vulnerability and occasional *naïveté* – a legacy of Harold's paternal dogmatism – would resound through his work for the next thirty years: *I think continually of those who were truly great* is the definitive statement of self-deprecation.

For the moment, however, its only outlet was the columns of *The Gower*. Indeed, it is the dominant voice in the last two editions with which Spender was concerned. For, though still silent on all matters sporting, 'S.H.S' came to excel at that other chore of the school magazine editor, the obsequious or sharply rebarbative internal comment on the school's full-dress plays and Christmas concerts. In March 1927, for instance, he reviewed two plays by Mordaunt Shairp, a teacher in the English department and an aspiring – but ultimately unsuccessful – professional dramatist.

The Bend in the Road had been given a single, Sunday-night professional performance at the Apollo Theatre in the West End on 30 January. Spender and his co-reviewer 'R.K.N.B.' duly turned up with their notebooks – and then turned in some dull and uncontentious copy about a 'startling' play and 'a very fine performance on the part of actors, author and the producer, Miss Edith Craig'.

Spender was not, however, so beholden to his betters when he gave his opinions of Shairp's other play *The Stranger*, which had been the school's Christmas production the previous December. Shairp himself had loudly puffed it in the previous edition of the magazine as 'more elaborate than anything we have attempted before [. . .] a step further towards the ideal of a School entertainment provided entirely by the School'.[83]

'S.H.S.' disregarded all that and described what he saw. The play's disarming simplicity did little to hide weaknesses in its construction, he wrote: 'Were it not for the anticlimax provided by the entrance of the Doctor, [the] rousing end of Act I and the contrast of the calm sanity of the beginning of Act II would be above criticism [. . .] It is a pity the epilogue was not a prologue.'

Fittingly and inevitably, the March 1927 issue of *The Gower*, the last to which Spender contributed, also included a couple of his poems. In all probability used as no more than a neat page-filler, 'To —, with Her Violin' was his third public essay in sonnet-form. It was a neat summing-up of his work to date. Solemn in mood, Spender offered to play his anonymous muse 'an archaic measure' or, if she preferred, to try to play something on 'Milton's instrument'.

Far more technically assured, 'A Byronic Fragment' filled more than a page and a half of the magazine. Its nine eight-line stanzas describe 'Don Juan in Hell' and 'The Solemn Service of Admission'. Ostensibly fragments from 'one of the later Cantos of the incomplete *Don Juan*' which had been 'discovered during the recent excavations and rebuilding at Newstead Abbey', they are presented as part of a (probably fictional) work-in-progress. 'Our Editor' was expanding them 'with the object of eventually completing Byron's work, only in a more edifying manner; a task for which he feels eminently qualified'.

This confidently up-beat squib brought to an apt and promising end the first chapter of Spender's literary career, for by the time it appeared he had already left U.C.S. He had long-since sloughed off his 'backwardness' and, as far as University College

School was concerned, matured into a committed, dedicated student. He had passed his General Schools matriculation examination in July 1925, entered U.C.S.'s élite 'Modern' sixth form (where he accompanied Derek Scott-Lowe to Greek tutorials in the headmaster's study)[84] and by the beginning of 1927 he had been offered a place at University College, Oxford.

He was gone, but not forgotten. In the Library his leaving-gifts —copies of *The Mercury Book* and the newly published *Satirical Poems* of Siegfried Sassoon — kept his name alive; while, as we shall see, *The Gower* continued to publish occasional dispatches chronicling his Oxford career. For the moment, however, it contented itself with a dignified 'Valete' which delicately caught the note of mutual sadness at his departure:

HOUSE NOTES ρ: Spender left us last Term, and we feel sure that we are even more sorry to lose him than he was at leaving.[85]

TWO

'Away from the Women at Last!'

In *The Backward Son* he called her Mrs Harding and gave her a comic, working-class way of speaking.[1] In *World Within World* – and, we must assume, in real life – she was Mrs Alger, general servant at The Bluff and the enthusiastic, broad-bosomed purveyor of countless calumnies.[2] Whoever, whatever, she was only one of many euphemistically labelled 'girls' who ran the lives of the Spenders both in Norfolk and in London.

Away from the women at last . . . Harold's boyishly triumphant cry on the beach at Sheringham must have drawn piping echoes from the throats of Spender, Michael and Humphrey. For, not quite rich enough for the uniformed obsequiousness of a butler, a footman, a coachman/chauffeur or any other male servant above the rank of gardener – apart, of course, from Harold's long-time secretary Captain Devoto – like so many others, the family was conspicuously hag-ridden throughout Spender's childhood.

In the climate of the time, a proper complement of maids, cooks, nurses and governesses was, of course, necessary. For a professional man like Harold in an age in which a general servant could be hired for 10s. (50p) a week (plus board) it was also affordable. But, particularly in the years before Violet's death, the Spenders do seem to have regarded the small army of lower-class misses who 'did for them' with what now seems unacceptable disdain. They were treated as little more than disposable accessories, and dismissed and replaced with bewildering rapidity. The majority were engaged (one assumes by Violet), but then abruptly dispensed with following the discovery of some 'unsuitability'.[3]

Only two stayed the course for any length of time. Bertha and her younger sister Ella had joined the family at Sheringham after leaving (or possibly being poached from) positions in a nearby house. They were to remain with the Spenders for the next fifteen years – and linger as a couple of off-stage Eumenides in Spender's life until the early 1940s[4] – forever battling against dust, unwashed hands and any sign of physical or moral slackness. After moving with the family to Hampstead they were virtually regarded – and certainly came to regard themselves – as honorary Spenders. The house in Frognal was 'home', they said; Ella was even reduced to floods of tears when one of the family cats died.

Thus, after the successive deaths of Violet and Harold, it was inevitable that the sisters came to play a key role in the household. Michael early on taught Bertha and Ella the deference due to him, but as far as the younger children were concerned they assumed the roles of benevolent despots, supervising every aspect of life. Bertha cooked the meals while Ella dusted and swept and acted as chaperone whenever one of their young charges ventured out. They paid all the household bills; and when, much later, Spender took to staying out late at night, one or other would sit up and await his return: even at the age of seventeen he was not trusted with a front-door key.

They were a formidable duo; but although Violet had good-naturedly referred to them as a single entity – 'Berthella' – even the young Spender realised that Bertha and Ella had separate and very definite identities. Bertha was, in her own way, a New Woman. Opinionated, *Daily-Mail*-reading, she dipped into Harold's copies of the latest works of Arnold Bennett, H.G. Wells and John Galsworthy. She went to the theatre and enjoyed the symphonies of Beethoven, whether heard on the wireless at 'home' or in the concert hall. Complementing her perfectly, Ella was more demure, less forthright. Like so many of her generation, she had lost her fiancé in the Great War and – although she was later to astonish everyone at Frognal by marrying the local postman – she had to some extent retreated into herself. With her frequently pursed lips but seemingly endless patience, the

children found her at once more lovable but more infuriating
than the outspoken Bertha.

For all their identification with the family, however,
'Berthella' were never truly instrumental in the upbringing of the
children. After Harold's death they quite literally became the
agents (often, the children thought, the secret agents) of Violet's
mother, the formidable Hilda Schuster. Hilda, although already
in her late sixties, had quickly assumed responsibility for the
well-being of her grandchildren. Bertha and Ella received their
instructions by telephone from her in the morning and called
back every evening to report on the children's progress. (Harold
had early on decided to subscribe to the telephone service: the
Frognal number, HAMpstead 3137, was included in his *Who's
Who* entry.)

Further circumscribing their influence was Mrs Schuster's
decision to appoint a younger live-in companion for the
children. Christine's needs seem to have been uppermost in her
mind in this. The shy, impressionable eighteen-year-old was
studying domestic science at college at this time and obviously
needed a confidante and chaperone. The younger boys too, their
grandmother decided, would benefit from the presence of a
responsible chum-cum-governess. And Hilda knew precisely the
right 'gel' for the job.

Never a woman to waste an opportunity, through her
impeccable social connections – she was after all the daughter of
the late Sir Herman Weber – she had already 'head-hunted'
Caroline, the niece of her old friend Helen Alington. Caroline
happened to be working in Lausanne in Switzerland in the spring
of 1926, but that was no obstacle for the indefatigable Hilda.
For her own part too, this unknown but putative governess was
so intrigued by the idea of mothering the four teenagers that she
immediately returned to London.

According to her memories of the months she spent at Frognal
(which Spender includes almost verbatim as a curious third-
person digression in *World Within World*)[5] Caroline was
initially interviewed by Hilda at Piccadilly Circus underground
station, then taken on to Hampstead to be introduced to her

charges. Only two were at home. Christine, was 'almost ill with apprehension and shyness'; while Spender, then seventeen, gave her 'the limpest of handshakes'. Unnerved, Caroline neverthe- less stayed on for tea, during which Hilda regaled her with tales about the two remaining members of the family: Michael was nineteen and 'very clever, oh so clever' (he had indeed just won a scholarship to Balliol College, Oxford); sixteen-year-old Humphrey was unfortunately away at boarding school.

Despite finding the whole domestic regime at Frognal (quite understandably) 'fantastic', Caroline accepted the position when it was finally offered to her. She moved in and rapidly became a sort of Mary Poppins to the teenaged but socially and emotionally infant Spender and Christine in particular. Respec- tively overcoming languid indifference and initial nerves, they soon grew to like and even love her. She was certainly very different from any other adult they had encountered. Free- thinking – shockingly, she wrote off the great J.A. as 'a mere businessman' – and half-French, she related to them as neither Harold and Violet nor even Bertha and Ella never could.

Spender drew her as compulsively as he had once drawn his father and one day summoned up all his courage to tell her that he liked the Elgin Marbles and the works of Michelangelo. From his recollection of the incident in *World Within World*[6] it is possible to deduce that this was also an admission that he was 'artistic', and all that that implied.

For all her benign, civilising influence, however, even Caroline was never more than a Miss Prism to Hilda Schuster's domineer- ing Lady Bracknell. Indeed, one of her principal duties was to ensure that Christine and Spender got themselves across London and down through Kensington Gardens every Sunday in good time for lunch or tea and what amounted to an afternoon interrogation by their grandmother.

———

Following her husband's death in 1924, Hilda had stayed on in the flat to which they had retired. No.33 Albert Court was on the fourth floor of a large mansion block only yards away from the rear of the Royal Albert Hall. The whole building was (and still remains) a monument to high Victorian style, with columns, dark panelling and potted palms adding to the gloom of the echoing common areas; but even in 1924 it was a good, 'fashionable' address.

Wealthy even when judged by the Spenders' comfortable, £2,000-a-year standards, within her spacious flat Hilda nevertheless lived under a regime of self-imposed parsimony which would have shocked and appalled the more socially conscious of her neighbours and fellow-tenants had they ever been invited beyond the front door. Except on the rarest of occasions the flat remained unheated, and its long corridors were lit by dim oil lamps to save electricity. Hilda herself rarely ventured down them, and camped out in one corner of the drawing-room where she sat, for preference, on a three-legged stool. Even when she was entertaining her grandchildren she – and they – ate little more than stale bread, mildewy cakes and bruised and rotting fruit.[7]

But, though not herself Jewish, and despite an undoubted eccentricity, after Harold's death she quickly became a sort of honorary *bubeleh* to her grandchildren, and to Spender in particular. (Psychologists might see a connection here with the fact that she had lost her favourite son, Alfred, in the Great War.) Intuitively, she had understood the ambivalence of Spender's relationship with Harold, the lack of real communication between the sensitive sixteen-year-old and his increasingly crusty father. Unobtrusively, she had also done her best to mitigate its worse effects, surreptitiously siding with her grandson against her son-in-law.

Now she had *carte blanche* to do with him as she liked. A thin, bird-like woman who only ever dressed in black, she was instinctively liberal, open, enthusiastic and indulgent. Following her son's death she had become a Quaker and seems to have spent more on a succession of lame ducks than she did on herself. It is hardly too much to say that Spender quickly became one of them; another bruised and wounded victim she could take to her bosom.

'Dear Stephen, say something quickly to shock me,' she would cry; and Spender would comply. Alone with her at the icy flat in Albert Court, he'd talk about religion, the books he had been reading, the paintings he admired and even sex in a way which would have been impossible with Harold or even Violet. In return, his redoubtable grandmother took him off to art galleries and, when Harold was safely out of town, to 'modern' productions of Shakespeare, Ibsen, Chekhov and even Strindberg at little clubs and theatres in outlying and distinctly unfashionable suburbs.

Inevitably, Spender became very close to her and would later cite his friendship with Hilda as one of the key relationships in his life.[8] Suddenly someone was taking him seriously. Hilda did not laugh at his ambition to be a poet, or perhaps an artist – she merely warned that in either career he would fall into bad company and quite probably starve – and despite her own misgivings she interceded on his behalf when his uncle J.A. Spender threatened to toughen Spender up with the imposition of something like Harold's no-treat regime. She was not shocked by the beginnings of his obsessive preoccupation with his German-Jewish roots. She was herself of mixed German and Danish blood; but what did mixed blood matter, Stephen – what did anything matter?

Maybe there would not have been this bond between grandmother and grandson if his mother, or even his father, had lived longer (although their marked similarity of temperament suggests that there would). Maybe things would then have turned out differently. As it was, however, during the six-and-a-half years which separated his mother's death and his own departure for Oxford, Spender's character was increasingly and effectively shaped by Hilda Schuster.

She made it her business to know exactly what he was doing, shamelessly exploiting the loyalty of 'Berthella', Caroline and a network of friends and contacts for this purpose. Sometimes it seemed to Spender that he could not do anything which would not, sooner or later, be reported back to his grandmother: *Dear boy, I hear that last week you were at Kew Gardens . . .*

His protests, however – if he ever got around to making them – were in a muted minor key. Bizarrely, his elderly grandmother was providing an entrée, or at least the entry-fee, into a seductive bohemian world of little theatres, struggling artists and lame ducks.

Thus Spender was content to put up with the ostensible indignity of accompanying her on a holiday in Switzerland. Since he records that this was just after his recovery from rheumatic fever, in all probability the trip took place in the summer of 1926, during the school holidays before his final, truncated year at U.C.S. His one-paragraph account of it in *World Within World*[9] yields little of interest, however; although the sheer reticence of its phrasing in itself suggests that the holiday (apparently Spender's first brush with 'abroad') was not the happiest of experiences.

She accompanied me on every walk ... Spender recalls nothing more than that Hilda was always by his side, proffering as lunch the uneaten bread rolls she had earlier removed from the breakfast table and relentlessly questioning him about 'personal relationships'. Spender was seventeen at this time and seemingly as worried about these (or the frustrating lack of them) as his grandmother. But how could he find them when she and her formidably correct circle never for a moment let him out of their sight? Harold and Violet had kept him from children who were rough; now, misguidedly, even Hilda was wrapping him in a cloak of Frognal respectability as he tried to savour the more adult pleasures of Europe.

———

It was the same nine months later. It was Hilda who suggested that Spender, having obtained his place at Oxford, should leave U.C.S. and spend the months between Easter and September 1927 living abroad with some suitable family and learning a 'useful' language. (Why do both the chaperoned holiday in Switzerland and the whole concept of this later foreign sojourn seem more suitable for a debutante in need of 'finish' than they do for an impatient, if immature, eighteen-year-old boy like Spender?)

Germany would be convenient, Hilda suggested, and, given his background, appropriate. Still under the influence of the half-French Caroline, however, Spender had other ideas. At the time – and much to his later chagrin – Germany and German did not interest him at all. He wanted to go to France and, if he had to learn any language, to learn French.

Hilda was appalled. To her and to many of her generation, France was the enemy and the root cause of all the suffering which Europe had undergone in the previous two decades. France was Paris, *boulevardiers*, the Moulin Rouge, immodesty, immorality and all the shockingly un-German *loucheness* of the Left Bank.

But Spender was insistent and slowly won his grandmother round: at any rate an acceptable compromise was reached. For young Stephen to stay alone in Paris was obviously out of the question. But her Quaker friends had assured Hilda that French provincial towns were quite different from Paris. Her grandson would not be in any danger if he stayed at, say, Nantes . . . where, it so happened, the Protestant *pasteur* would be very willing to accommodate the grandson of *la quakeresse anglaise*.

Chaperoned by Hilda and Humphrey, then, it was to Nantes, a port and semi-industrialised provincial capital on the estuary of the river Loire (and as far as his grandmother was concerned a satisfactory 250 miles south-west of Paris) to which Spender travelled in the spring of 1927.

After the departure of Humphrey and his grandmother, however, France did not live up to his expectations. Nantes itself proved to be grey and provincial. Many of its inhabitants seemed equally dull; nothing like Caroline at all. Drunks lay senseless in the streets of the port area, while in the nearby countryside the 'peasants' were quite different from the country-people of the Norfolk of his childhood. At the Lycée Clemenceau, where Spender attended some lessons – including what he felt was, for his sole benefit, an unnecessarily apologetic course on the Napoleonic wars – his fellow-students were lumpish and crude, their scatalogical comments about menstruation and the female body even worse than the stone-like words of the rough boys of Sheringham. Frequently almost incapacitated by hay-fever, not even the *pasteur* could lift the gloom. Naturally melancholic, if anything he actually increased it by regularly coming out with doleful couplets from Baudelaire and other French writers in honour of *le jeune poète anglais*.

Soon Spender was as lonely and as desperately homesick as he had ever been during his pre-school days. Nantes – and, for all he knew, the whole of the rest of France – was insufferably 'bourgeois', he believed (and it was to be several decades before he could rid himself of this notion). In a vain attempt to overcome his loneliness he retreated into himself, just as he had at the O.S.H. In his mind he created a variety of imaginary companions, beautiful young poets and *sympathiques* French youths, with whom he fantasised engaging in all manner of homo– and heterosexual acts in the fields and under hedges.[10] He cried; he took himself off for protracted walks in the countryside or along the banks of the Loire – and he wrote long anguished letters home to Caroline and civilisation.

It was these which persuaded those back at Frognal that all was not well. Finally, Spender's pleas were acceded to, and he was removed from Nantes and the snuffling *pasteur*. Caroline knew of a *pension* outside Lausanne in Switzerland and, for all that it involved a journey across the entire breadth of hostile France and even a dangerous change of trains in Paris, it was decided that Spender should go there.

He was himself a very willing party to the decision, not least because of the link between Lausanne and Caroline. And, almost unexpectedly, for various reasons he found the *pension* entirely to his liking. It offered spectacular views right across Lake Geneva (Lac Leman) to the distant peaks of the Bernese Oberland and the southern Alps. (These, together with memories of that Lake District holiday ten years previously, were later to contribute to his own, specific *parole* in the mountainous *langue* of what would come to be called the Audenesque.)[11]

More immediately, this stay at Lausanne also brought Spender into violent and abrupt contact with the ambivalent sexual feelings of which he had been aware for the previous couple of years. Among his fellow-guests at the *pension* was another English boy whom in *World Within World* he refers to as 'D—'.[12] He was 'beautiful', but no rival to the Shelley-Ariel fantasies of the lonely days at Nantes and certainly no early precursor of the Truly Great. Nevertheless, Spender was obsessed by him. Upper-middle-class but unintelligent, provocative but not quite 'rough' enough to jump-start his already overheating libido, 'D—' remained a thoroughly unsettling presence.

Fain I would climb, but fear I should fall . . . Ostensibly so well suited, the pair spent a fair amount of time together, certainly enough for Spender to come to a patronising, and ultimately selfish, assessment of 'D—' 's 'weaknesses'. Although, if we are to believe *World Within World* – and in this instance there seems no reason not to – nothing happened. In the parlance of the day, no 'real friendship' developed between them. Sheer chance had brought them together; nothing should have been more propitious, except that Spender was trapped in the *cul-de-sac* of his own emotions. Lausanne meant Caroline (then, coincidentally, seriously ill in a London hospital) and, indirectly, the mother he had hardly known. How could he now renege on all that? He admitted to himself that he was attracted to the powerfully available 'D—'. He knew that this was passion, as far as it went . . . but he could not bring himself to take it any farther, and at some time before the early autumn he returned to London to prepare himself for Oxford.

———

Much has been written about the Oxford of the 1920s. Then – or so the story goes – the university was, quite literally, the second home of the so-called Brideshead Generation. So it was, particularly in 1922 and 1923 and 1924.

They were the years in which (as Humphrey Carpenter

marvellously recounts in his study of *The Brideshead Genera-tion*) the likes of Harold Acton, Brian Howard, Cyril Connolly, John Betjeman, Evelyn Waugh and a whole tribe of wealthy, Eton-educated young men gave set-piece luncheons for thirty of their friends. They were the years Waugh later recalled in *Brideshead Revisited* when no one set much store by academic work – having completely exasperated his tutor, Waugh himself spent a 'blissful period' in which he received no teaching at all – and everyone who was anyone was bent on pleasure, fun and making his mark. It was, after all, Acton who invented or at least popularised the wide, flapping trousers which became known as 'Oxford Bags'.

There were drinking clubs, dining clubs, luncheon clubs, magazines, country-house weekends and parties, parties, parties. The cosmopolitan Acton was very much the *genius loci*. From his fussy, cluttered rooms in a hitherto unfashionable neo-Gothic extension to Christ Church college ('The House') he masterminded a resurgence of the camp Victorian values which had abruptly disappeared from Oxford in the weeks following the trial of Oscar Wilde in 1895. Suddenly, under his tutelage the university became a private joke, its most cherished institutions demeaned with silly names: to Acton and his cronies the Union was the 'Ugger' and the Martyrs' Memorial in the middle of St Giles the 'Maggers' Memugger'.

The languid indifference of the monied nineteenth-century undergraduate was rather laboriously aped on the pages of Acton's magazine *Oxford Broom* (a successor to his earlier *Eton Broom*) and at the Hypocrites, a student club in St Aldgate's. Originally no more than the haunt of oiks with 'unshaven chins and beer-stained corduroys',[13] Acton quickly tinselled and transformed this 'ramshackle' establishment into a more suit-able meeting-place for his kind of people. Its drag parties quickly became famous – then notorious; and, to all but the most *au fait*, Acton's set equally quickly became almost indistinguishable from the more ordinary neo-Aesthetes who minced up and down St Aldgate's and The High. It was all very bewildering:

> I used to think they passed away
>   With rather naughty '99,
> Those gaudy insects of a day –
>   Your pardon, the mistake was mine.
> O, la la! the Aesthete!
> I've met one in the street . . .
> I'm glad there's someone still who '*yearns*',
>   And dotes on Dowson and on Wilde . . . [14]

Even more than money, homosexuality was, of course, at the root of it all. Despite the existence of a few discreetly placed women's colleges, in the twenties Oxford was still a predominantly male enclave. 'Real friendships' flourished, just as they had always tended to in public school dormitories. And even undergraduates who were temperamentally unsuited to it (like John Betjeman, who went up to Magdalen College in 1925) found that, in Alan Pryce-Jones's words, it was '*chic* to be queer'.[15] According to Tom Driberg, it was not uncommon to see even Evelyn Waugh 'and another [man, rolling] on a sofa with (as one of them said later) their "tongues licking each other's tonsils" '.[16] (The sexually rapacious Driberg, who had been at school with Waugh, predictably went one better and, while a student at Christ Church, maintained a relationship with a young don he had met in a public lavatory.)

Acton and his set were dubbed 'girl men' (a reference to Proust's 'men-women'?) and by 1925 had become a well-known Oxford phenomenon. So much so that in October that year *Cherwell* – with the more Acton-allied *Isis*, the most widely read of the university's plethora of student magazines – felt able to publish a magnificently ironic diatribe under the headline 'GIRL MEN AT CAMBRIDGE':

> Oxford is not easily roused, [it declared] but she cannot afford
> to lose her only claim to public attention. Girl men are hers,
> and hers alone; they have provided three dozen special
> reporters with their daily bread for at least six months. [. . .] I
> received a cutting from a newspaper in India in which an
> eyewitness described how he actually saw one undergraduate

produce a stick of lip-salve and paint the lips of his companion! Shall Cambridge take this away from us? Never![17]

By October 1927 when Spender arrived at University College (despite the name, there was no connection with either University College London or the University College School) 'the Acton period' and the Brideshead Generation were little more than memories, albeit fond ones in many quarters. Acton and his circle had for the most part already abandoned the dreaming spires of Oxford and left with – or in many cases without – their degrees, to peddle their special brand of champagne-scholasticism among the more seductive flesh-pots of London. Acton himself went down in 1925 with an inglorious Fourth in Modern Languages. Waugh, Connolly and Anthony Powell all took Thirds, while Brian Howard failed altogether first time round and John Betjeman was actually sent down for repeatedly failing the compulsory biblical test familiarly known as 'Divvers'.

Things had calmed down – 'gone dead', according to Brian Howard. The colleges and quads were quiet. The proctors had moved in on the Hypocrites. The Oxford Bags were not *quite* so baggy, and Acton was no longer to be heard reciting his own poems through a megaphone. (His first collection *Aquarium* had been published early in 1923, when he was still in his second term.) Nevertheless, like a pint of beer which has lost its head – or, more appropriately perhaps, a glass of champagne which has lost its bubbles – beneath the surface in 1927 things were very much the same as they had been in 1924 or 1925. The breathless hush on the High was broken by the wheezing of the steam-lorries whose to-ing and fro-ing from the industrial plants on the fringes of the city took no account of term dates, and still less of what even the new-conservative class of '27 regarded as the elastic division between night and day. [18]

But there were still public school cliques, exclusive supper clubs and a social hierarchy every bit as elaborate as those pertaining in London or the grander country houses. Indeed, it was to take another twenty years before there was any discernible change in the demographic profile of Oxford (and Cambridge) students – and another thirty before that change could even begin to be called fundamental.

Many of the members of that class of '27 were thus quite prepared for the brilliant world which still existed beyond their 'oaks', the doors of their 'sets' (of rooms) which *could* be firmly closed, or 'sported', against all callers and the cocktail-and-conversational lure of the Brideshead side of things. 'Oxford was all that I expected – and more so,' Hugh Corbett-Palmer, who arrived at New College in 1927, recalled. 'We'd been groomed for the Brideshead life; although after public school all we really responded to was the freedom.' That was intoxicating enough. But everyone knew that the spirit of Acton was still close to hand: ' "Brideshead" was no more than a short train ride away. Oxford was an extension of London, and vice versa. We *relied* on the 10.58 back from Euston.'[19]

Inevitably though, Spender found himself totally at sea during his first few weeks at Univ. Despite the fact that his elder brother Michael had gone up to Balliol two years ahead of him and must have told him something about what lay in store – it is pleasant to imagine Michael arriving home for 'vacs' sporting Oxford Bags in just the same way in which he had earlier worn the O.S.H. blazer – Spender was later to admit that university life was not quite what he had imagined or hoped for.[20]

Michael was, anyway, out of touch with the 'real' Oxford. Not only was he a physicist and studying engineering, he frequently castigated his brother's 'inefficiency' and general lack of what he would have been far too academic to have called common sense:

Compared with his brothers, Michael appeared rugged and masculine and altogether less sensitive, but he had his share of the Spender good looks. Christopher [Isherwood] had met him briefly before this and had then been inclined to accept

Stephen's view of him. Stephen, the hypersensitive, had made fun of Michael for having claimed that he had never in his life held a subjective opinion. Michael certainly was a pragmatic type of scientist who made a cult of efficiency and despised the lack of it in others. However, he was also aware of his own limitations and more modest than Stephen would admit.[21]

In *World Within World* Spender rather disingenuously implied that he was expecting Oxford to be a classless, meritocratic fraternity, and went on to describe how shaken he was when he found himself among 'public-school boys', and actually rubbing shoulders with a prince, a count and an American Rhodes scholar. Charles Ryder felt similarly *declassé* at a luncheon-party given in Sebastian Flyte's Oxford rooms in Waugh's *Brideshead Revisited* (1945): 'There were three Etonian freshmen, mild, elegant, detached young men who had all been to a dance in London the night before, and spoke of it as though it had been the funeral of a near but unloved kinsman. Each as he came into the room made first for the plovers' eggs . . .'

Spender's unpreparedness was, however, only another illustration of his *naïveté*. By his own admission, in the autumn of 1927 the blond, six-foot-two-inch, rather attractive eighteen-year-old who arrived at Oxford — where Louis MacNeice thought him a 'towering angel not quite sure if he was fallen'[22] — was curious, elated, but also humourless, self-conscious and guilt-ridden.[23]

More so even than an 'ordinary' freshman like Corbett-Palmer, then, he was plainly going to be no new Acton. He had neither the money, nor, at least at the beginning, the nous to cut a dash. While Corbett-Palmer assiduously sought out 'congenial places to drink' (students were still forbidden to enter public houses) and ways to circumvent his college's midnight curfew, Spender was too nervous even to enter a pub unaccompanied.

To start with, this insecurity seems only to have been compounded by his membership of the large but relatively undistinguished University College. He might have consoled himself with the thought that the poet Percy Bysshe Shelley was

Univ's most famous son (although in 1811, like some proto-Betjeman, he too had been thrown out of Oxford before taking his degree!) but socially, geographically and intellectually in 1927 Univ was rather out of the swim of things.

It was at the wrong end of the High Street — only Magdalen was farther off the House-High-and-Aldgate's track — and, if anything, it had a reputation for hearty sporting endeavour rather than academic or cultural distinction. It was the natural home of Waugh's 'muddied oafs' and 'flannelled fools' rather than a sequestered ivory tower for sensitive poets. Somewhat irreverently it had even been dubbed 'the pub on the High'; Acton would never have been seen dead on its lawns, or anywhere else for that matter. In Spender's time it did still accommodate one or two of Acton's sort of 'aesthete' — you could recognise them because they called each other 'dear' — but they had long-since been marginalised by its rowing-and-rugby, beer-swilling, First XV ethos as much as they had by time. One year Univ alone provided six members of the Oxford rowing Eight.

Because of all this, Univ was only (in Spender's word) a 'middling' college. It was a seat or two below the salt from the likes of New College, Balliol, Magdalen, Christ Church and even 'respected' smaller colleges such as Wadham and Oriel, but still a definite cut above then unfashionable places such as Keble and Brasenose.[24] Hugh Corbett-Palmer agreed with this assessment, independently volunteering that, in the late twenties, 'the real Oxford' (Spender calls it 'the University') comprised 'Magdalen, the House [Christ Church] and New; all the bright chaps were at Magdalen — and Balliol, of course.'[25]

Inter-college rivalries and pretensions were important: only a few years earlier Evelyn Waugh had hated the social obscurity of his own Hertford College ('respectable but rather dreary') while Compton MacKenzie had already sealed the fate of the hapless Lincoln College. In *Sinister Street* (1914) he had had a student ask: 'I don't know where Lincoln is. Have you got a map or something?'

But, as ever, for Spender there were further, personal

resonances to all this. It cannot have escaped his notice that he was up at Univ, just as his father had been before him: meanwhile, his elder brother was amongst the stars at Balliol – just as his father's elder brother had been. (Making matters even worse, Spender's cousin was hob-nobbing with half a dozen Old Etonians at New.) Was Spender too to be condemned to a second-fiddle role, another plodding Harold to Michael's eminent J.A.?

He seems to have floundered, confronted by the seeming inevitability of it all, in his first few weeks. But thereafter, something of the spirit which had carried him through his time at U.C.S. began to make itself felt. It is even discernible in the columns of *The Gower*, whose anonymous or pseudonymous spies regularly sent intelligences back to U.C.S. on the doings of their fellow Old Gowers. Thus, as early as December 1927, 'O.U.O.G.' (Oxford University Old Gower) was reporting that:

> Forrester is in the quiet stage of Oxford intellectualism, seeking truth in the smoky recesses of the coffee hells. In the rampant stage is S. H. Spender, incompatibly of Univ. He doesn't care for it, but works off something to do with his psychology by writing for the *Isis*.

Spender could only have been at Oxford for a matter of weeks when that copy was written. But the fact that he was 'rampant' at all suggests that very soon after his arrival he had once again felt the gnawings of fame. Acton, Howard and Connolly had used Oxford and *Isis* to make their mark – well, so could he; and he was certainly not going to let Michael stand in his way. (In this connection, it is perhaps not irrelevent to note that in the later, strongly autobiographical poem 'The Furies'[26] Spender twice implicitly described himself as the 'only son'; once, indeed, as 'the handsome only son'. Nor can it have been entirely coincidental that, when – still later – he came to organise the *Collected Poems*, he used 'The Furies' as the centre-piece of a section entitled 'Ambition'.)

He was not one of the 'public-school boys', compared with whom he still felt inferior, but he quickly and surprisingly efficiently succeeded in creating his own image. In *World Within World* he describes how he put up prints of paintings by Van Gogh, Gauguin and Paul Klee in his noisy rooms overlooking the High, took to wearing a provocative red tie and, whenever the weather was good enough, made sure he was seen sitting on a cushion in Univ's honey-coloured quad reading poetry.[27] It was, he knew, pure affectation. But it served its purpose; it got him noticed. He survived a half-hearted attempt to break up his rooms (he read William Blake's poetry aloud, to the bewilderment of the intruding hearties who did no more than chop up his red tie) and emerged intact to carry on playing what he claims he knew all along was a 'role'.

Henceforth, Spender decided, he was to be the 'mad Socialist poet';[28] all red ties and revolutionary talk, his own man and no quarter given to history or fashion. In July 1929 he began keeping a journal, the first paragraphs of which he reproduced in *World Within World* (and subsequently in *The Temple*). His only purpose in life was to write, he told himself. Shamefully, he was too dependent on other people, too worried about what they thought or did. He had to make himself an independent, sentient being and put all his thoughts down on paper.

When, with Louis MacNeice, Spender co-edited *Oxford Poetry 1929* this separateness was again apparent. An otherwise blank page in the book announced:

DEDICATED

Neither to 'POESY'
Nor to the 'ZEITGEIST'

But it was not an easy game to play – ideally, Spender should have been a thorough-going Acton, with funds and friends to match – and how long he should continue playing it, and quite how far he really believed in it, were questions which were to exercise, irritate and finally defeat him over the course of the next decade.

‗‗‗‗‗‗

As the weeks went by and term succeeded term – Michaelmas giving way to Hilary, Hilary to the long warm days of Trinity – Spender began to relax into the sybaritic (post-) Brideshead side of things, adapting it as necessary to suit his own style and pocket. He read poetry; Shakespeare and the other Elizabethans, Blake and the Romantics, T. S. Eliot and the moderns; 'little else'. He went for long, lonely bicycle rides in the countryside. Occasionally, when he could find someone to go with him, he ventured into a discreet pub and got discreetly drunk. 'Cornflower' noticed all this and dutifully reported back to the editor of *The Gower*:

> Univ, incidentally, also contains, as best it may, an O.G. [Old Gower] trio – the aforementioned Langdon, together with Spender and Holmes. Of these latter, the first aspires both physically and mentally, and is so bracing . . .[29]

Work did not particularly interest him; nor did he enjoy it. He had come up to Oxford with the intention of reading History, but quickly discovered that the plethora of dates and facts he was obliged to learn conflicted with his new *soi-disant* role as a creative artist: as well as bombarding *Isis* with material, at this period he was experimenting with some (now apparently lost) stream-of-consciousness prose pieces inspired by James Joyce's *Ulysses*[30] – few dates and facts in that! (One wonders, incidentally – Spender does not say – how he had come to read *Ulysses* by 1927. First published in Paris in 1922, the novel was banned in Britain and the United States until 1937. 'Samizdat' versions were circulating among the literati during the twenties – Virginia Woolf famously described it as 'the scratching of the pimples on the body of the bootboy at Claridges' as early as August 1922 –but it is difficult to imagine how Spender could have got hold of one.)

Disillusioned by History, he should, he knew, have changed

Schools and read English; but for some reason he did not. Instead, he opted for Politics, Philosophy and Economics (P.P.E.), a subject requiring an even greater application of discipline and logical thought than History. He hated it, and in particular the reductionist way in which John Stuart Mill, Locke, Hume, Kant and all the rest were knocked down in tutorial after tutorial.[31] Nevertheless, he ploughed on; it was too late to change again.

Years later he was to admit that he had always been 'ineducable' – no matter that at the time he was speaking he was Emeritus Professor of English Literature at University College London. He regretted the fact, but went on to explain that right through his life he had been able to absorb only those things which had interested him.[32]

Meanwhile, after facing out the Univ hearties he discovered that he had acquired a certain position within the college. If he was not exactly popular, Spender was at least tolerated and began making friends at Univ – the college's ineffectual Master, the pioneering educationist Sir Michael Sadler, disapproved of his students having too much contact with men from other colleges.

Archie Campbell, Sidney Thorp and Alec Grant, all of whom are mentioned in World Within World, were second- or third-year students. Thorp, who was reading philosophy, introduced Spender to the work of George Santayana. With more lasting effect, Grant first made him read D. H. Lawrence; not just his novels (whose castigations of effete 'namby-pamby young men' such as Gerald Crich in Women in Love nevertheless put extra iron in the soul of the mad Socialist poet)[33] but also the Lawrentian exotica, books such as The Fantasia of the Unconscious.[34]

Away from Univ, there were other friends with whom he could truly be himself – or, more precisely, the self he had so recently created. Figuring rather luridly among these is the provocative, promiscuous blonde he calls Polly in World Within World. He inherited her from Michael and the science set. She wanted to get to know a poet and certainly got to know Spender sufficiently well for him to take her to Frognal to meet Caroline, who didn't approve of her short skirts and free talk. There may have been a sexual element in the relationship – Spender is at his most 'poetic' in his description of it – but it seems unlikely. 'I never went into that garden,' he writes in *World Within World*.[35]

He is almost as opaque in his descriptions of his male friendships. In his account of his relationship with his brother's friend Christopher Bailey (whom, coincidentally, he had known slightly when they were both at the O.S.H., Holt) Spender says little more than that the hearty, masculine, beer-swilling Bailey treated him with gentleness and delicacy.[36] Indirectly, however, he leaves clues that theirs was more than a casual acquaintance. He certainly visited Bailey at his lodgings and, even more pertinently, was in the habit of showing this loud, extrovert scientist copies of his latest poems, presumably before he dropped them off at *Isis* or read them at the University Poetry Society, of which he had become a member. ('Your typing has certainly improved,' Bailey rather laconically commented on one occasion.)

The description of his relationship with 'Tristan' is treated even more warily – as indeed the unacknowledged deployment of yet another pseudonym would suggest. In reality, Tristan was Gabriel Carritt, who had come up to Christ Church (from Sedbergh School) at the same time as Spender, in the autumn of 1927. Or maybe it would be more accurate to say that he had come *back* to Oxford, for he was the son of a philosophy don – and one of Spender's tutors – at University College. Edgar Frederick Carritt had been a fellow of the college since 1898; and, as its Praelector in Philosophy and Librarian, Gabriel later recalled, he had long-since 'learned to accept unserious students like Stephen'.[37]

Almost in the manner of a medieval morality play, in *World Within World* Spender depicts Carritt as Bailey's exact opposite. He is melancholic, moody and self-deprecating. 'We're just piddling undergraduates and everything we do or feel is without any importance,' he says, gripping Spender's arm as the two of them set out on another long, private walk. 'If we write, we write undergraduate stuff; if we fall in love, we're just undergraduates in love.' To an almost absurd degree, he comes across as a personification of the real Spender; timid, easily intimidated, deeply insecure. In that morality play he would be the hortatory voice of Reason (or, given his philosophical upbringing, Logick): 'What I like about you is that I feel you're like me. We aren't clever, we aren't brilliant, we're just ourselves, and we know we're just little undergraduates.'[38]

The trouble is that, by all accounts, the real Tristan was not like that at all. Carritt was 'full of awe' when he returned to Oxford as a freshman, but soon found his place and indeed became something of a hearty. He played rugby (he had been captain of the Sedburgh XV) and even rode out with the Berkshire hunt. As contemporary photographs confirm, he was also extremely good-looking, with straight dark hair, dark eyes, a full mouth and what W. H. Auden always thought of as a 'snub-nose'.

Is it too fanciful to suppose that Spender saw in Carritt an early manifestation of the Truly Great? From the evidence given above, the case is hardly convincing; but once again Spender's account begins to make more sense when seen in context.

In his biography of Auden, Humphrey Carpenter revealed that he (Auden) was besotted with Carritt. He would visit his rooms late at night, take him on walking holidays, and write poems for and about him — but all to no avail: Carritt firmly but politely refused his explicit sexual advances. (One of the poems, inscribed 'For G.C.' included the phrase 'we sit lax. In close ungenerous intimacy'.) Spender alludes to all this, and to his own relationship with Carritt/Tristan, when he tellingly but typically guardedly notes in *World Within World* that his relationship with Carritt was as frustrating as Auden's.[39]

It is likely, then, that the *World Within World* account of the 'Tristan' affair is no more than the recollection of the resolutely straight Carritt's tactful, final but none the less painful put-down of the naïve Spender: 'I'm sorry, Stephen. I like you terrifically, old man. We can still be friends. Actually, we're very much alike'

... Such a scenario certainly explains the puzzling opacity of references in *World Within World* to Carritt's wanting only 'an *ordinary* warmth' from his friendship with Spender.[40] It also throws a different light on the barely concealed pique which, as we have already seen, underlay Spender's diagnosis of 'D—''s 'weaknesses' and which was now beginning to corrode his relationship with Carritt.

Carritt's words had struck home and effectively destroyed the façade of the mad Socialist poet. But while acknowledging this, Spender makes it very clear that, even as Carritt was speaking, he was disagreeing with every syllable. Far from seeing himself as just another 'piddling undergraduate', he was by then convinced of his own uniqueness and his very special simplicity. He politely forbore from telling Carritt any of this, he wrote, for fear of hurting him and destroying their relationship. Venal though it seems, Spender also implies that there was another reason for his persevering with the tormenting relationship with Gabriel Carritt — and indeed for maintaining his ostensibly unlikely friendship with Christopher Bailey. Carritt was a conduit to, and Bailey a great friend of, the man Spender most wanted to meet: a third-year student at Christ Church whose name was Wystan Hugh Auden.

There are good grounds for arguing that, if anyone did, it was W.H. Auden who picked up Harold Acton's torch at Oxford in the mid-1920s. Acton and, more particularly, his friends — they had cheered him down from the 'Varsity with cries of '*après toi le déluge*'[41] — may have winced at the notion, but imperceptibly, the times had changed.

Auden had no real money, and he had not been to Eton. Nor, with his untidy 'tow-coloured' hair and almost albino complexion, could he ever have been considered good-looking. However, by about 1927, along with tyros such as Richard Crossman and Rex Warner,[42] he seemed to embody the new *Zeitgeist*. (Even his nick-name 'Uncle Wiz', though probably

derived from his christian name, had connotations of wizardry
and the supernatural.) Everyone was struck by him, not least an
old friend from prep school days, a certain Christopher
Bradshaw-Isherwood (then inconveniently up at Cambridge,
and reading chemistry of all things). In his later autobio-
graphical novel *Lions and Shadows* (1938) Isherwood was to
describe a young Oxford poet whom he called Hugh Weston:

> He had grown enormously; but his small pale yellow eyes were
> still screwed painfully together in the same short-sighted scowl
> and his stumpy immature fingers were still nailbitten and
> stained – nicotine was now mixed with the ink. He was
> expensively but untidily dressed in a chocolate-brown suit
> which needed pressing, complete with one of the new
> fashionable double-breasted waistcoats. His coarse woollen
> socks were tumbled all anyhow, around his babyishly
> shapeless naked ankles. One of the laces was broken in his
> elegant brown shoes.[43]

Certainly, it was by the sheer power of his personality more
than anything else that Auden came to dominate the under-
graduate literary scene during his second and third years at
Oxford. 'His sayings were widely misquoted,' recalled his tutor
Nevill Coghill. 'Well, anyhow, that's what Wystan says,'
students announced to their own tutors. He was 'organised so
well,' Acton himself recalled. Nevertheless, everything about
Auden –and not least his clinical, matter-of-fact brand of
homosexuality – only emphasised how much things had
changed on the departure of the old, neo-aesthetic order.

John Betjeman, whose sojourn at Oxford overlapped with
those of both Acton and Auden, later recalled that Auden

> represented the new type of Oxford undergraduate. I was the
> old type, trivial, baroque, incense-loving; a diner with a great
> admiration for the landowning classes and the houses and
> parks in which they were lucky enough to live. Wystan was
> already aware of slum conditions in Birmingham and mining
> towns and docks. But he combined with this an intense interest
> in geology and natural history and topography of the British

Isles. He liked railways and canals and had a knowledge of Bradshaw's [railway] timetables.[44]

It was Auden's eccentric brilliance which made Spender so determined to meet him. But, despite his assiduous cultivation of friendships with such likely go-betweens as Carritt, Bailey (and even Michael, who had been a contemporary of Auden's at Gresham's School, Holt) the longed-for introduction was endlessly delayed. Spender even suggests that his friends wanted to stop the meeting and actively sought to keep him away from Auden.[45]

In a way they succeeded. He never did meet Auden through their ministrations; and indeed it is fascinating to speculate how his own life would have turned out – and how the literature of the 1930s might have differed – if Spender had not unexpectedly run into Auden at a luncheon party given by his old Univ chum, Archie Campbell. For, from that afternoon dates the friendship which, more than any other, was to shape Spender's life in the next forty years and a connection which will, inevitably, define his eventual place in the literary history of the mid-twentieth century.

By the time of their meeting, Wystan Hugh Auden (who had arrived at Christ Church in the autumn of 1925) had already encountered and befriended the other central members of what would, very shortly, explode on the jaded palate of post-Bloomsbury London as 'the Auden group'.

Ironically, however, they were never much of a group. Auden, Spender and Cecil Day-Lewis were not actually together in the same room until just before the Second World War, when they made a radio broadcast. Much to the irritation of biographers and literary historians, there does not appear to be a single photograph in which they are depicted *en partie* with Isherwood and Louis MacNeice, the other two members of what Auden referred to as his 'Gang'. Indeed, the first shots of Auden, Spender and Day-Lewis together date from as late as 1949 – from exactly the time when the gang was being up-staged by the shocking poetic novelty of the Apocalyptics and The Movement and the arrival of poets like Peter Redgrove, Peter Porter and Edward Lucie-Smith who – irony of ironies! – even called themselves The Group.

Day-Lewis had (like Rex Warner) gone up to Wadham College in 1923. MacNeice, an acquaintance rather than a friend of Auden at this period, had arrived at Merton in 1926 – the year after Isherwood had gone down from Corpus Christi College, Cambridge, having spectacularly ploughed in his Finals by answering all the questions in either limericks or blank verse.

The very fact that he was younger than Auden and the others,[46] and the last recruit to the gang, may account for what immediately became, and always remained, Spender's subservient role *vis-à-vis* Auden – although, as we have already seen, his own natural feelings of personal inadequacy probably had as much to do with it. Within hours of meeting him, he had ceded to Auden the role of *miglior fabbro* (with even less irony than that with which T. S. Eliot had hailed Ezra Pound in the dedication to 'The Waste Land') and found his place as a willing acolyte, or 'handmaiden'.[47]

It should perhaps be noted here that, in his biography of Auden, Charles Osborne asserts (though without citing his authority) that, at about this time, Auden 'enticed the virgin Stephen into his bed'.[48] There are no public primary or secondary sources for this story; nor even hearsay accounts of Auden recounting it with all the glee with which he used to describe his somewhat similar experience with Betjeman. It does, however, have a ring of truth about it; and for both Auden and Spender it has a certain quasi-mystical correctness.

If Auden really *did* bed and deflower Spender at this period, it would explain much in their later relationship. In the present context, it might even account for the fact that Spender's descriptions of Auden at Oxford are, as Osborne puts it, 'the most extensive and most memorable' of the half-dozen or so which have appeared.[49] They, and principally the long account of their first meeting which is one of the chief set-pieces of *World Within World*, are certainly longer and more detailed than the equivalent passages in, for instance, Day-Lewis's autobiography

The Buried Day, MacNeice's *The Strings Are False* and even Isherwood's extensive autobiographising. They are also among the earliest, and it is sometimes possible to see something of Spender's hero-worshipping – the odd detail, the rather hind-sighted attribution of eccentric 'greatness' – reflected in later works. (It is worth noting too that when *World Within World* first appeared in 1951, in Britain at least, Auden's reputation was not high. He had fallen from his pre-war pre-eminence, and it would be two decades before he was accorded Grand Old Man status. Spender, even then enjoying what we might call inter-national semi-eminence, was well-placed to give his friend a 'leg up'.)

In essence, Spender recalls in *World Within World* that at that first meeting in Campbell's rooms Auden had virtually ignored him, belittled his taste in poetry, but then suddenly invited him to call at his own rooms in Christ Church. Primarily because of what comes next, 'Peck V.5' – that oak-panelled 'set' on the north-west corner of the first floor of Peckwater ('Peck') quad – has become one of the most famous 'digs' in literary history. Spender and other visitors have memorably described how rough sackcloth curtains were always kept drawn over the tall windows; how Auden kept a Meccano sculpture on his mantel-piece alongside a half-mildewed orange which apparently reminded him of the decline of the West; how a loaded gun – probably no more than a starting-pistol – lay on his desk; and how, somehow, he had smuggled in a piano on which he would thump out tunes from *Hymns Ancient and Modern* with more gusto than accuracy.

Visiting Auden was 'a serious business'. Appointments were necessary, and even then no visitor quite knew how he would find his host. Some days he'd sport a monocle, others a pair of glasses. When he was working he could well be wearing a journalist's green eye-shade. Conversations took place across his desk, with a single table lamp providing little relief from the eerie, daytime dark. Even then he deployed a scientific, philo-sophical, psychological vocabulary, and interrogated rather than conversed with his friends, frequently reducing them, their parents and even Nevill Coghill to uneasy silence by his formidable directness as much as his precosity.

John Betjeman was quickly disabused of the idea that he was the only man in Oxford who read the lesser Victorian poets. He soon learned to his cost that Auden could, for instance, match him line for line on Ebenezer Elliott and Philip Bourke Marston.[50] Other friends were bombarded with questions about their sex-lives, while Gabriel Carritt's mother was once tartly informed that a cup of tea she had made tasted 'like tepid piss'.

Spender too soon came to realise that Auden was a force to be reckoned with; and – quite as much as the fact that they actually refer to Auden by his real name – his accounts of his frequent humiliations at the stubby, nicotine-stained, nail-bitten hands of the *miglior fabbro* do much to give his reminiscences of their first meetings an obvious authenticity.

On one occasion Auden asked him to name his favourite contemporary poet. 'W—', Spender hazarded (once again, *World Within World* is not entirely frank). A 'little ass', Auden replied. Later there were to be further illuminations. Spender was reading all the wrong things: one poet he admired 'had the mind of a ninny', another was 'up the wrong pole'. Edmund Blunden was 'not bad'; but Spender should really be reading Gerard Manley Hopkins, Edward Thomas, A. E. Housman and T. S. Eliot . . .

Within a matter of weeks, of course, he was. Auden had completely taken him over. (How often did he write? he once asked Spender. Rather proudly Spender announced that he knocked out something like four poems a day. But then, on hearing that Auden took three weeks merely to finish one, he immediately fell into line – and accepted the eighty-four-fold drop in productivity.) Indeed, it is hardly too fanciful to say that, in Spender's eyes at least, the twenty-one-year-old Auden was a messiah, the coming man at whose feet he would willingly sit – especially when Auden made it plain that he wanted Spender as part of an Oxbridge Cabinet of the Talents which he was sure would breathe new life into the moribund worlds of British art and literature.

Auden was naturally the premier-in-waiting. His friend Robert Medley would be The Artist. Isherwood would be The Novelist. Spender and Cecil Day-Lewis would have seats at the table, while jobs would be found somewhere for the likes of Louis MacNeice and another Oxford poet, Bernard Spencer.[51]

What fun they all had, plotting and scheming this aesthetic *putsch*! Inspired by Auden's scientific certainties, the poets purged their vocabularies of the comfortable clichés of their Georgian fathers and wrote instead about the world they thought they knew. All must have been route-marched down to St Ebbe's — not a college but the site of the Oxford municipal gasworks. Its angular, prefabicated buildings were, according to Auden, the most beautiful sight in Oxford: similarly, a visit to the local dog-track was the *only* way to spend an evening . . .

Following Auden's lead, echoing his master's voice, Spender in particular began deploying the awkward, if memorable, language which in a few years would lead to the group's being caricatured as 'the Pylon Poets', after the title of one of Spender's poems.[52] In an untitled but frequently reprinted poem first drafted in January 1928, Auden had written:

> At Greenhearth was a fine site for a dam
> And easy power, had they pushed the rail
> Some stations nearer.[53]

Some months later Spender easily bettered that in, of all things, a love poem. Needless to say, by then he too had dispensed with such things as titles; but a poem now listed as 'Acts passed beyond' in the *Collected Poems* (an earlier version appeared in *Oxford Poetry 1929*) shows just how tenaciously he was even then embracing the 'Audenesque'. Gone was all the Miltonic, Wordsworthian rhetoric. In its place had come St Ebbe's: Spender hoped he could muster sufficient love to run a factory, power a city or drive a train.[54]

At any other time, these adolescent, undergraduate *folies de grandeur* would have been seen for what they were. But as Harold Acton had observed, Auden and the Gang were 'organised so well'. It was therefore inevitable that Spender had somehow acquired for five pounds a small hand-operated Adna printing press.[55] This was to lift them above the obscurity of the pages of *Isis* and make even their dutiful obeisances to the annual anthology of *Oxford Poetry* all-but redundant. They could be *published* poets, not just among the also-rans who contributed the odd sonnet or love-lorn lyric to the indulgently edited student rags.

And soon, famously, they were. Back at Frognal for the summer vacation of 1928, Spender laboriously printed a selection of his work – which he rather tentatively called *Nine Experiments* – and then, romantically revelling in the fact that he was absorbing his mentor's words through the ink on his fingers,[56] set about producing the first 'professional' edition of Auden's poetry. As the slightly cockeyed typesetting and an appreciable number of typographical errors which escaped Spender's notice suggest, it was a tricky business. The press refused to ink the type evenly and then broke down completely so that Spender had temporarily to abandon the project and get the book completed and bound by the Holywell Press when he returned to Oxford in the autumn.

With a bright orange dust-jacket, the tiny volume (it is barely six inches high) appeared in an equally tiny edition. Figures vary, but the print-run seems to have been no more than about forty-five, at the very most. Because of this, copies of the book, whose title page simply announced

---

W. H. Auden

POEMS

S.H.S. : 1928

---

and which were originally distributed to family and friends — although A. L. Rowse was made to pay for his — are among the most sought-after treasures of twentieth-century publishing. The curators of the Berg Collection at the New York Public Library allowed the present author to examine a copy only after taking up references from the vice-president of a prominent Fifth Avenue publisher. Inevitably, however, it is the name of the author rather than the shy initials of the 'publisher' which gives the book its value. At the time of writing I have been unable to discover the whereabouts of any copy of Spender's own *Nine Experiments*, that other volume which was so laboriously produced in the bedroom of a house in Hampstead during the long vacation days of the late summer of 1928.

Il miglior fabbro indeed . . .

———

By the time that Spender finally collected the finished copies of *Poems* from the Holywell Press, its author was abroad. At the end of Trinity Term 1928 Auden had completed his three years at Oxford — and, inevitably perhaps, like Acton and so many of his group, emerged from the Examination Schools with a rather poor third-class degree in English. Within a matter of weeks he had also left Britain, and was living as an unhappy paying guest in the very respectable home of a middle-class family in a middle-class suburb of Berlin.

Back at Oxford in the Michaelmas Term of 1928, Spender realised that the Gang was suddenly little more than a memory. Auden, its presiding genius, had gone down and away. Louis MacNeice was still around, it was true; Cecil Day-Lewis (who actually went down in 1927) was also just around the corner, but as a member of 'the town'. Rather sheepishly, he had accepted a teaching post at Summer Fields, a prestigious prep school on the Banbury Road.

Isherwood, partly because of his original isolation at Cambridge, partly because he was 'The Novelist' in a world of poets, was as yet a distant figure, whom Spender had met only once or twice in Auden's rooms the previous year. Indeed, as well as trying to write The Novel (and his first, *All the Conspirators*, did appear in 1928) he had now persuaded himself that he actually wanted to be a doctor, and embarked upon a course in medicine at St Thomas's Hospital in London. It didn't last long. 'The door of the operating theatre [. . .] led him nowhere,' he wrote in his third-person autobiography *Christopher and His Kind*. 'Within six months, he had given up medicine altogether.'[57]

Thus, Spender perforce began to move in slightly wider circles. He established what would be a life-long friendship with Isaiah Berlin, and almost accidentally found himself at the centre of a sub-group or neo-Gang. He became much thicker than Auden ever had with MacNeice and began encouraging a new generation of Oxford poets which included the likes of Bernard Spencer and Arthur Calder-Marshall.[58] He was, it seems, remarkably loyal to both.

Two of Calder-Marshall's poems and one of Spencer's were included in the 1929 edition of *Oxford Poetry* which Spender and MacNeice edited for Basil Blackwell, the Oxford bookseller and publisher. (By contrast, the young editors allowed themselves four poems apiece.) Other contributors included Dick Crossman, his future Labour Cabinet colleague Douglas (later Lord) Jay, E. J. Scovell and Hugh Corbett-Palmer.[59] When the reviews appeared the latter two were singled out for special notice in the influential *Manchester Guardian*. But MacNeice was written off as having achieved 'little but a cleverer than clever strut.' Even more gallingly, Spender was not so much as mentioned.[60]

This may have had something to with the fact that his four poems[61] were all about or at least suggested by what we shall see was his climacteric relationship with the student he called Marston: each was in its way mawkishly lovelorn while 'lesser' poets such as Corbett-Palmer (also, incidentally, homosexual) had, in the words of the *Manchester Guardian*'s anonymous reviewer, 'the wisdom, and the power, to be original in the best way'.

But it would be a mistake to think of these rather limp

offerings as representing the Spender whom his contemporaries knew in the post-Auden days of late 1928 and 1929. As far as they were concerned, in life if not in art, it was he rather than his co-editor MacNeice who had the cleverer than clever strut. In the summer of 1929 the ever vigilant O.U.O.G. reported back to *The Gower* that a 'very lofty' Spender was enduring 'the worldliness of Univ' and writing 'extremely free verse' for the Poetry Society.[62] Quite how free it was is now impossible to ascertain since none is included in the *Collected Poems*, but a few months later Dick Crossman was forced to tell the *versifier libre*: 'My dear Stephen, I don't understand your work now-adays at all.'

By all accounts, too, Spender was becoming something of a 'character'. He has himself admitted that during his final terms at Oxford he was 'crazy', but crazy in a markedly self-serving way. Reading books like the works of Dostoevsky – he identified himself with the character of Aloysha in *The Brothers Karamazov*[63] – brought kudos and a certain credibility. One night in June 1930 he impulsively decided to sleep out in the quad at Univ where a marquee was being erected for the annual Encænia celebrations ('Commem') and was astonished when, instead of throwing things at him as they would once have done, two hearties came out to join him.

The Gower's spies could not have heard about that little jape, but they were hardly short of other Spender stories:

> When such widely differing figures as the Scholar Gypsy and Charley's Aunt find in Oxford their natural setting, a dozen Old Gowers should have no great difficulty finding niches somewhere between the two. In fact, even Spender has decided that this range offers possibilities; and after having spent two years as a voice crying in the wilderness (albeit edging nearer and nearer to civilisation), he now appears weekly in a dinner jacket, and reads the Minutes as Secretary of that most efficient and most constitutional of societies, the [Oxford University] English club.[64]

Three   months   later   another   O.G.   sneak   reported   with barely concealed irritation, – or was it awe-struck wonder that an Old Gower had discovered his 'uniqueness in time and space'? – on the less endearing side of the Spender persona:

> Spender sometimes recognizes our deferential salute with a gentle nod and pleasant smile. Occasionally, however, he strides by, his eyes turned prophet-like to the skies, as if seeking to probe their inner mystery. He still wears a dinner jacket at the English Club.[65]

Outwardly, it was all very Acton; but, unlike Acton, Spender was boxing above his weight. And mixing with the 'smugs' (just as his father had done) and muscling in on the social whirl of 'the University' – 'Me, just a piddling undergraduate? I'll show them!' – soon had the inevitable consequences. Not surprisingly, Spender (who had to live at Oxford on a relatively modest allowance of £350 a year) suddenly found himself in debt. As early as January 1929 he had had to sell off some of his books to clear a £17 overdraft.[66]

Fundamentally, however, Spender's posturing at the English Club and self-conscious parading around the streets was only part of the continuing strategy to get himself noticed, for preference in the wider world beyond Oxford and the black-tie eminence of the English Society. (We cannot blame him for this; for two centuries and more British public life has been dominated by those who first came to prominence as Oxford or Cambridge 'characters'.)

Nine Experiments had hardly set the world on fire – nor, to be fair, had Auden's *Poems*; and in all probability neither was ever really intended to do so. But now, beleaguered though he was at Univ, Spender was at least managing to get himself talked about in literary circles. During his second year he had begun submitting poems and short stories to London editors – typically, a poem fired off to Wyndham Lewis at his short-lived magazine *The Enemy* was accepted, but then nervously retrieved for further work – and he was now starting to tout round for book reviews and more general commissions from literary and political magazines.

It was eventually the venerable *Spectator* which gave him his debut as a proper, professional writer. In August 1929 it carried his first published article, an essay rather prophetically entitled 'Problems of the Poet and the Public'.[67] Ultimately of rather more importance, however, was the appearance the following year of his first collection of verse, a slim volume entitled *Twenty Poems* which was published by Basil Blackwell in Oxford. It caused something of a stir in and around the university, but was rather upstaged when, within a few months, T. S. Eliot and the London publishers Faber & Faber (of which Eliot was a director) produced *Poems*, W. H. Auden's first collection.

In his more private moments, Spender remained just as mixed up as ever. His poem 'Never being, but always on the edge of being'[68] with its desperate demand for romantic fulfilment dates from this period. So too does his curious announcement that he found Philip Snowden, the Labour Chancellor of the Exchequer of the day, 'incredibly beautiful'.[69] Psychologists could doubtless make much of the fact that Snowden was born in the same year as Harold (1864) — which means that in 1929 he was fully sixty-five years of age.

Quite apart from his personal difficulties with 'Tristan' and others, much of Spender's confusion and unhappiness at this time seems to have stemmed from Auden's departure. He was becoming impatient with what, for all the dinner jackets, now appeared to be an endless and essentially lonely exile in Oxford. In the spring of 1930 he was damning the city and looking for some means of escape.[70] A few months later things had got even worse. In a letter to Isherwood he described the rain and a Sunday gloom which seemed to encapsulate his own personal, literary and sexual frustration.[71]

After Auden's flight to Germany, Isherwood had become a sort of Auden-surrogate: at least he was only in London! Four years Spender's senior, and already a published novelist, he offered a new and promising link with the real world. Almost inevitably, therefore, and quite possibly as a result of some wry, long-distance match-making by 'Uncle Wiz', a close friendship soon developed between the two men. Spender was concluding his letters to Isherwood with 'Love, Stephen' by 1929; eighteen months later this had escalated to a more characteristic 'With Best Love, Stephen.'

Inevitably, too, The Novelist emerged as the dominant partner, a mentor as influential as the Auden he replaced. Briefly, at the end of 1928, Spender had even gone as far as to forsake poetry in order to start work on a novel of his own. (It was to be published – in heavily revised form – as *The Temple* some sixty years later.)[72] From then on he also sent Isherwood – and through him, Auden – drafts of short stories and poems, and began spending more and more time in London to be with him. Sometimes, like Hugh Corbett-Palmer, he relied on the 10.58pm train back from Euston; more often he made a weekend of it and stayed over at Frognal.

For the twenty-one-year-old Spender, Isherwood was (as for the rest of his life he was to remain) congenial company. But with all his talk about how Oxford, Cambridge and the comfortable, country-house England from which he (and, to a lesser extent, Spender) had sprung were the enemies of the writer, he was also what most parents at the time would have regarded as a dangerous, unsettling influence. Harold and Violet would certainly have seen him as much. But Harold and Violet were dead. Spender was his own man – at least on paper – and lapped up everything Isherwood said. At this time he could well have written a book entitled *My Guru and his Disciple*, just as Isherwood was to in 1980, chronicling his later relationship with the Swami Prabhavananda.[73]

He could even have taken Isherwood at his word and 'chucked everything up'. He didn't, of course; he made a wholly typical fudge. Despite all Isherwood's blandishments Spender remained at Univ, hating but enduring 'the University', putting in the bare minimum of work, turning up for as few seminars as he could get away with – but still presenting himself in June 1930 for his all-important Finals.

Still more, perhaps, than for Hugh Corbett-Palmer, Gabriel Carritt and the rest of the class of '27, literally and metaphorically this ritualised oblation (even today Oxford undergraduates are required to wear gowns in the 'Examination Schools') was for Spender only the beginning of a long, hot summer. He knew he had not done enough work; he knew too how Isherwood had cocked a snook at the whole intellectual edifice of Cambridge. And yet he still went into the Schools:

> . . . In spite of the heat [. . .] KELLY, BAXTER, LANGDON, SPENDER, and DRAGE are, to the best of my belief, to be daily seen among the throng who frequent the Examination Schools; so that their appearances in a private capacity have been few and far between. SPENDER has nevertheless found time to publish a volume of poems, which will, no doubt, enhance his already considerable European reputation.[74]

The Gower's Mr Gossip Junior had evidently seen a copy of *Twenty Poems*; but his rather catty reference to Spender's 'considerable European reputation' is much more likely to have been motivated by Oxford gossip about his vacation forays to Germany. And those too were suggested and even facilitated by Isherwood.

THREE

Songs of Innocence and Experience

For all the civilisation, sophistication and downright eccentricity he tried to affect after Auden's departure, there is no reason to believe that, even in his final year, Stephen Spender cut a particularly distinguished figure in Oxford literary circles. Hugh Corbett-Palmer recalled: 'I never thought he was particularly attractive, although some other people were attracted by him. To me he was just like any other undergraduate, but he did have a good figure.'[1] For all his dinner-jackets and hob-nobbing with the likes of Walter de la Mare, Edmund Blunden and J.C. Squire at the Oxford University English Club, he seems to have been no more prepossessing than the poet Stephen Savage, whom the narrator of Christopher Isherwood's early autobiographical novel *Lions and Shadows* first met in his friend Hugh Weston's rooms. And, indeed, Spender himself has confirmed the accuracy of a frequently quoted passage in which Isherwood described how Savage

> . . . burst in upon us, blushing, sniggering loudly, contriving to trip over the edge of the carpet – an immensely tall, shambling boy of nineteen, with a great scarlet poppy-face, wild frizzy hair, and eyes the violent colour of blue-bells.[2]

Spender both looked and behaved like a 'boy'; and his blond, flush-cheeked gaucheness initially did as little for Auden and Isherwood as they had for Corbett-Palmer. Dropping in from London, Isherwood was at first actually rather irritated by him. 'You blushed for him, you squirmed at his every *faux pas*; you wanted, simultaneously, to kick and protect and shake him,' he noted.[3] Making matters even worse was the fact that Spender was subject to embarrassingly frequent and disconcertingly violent nose-bleeds at this period. In *Lions and Shadows* Hugh Weston dubs Savage 'the fountain' because of them.

Maybe it was because they had both been to public (though different) boarding schools; but by the time they arrived at university, in stark contrast to Spender's disoriented confusion, both Auden and Isherwood thought of themselves as men and had long-since put away such childish things as nose-bleeds and adolescent insecurity. Auden, as we have already seen, was from early childhood possessed of an extraordinary self-confidence. Isherwood also had a fairly precise notion of his place in the scheme of things.

Inevitably then, Spender – still unsure of quite who or what he was, and continually casting around for role models in life in just the same way as he was in art – had uncritically adopted them both. As even he recognised, he always did everything his friends told him to do.

Perhaps for no other reason than that he was Auden's chum, Isherwood had quickly been elevated to a pedestal only fractionally lower than Auden's. He had become a confidant and, more thrillingly still, a creature of the imagination when, somewhat obscurely, Spender chose to visualise his new friend as a sea captain, a naval commander who had asked for him as an adjutant.[4]

The boyish need to 'hero-worship' was a central feature of Spender's character. We have already noticed it in his ambivalent thoughts about the children who were rough, his frank subservience to Auden and his tortured relationship with Gabriel Carritt. It stemmed from his feelings of inadequacy as a child and prep-school boy and was to be of crucial importance in his personal and emotional development throughout the 1930s. But there was another side to Spender's special attraction to Auden and Isherwood.

They were both homosexual. What's more, even when he first knew them, they were both, in the police-court phrase of the time (when homosexual acts were of course illegal in Britain) '*practising* homosexuals'. Occasionally, they even slept together: not because they were physically drawn to each other – they weren't – but because for Auden and, one suspects, for Isherwood too sex was a normal, natural, inevitable and 'adult' aspect of friendship. They had none of the hang-ups which hobbled (and were to continue to hobble) Spender. They were not attracted to girls, as Spender increasingly was, most notably to Polly, his fellow-undergraduate, and their frank, unembarrassed sex-talk simultaneously appalled and excited him.

Paul Schoner, the strongly autobiographical hero of *The Temple*, also felt this *frisson* – and never more so than on the occasion when the intimidatingly forthright Oxford poet Simon Wilmot asked him straight out whether he was still a virgin – or, in the university slang of the times, a 'Verger'. Blushing furiously, he had to admit that he was.[5]

Why couldn't he be like them? As he returned to Oxford for Hilary Term at the start of 1929 Spender arrived at the first real crisis in his life. Socially, sexually and psychologically he had driven himself into a cul-de-sac. He was twenty years of age and, possibly as a result of Auden's 'psychological' probings, he was beginning to confront the issues which were to dog him for at least the next ten years. To appreciate their crucial influence upon him as an individual and a writer we must, however, briefly return to University College School, Hampstead.

━━━━━

Shortly after the 'liberation' brought about by Harold's death, Spender had written a poem which was eventually published in the December 1926 edition of the U.C.S. school magazine *The Gower*. Although 'To J— H—' is still derivative in form – it is defiantly subtitled 'A Sonnet in the Miltonian manner' – it is the first of those early poems of Spender's which have survived that displays something of the later preoccupations we have already identified in 'Rough'/'My Parents'.

Extraordinarily for a poem published in a school magazine, it is a blatant, breathless apostrophe to another boy – and significantly one who, unlike Spender, was athletic, extroverted

and pleasure-seeking. In all probability this paragon was S.J.M.
Heath, the friend of Spender's fellow O.T.C. Lance-Corporal,
R.N. Hetherington. The poem was certainly inspired by a fight
or tussle in which Heath beat 'Heth Ring Ton'; but now its
significance lies less in Spender's almost orthodox hero-
worshipping of Heath than in his intense desire to be *like* (rather
than *with*) him. Emotionally, it can be placed somewhere
between 'Rough'/'My Parents' and that other much antholo-
gised early poem 'The Truly Great'.[6]

But like them (and, for exactly the same reason, like much of
W.H. Auden's early work) it is fundamentally dishonest; a
careful, sculpted carapace of Art concealing a scared, cowering
centre. There is more than a suggestion of homo-eroticism, but
even this is somehow excused by Spender's adoption of the
'Miltonian' manner. It was a convenient device, as useful to him
as it must have been to the editors of *The Gower* and the school
authorities when they came to authorise the poem's publication.
Seen in context, the poem's opening imprecation 'H******!' and
the use of words such as 'Lover' and 'Thou' must have made a
literary kind of sense.

For its adolescent author, however, they were the truth – or as
much of that truth as he dared reveal at this time. It seems
inconceivable that the poem was written out of anything but an
intense, unrequited admiration for Heath. (One wonders what
he felt, confronted by the so easily penetrated blanks and
asterisks, when the poem appeared in *The Gower*.) Indeed, it is
impossible now to see 'To J— H—' as anything other than
Spender's first (or first-known) attempt to come to terms with his
own nascent homosexuality.

He was seventeen when he wrote it, and we know that, for all
their intensity, his friendships up to this period (and indeed
throughout his time at U.C.S.) remained frustratingly platonic.[7]
Heath, like the rough boys of his early childhood, was just
another Ideal, set on an unclimbable pedestal of desire.

Back at home, however, in the emotionally charged days and
weeks and months after Harold's death, Spender had begun to
indulge in convoluted fantasies of being up there among the real

men, the truly great. Masturbation seems to have provided a physical release,[8] – as it was to continue to do throughout his time at Oxford.[9]

In truth, there wasn't very much alternative. Even if we discount Charles Osborne's Auden-Spender story; even if we allow for a few unrecorded, fumbled and ultimately futile one-night stands, Isherwood's *Lions and Shadows*, his later, franker, *Christopher and His Kind* and all the other publicly available testimonies of the period bear out the *World Within World* idea that, for all his posing, Spender was a frustrated, sexually labile inadequate for most or all of his undergraduate years.

━━━━━━

We have already seen how, by his own admission, the reality of his relationship with Gabriel Carritt brought him face-to-face with his own nature. Confronting this reality, as he did, we must now turn to his immeasurably greater infatuation with the fellow-student he called Marston. Not only was it of eclipsing importance to him at the time – the 'Marston' poems make up a good half of his first properly published volume, the *Twenty Poems* which Basil Blackwell produced in Oxford in 1930 – it has continued to resound through his life. For that reason, perhaps, Spender has found it necessary to preserve for more than sixty years Marston's true identity.

Why? And indeed why 'Marston'? That is the simpler question, for the name does have some literary provenance. John Marston (1575?–1634) was a Jacobean dramatist and the friend and collaborator of both Ben Jonson and John Webster. *Eastward Hoe* was written by Marston and Jonson (with George Chapman); Marston's better-known comedy *The Malcontent* was embellished by Webster in 1604. Furthermore, we have already seen that the work of another Marston, the blind sonneteer Philip Bourke Marston (1857–87), was enjoying something of a vogue – among the Betjeman-Auden circle at least – in the Oxford of 1927. In addition, it may not be entirely irrelevant to note that, while there are towns called Marston in

Cheshire, Herefordshire, Lincolnshire and Warwickshire, there is also a village of the same name only a couple of miles north of Oxford.

Of Marston the man, Spender – as usual – reveals tantalisingly little. He is an abiding though insubstantial presence in both the early poems and *World Within World*; his name is the fifth word in the 'English Prelude' to *The Temple*. But, even in comparison to Tristan, he is a vague figure – possibly deliberately so. Spender records that he first met him during his second term at Oxford and that Marston was also a Univ man.[10] He recalls that he was not conventionally attractive[11] and that he had close-cropped hair[12] – but, physically, that is as much as we get.

By now, however, it is enough; we can read the signs, we know what is coming. Marston is another hearty; another Heath, another Tristan. He was not particularly talented or more than averagely intelligent.[13] He played games and even had a pilot's licence.

The Temple's Marston is rather more fleshed-out than *World Within World*'s. He is the son of a Harley Street surgeon and goes on to box for the university[14] in addition to all his other accomplishments. (In the *Collected Poems* 'Marston', one of the three 'Marston Poems' which have survived from the 1930 *Twenty Poems*, contains the rather repellent image of a boxer punishing 'a nigger'.)[15]

Spender first noticed him in the college quad[16] – or was it on the Oxford train?[17] – and promptly fell in love with him. There is no other way of putting it, and certainly no other way of explaining Spender's subsequent behaviour. Overcoming his still-disabling shyness – this was the early spring of 1928 – he consciously decided to get to know him. Boldly, he invited him out for a drink. Then, initial contact established, he began calling on him in his rooms and even aping the manners of the Univ hearties in an attempt to impress him. In a way that is startlingly reminiscent of *The Backward Son*'s account of how Geoffrey Brand feigned an interest in stamp collecting and the Arsenal football team as a survival tactic, he also did his best to mug up on boxing and Marston's other sporting passions, flying and skiing.

Marston apparently put up with these heavy-handed attempts at friendship. Surprisingly perhaps, he even agreed to accompany Spender on a walking tour in the west of England one Easter vacation; during another, rather later, holiday he went so far as to invite Spender to stay at his home.[18] Indeed, Spender's relationship with Marston, such as it was, seems to have been far more dogged and long-lasting than his accounts in either *World Within World* or *The Temple* would suggest. If we can believe the former, it began in the spring of 1928, during his second term at Oxford — but there is documentary evidence to prove that Spender finally let the relationship lapse only at the end of 1930.[19]

Even in its earliest stages, however, it was never easy. It should have foundered — and very nearly did — during the walking tour, which seems to have taken place during the Easter vacation of 1929. That was, of course, all Spender's idea. Marston loved the West Country: then they must go there; what about a walk along the river Wye; five days or so in March or April?[20]

The whole trip was a painful, embarrassing failure. The two had hardly got out of the bus which had brought them from London to Ross-on-Wye when it became apparent that they had nothing in common. Even casual conversation proved a strain as nerves got the better of Spender and he gabbled away, incoherently parroting his new-found knowledge of aircraft, yachts and even razor blades.[21] Marston just walked doggedly on.

Affairs took a turn for the worse — if that was possible — on the second day. Marston complained of stomach ache; Spender became over-solicitous, worrying about whether they should try to find a doctor. Eventually Marston's patience snapped. 'Oh, do shut up,' he cried; 'you fuss over me like an old hen!' — and promptly went off to relieve himself among some nearby trees.[22] Stung by Marston's words, Spender nevertheless recognised their truth. In his desperation to maintain what one part of him could even then see was a doomed relationship, he knew he was embarrassing, irritating and boring Marston. In his more honest moments he could see that he was even boring himself.[23]

But on and on they walked, following the wide meander of the river Wye south from Ross-on-Wye through the unexpected

14

grandeur of Symonds Yat and on to Monmouth. Spender took photographs.[24] One day the boredom and mutual irritation was broken by a farm dog which followed them for several hours.

That evening they agreed to stay overnight at a Monmouth-shire boarding-house, and then discovered that they would have to share the same bed. Not surprisingly, neither slept very much and the following morning they had breakfast together in uncomfortable silence.[25]

A glance at the map suggests that in all likelihood it would have been later the same day when, sulky and confused, the two nineteen-year-olds reached the ruins of Tintern Abbey. But there, intellectually at least, Spender was on home ground – and, just as his father Harold would have done, he immediately reached for his Wordsworth. Insisting that Marston sat and listened as he read aloud from 'Tintern Abbey' was, however, probably a mistake:

> For thou art with me here upon the banks
> Of this fair river; thou my dearest Friend,
> My dear, dear Friend; and in thy voice I catch
> The language of my former heart, and read
> My former pleasures in the shooting lights
> Of thy wild eyes.[26]

By the time they reached Tintern, they were near their journey's end (which must have been Chepstow, where the Wye joins the wider river Severn and buses and trains leave for London). Both, in their own ways, were understandably ready to go home. Physically, the walk had not been demanding – no more than thirty miles spread over five days – but emotionally they had travelled much farther than that.

Once again, they caught the bus. Chastened and depressed, Spender was still doggedly looking for some 'sign' from Marston. Now he invested everything in the manner of departure. When they reached London, they changed to the Underground. Marston, Spender knew, had to get off before him – would he look back and wave? Bleakly, in *World Within World* Spender recalled that he did not.

Extraordinarily, however, the spectacularly unsuccessful so-journ on the Wye did not mark the end of Spender's infatuation with Marston. The one-sided affair seems to have lumbered on for another eighteen months, overlapping with marginally more successful flings as Spender continued to wait for that elusive sign. If we are to believe *The Temple*, Spender even contacted Auden for his advice on how to hurry things along. An episode in the novel certainly describes an occasion when, after a chance meeting with Marston, Simon Wilmot, the poet and *soi-disant* pseudo-Freudian psychoanalyst, gives the hapless Paul his view of what had by then become a complete emotional impasse.[27]

Typically, however, Spender still saw light at the end of the tunnel.[28] He continued to visit Marston in his rooms; he still caught his breath every time he glimpsed him in the quad – and now he began pouring out his frustrations in poems and a stream of letters to Isherwood. Happily, many of these have survived and suggest that, ironically enough, it was the protracted affair with Marston which brought about Spender's infinitely longer-lasting friendship with Isherwood.

The twenty-five-year-old novelist certainly became something of a referee or emollient in the youngsters' relationship at about this time. He joined them for a weekend in the spring of 1930 and seems to have tried to bridge the chasm which divided them. He contrived to give each a private talking-to in what appears to have been the best Uncle Wiz manner. Spender appreciated it, but the reassurance he received from Isherwood was not reciprocated when he the tried to have his own similar heart-to-heart with Marston.[29]

And so things remained all through the spring and early summer of 1930, as Spender fractiously and ineffectually prepared for his Finals. It was only in the autumn that he brought things to a head. He wrote to Marston, explicitly describing his feelings for him (the letter has apparently not survived) and suggesting that if Marston could not respond to them, reciprocate them, then perhaps they would be better off severing the friendship altogether.[30]

Commendably, Marston played down Spender's melo-dramatic posturing. They were members of the same college, and when all was said and done even the university was a small community; they couldn't avoid running into each other, he replied. He also insisted on seeing Spender to talk things through.

No, he couldn't return Spender's feelings, he said when eventually they met – formally, and by appointment – in an Oxford teashop; but that did not mean they couldn't remain friends. Maybe Spender could explain things and even 'make him understand'. Apparently against his better judgement, Spender tried to do so. Intellectually at least, he succeeded; Marston later told Spender that that was the only time he had not been thoroughly bored by him.[31]

For Spender, however, it was an unwanted, Pyrrhic victory. Against all practicality, he reiterated his demand that he and Marston should not meet again. That was only going to prolong the agony: merely passing him in the college porter's lodge or glancing him across the dining hall was unendurable, he wrote to Isherwood.[32] The need to escape or at least cut his losses was now paramount in his mind. Several months earlier he had concluded a draft of 'Saying "Good Morning" Becomes Pain-ful', a now discarded poem which was originally published at the end of the 'Marston' poems in *Twenty Poems* with the request for a formal, definite break in the relationship.[33]

More than half a century on, the whole sorry business with Marston now seems no more than a storm in a tea-cup, an undergraduate – even adolescent – experiment no better and no worse than thousands of others before and since. And yet for Spender its impact was shattering. Once again he had made what was plainly a pitch for physical experience, only to limp wounded and disappointed from the field. That at least is the impression he gives in *The Temple*; and there are good grounds for believing it to be true. In his introduction to a recent collection of the photographs taken by a German friend at this time (a short essay which was in all likelihood written shortly after he completed his revisions to the novel in April 1987) Spender admitted that the first half of *The Temple* was closely based on autobiographical events and indeed drafted only months after they occurred.[34]

We should, however, be careful of taking it *too* literally. Not only does Spender disingenuously warn against that – he has variously called *The Temple* a work of memory, fiction, hindsight[35] and autobiographical fictionalising[36] – he also opts to maintain the Marston pseudonym. In addition, he creates new ones for his friends the poet Simon Wilmot (Auden) and the novelist William Bradshaw (Isherwood). On the other hand, he gives his alter ego the suitably German-Jewish name of Paul Schoner; and it is probably no accident that in German the adjective *schön* means lovely, fine, or beautiful – we have already noted that in 'The Furies' Spender had described himself as 'the handsome only son'.[37]

Bearing all this in mind, it is still obviously significant that *The Temple*'s Paul is completely debilitated by his relationship with Marston. Blushing furiously, he blurts out to the Dean of his Oxford college that he is in love with him. And after the Wye episode he confesses to one of his German friends that he is still a 'Verger' in a passage which seems to come closer than anything else which Spender has written to explaining the emotional complexity of his feelings for Marston.[38]

It is now impossible to say whether Spender really did remain a 'Verger' until as late as the summer of 1929. *The Temple* certainly belies Charles Osborne's theory. But it is beyond doubt that, in one part of his brain at least, he was at this period intent on dispensing with such a bourgeois legacy. Part of the problem was that, as we have seen, he had been taken up by Auden and Isherwood – or at least hitched a ride on their intellectual gravy train – on the strength of his credentials as a homosexual. Now it

seemed that he was, quite literally, failing to perform. Something
had to be done; and in the very nick of time Spender seemed to
have found both that something, and what looked like a way out
of his personal and sexual cul-de-sac, in the spring of 1929.

Once again Isherwood appears to have been instrumental in
leading him to it. He had gone out to Berlin to see Auden in
March 1929 and returned convinced that Germany was a
never-never land where all the obstructions and complexities of
life were cut through.[39] He had actually first been to Germany
the previous year, when he went to stay with a relative who was
the British consul at Bremen. But that had been little more than a
duty-visit; there were family obligations to be observed and he
was on his best behaviour.

In 1929, however, it had all been different, he told Spender.
Isherwood knew what he was getting himself in to – and could
hardly wait to get into it. *Christopher and His Kind* effortlessly
catches his urgency, and something of the Berlin-fever which had
by then infected the British homosexual bourgeoisie. Isherwood

> . . . was in such a hurry to make this journey. It was Berlin
> itself he was hungry to meet; the Berlin Wystan had promised
> him. To Christopher, Berlin meant Boys.[40]

Once again we see the hand of Auden at work; and the
familiar chain of Isherwood and then, tardily, Spender following
its beckoning. Spender was certainly excited by Isherwood's
descriptions of his experiences at a Berlin 'boy-bar' called the
Cosy Corner to which Auden had taken him; at Luna Park, at
the Wellenbad pool and at the city's other resorts. He began
learning German and by 22 July 1929 like Paul Schoner in *The
Temple* he had got himself to Hamburg in northern Germany.[41]

Hamburg proved to be more like Isherwood's Bremen than
the much fabled Berlin, however. Arriving on the train from the
port of Cuxhaven, Paul Schoner was as disappointed as Spender
had been when he arrived at Nantes three years previously. He
noticed only slums, tenements, backyards and poverty.[42] Nor
was that the only similarity. Where Spender had felt uncomfort-

able as the pastor's lodger in Nantes, now he was stifled by the formality and super-Frognal affluence of the house in the 'millionaire district' south of the city in which he was to stay. A Matisse, a Derain, a Van Gogh and an early Picasso hung in the baronial entrance-hall. His bedroom was similarly baroque, with thick carpets and opulent, over-powering furniture.[43] He felt suffocated by the sheer bourgeois niceness of it all.

Even more of a problem, he soon found that his host was as priggish as anyone he had encountered at home. He was the pallid, unerringly correct young Jew whom, in *World Within World*,[44] Spender calls Dr Jessell. Inevitably, he reappears in *The Temple*, this time more savagely caricatured as Dr Ernst Stockmann, a cold, calculating and arrogant young man eerily devoid of life.[45] In actual fact his name was Erich Alport.

Spender had originally encountered him at Oxford, where the two had been introduced by Univ's 'sympathetic' young Dean who guessed that they might 'get on'. Alport was a few years older than Spender and on that (and many another) occasion was sporting a Downing College, Cambridge blazer. In his slightly pedantic English, he talked about the poetry of John Donne, praised some of Spender's own Marston poems (which the Dean had shown him) and insisted on taking Spender and a few other friends to lunch at the Mitre Hotel. For Alport this time, it was a case of love at first sight – and an hour later he suggested that his new English friend should come out to stay at his family's home in Hamburg. Needless to say, Spender accepted with alacrity.

As the day of his departure approached, however, he began to have doubts. He barely knew Alport; he was setting off for a foreign country of whose language and culture he was still comparatively ignorant. Disingenuously, he also seems to have failed to recognise his host's motives in inviting him in the first place.

His sense of unease increased as the train pulled into Hamburg. He wondered whether he would even recognise the young *Herr Doktor*. He did, of course; but, right from the beginning, relations between them were brittle and artificial.

Remembering Isherwood's stories of his exploits at the Cosy Corner in Berlin, Spender was intent on making the best of his time in Hamburg. He wanted to do little more than slope off to the enticing *Lokalen* and *Weinstübe*, the beer-halls and boy bars in the working-class district of Sankt Pauli, between the Freiheit and the port. Like Paul in *The Temple*, he was after '*gemeine Leute* – low people'. But Alport had other ideas for him. A combination of his fear of his mother and his own deeply engrained guilt about his true sexual proclivities expressed itself in a preoccupation with form and propriety – the very things Spender had come to Germany to escape! – and he insisted on entertaining the *Engländer* with full-dress family dinners and further earnest conversations about literature and music.

In a later essay Spender recalled how, in many ways, Alport unwittingly made his stay in Hamburg even more frustrating than his holiday in Nantes. There, he had had only imaginary companions. Now, everything was so close! Everywhere he looked he saw the 'nihilism, sophistication and primitive vitality' which Isherwood had promised. At the swimming pool – the *Schwimmbad*, Hamburg's mini-Wellenbad – sun-tanned boys, nude or semi-nude, strutted like kings.[46] He and lesser mortals could only stand back and admire these personifications of the Truly Great.

Not unnaturally, he soon came to see the chronically repressed Alport as his 'jailor'. He felt he was imprisoned in the claustrophobic correctness of the Alports' house and developed a loathing for all that it and Erich represented.[47]

There were, however, some consolations. Alport's friends were charming – far more charming than Alport himself – and quickly made his English guest welcome. In their eyes Spender was nervous and inhibited, '*nicht schön, sondern interessant; unschuldig*'.[48] They giggled incessantly at his stammering attempts to speak German – but they nevertheless invited him to their parties and took him out on swimming and boating expeditions.

Spender quickly became particularly fond of one of these boys, and drastically altered his holiday plans when he found that his affection was apparently reciprocated. In any case, by the middle of August he had left, or been asked to leave, the Alport house. Erich's parents did not like him, believing him to be a bad influence on their son. '*Der Engel; der unschuldige Engel-länder*', they called him; the innocent, unfallen English angel. But Frau Alport was under no illusions. Spender was falling, she thought; and she was determined that he was not going to take Erich down with him.

Accordingly, Spender installed himself in the Hotel Minerva (where apparently he was joined by his grandmother, the indefatigable Mrs Schuster).[49] He was happy and in love, he confided to Isherwood. He had discovered German poetry, particularly that of Hölderlin and, appropriately, the rather mystic pantheism of Rainer Maria Rilke. Anxiously waiting for the beginning of September when he would be leaving for a walking tour along the river Rhine with his new German friend, he wrote long letters to Auden and other friends.[50] He had his portrait painted and killed time by writing a story and taking more German lessons. Entirely against his better judgement, he also agreed to spend a final weekend at Altamunde on the Baltic coast with Erich Alport.

Alport was strongly attracted to him, he had finally realised; and this only added to the awkwardness of the situation. In many ways it was the complete reverse of his relationship with Marston (at one point in *The Temple* Paul even echoes Marston when he accuses Ernst of fussing over him like an old hen).[51]

The Temple takes up the story. Paul is repelled by Ernst – and tells him so in a frank exchange of views – but nevertheless he finds himself slipping into Ernst's bed on their first night in a crowded hotel. They have sex of a sort, but needless to say, it is a joyless union, guilt-ridden and obligatory, during which Paul can do little more than lie back and think of what Simon Wilmot would have done in a similar situation.[52]

The next morning Paul rises early and goes out on to the deserted beach. Alone, he strips and goes for a swim in the flat, mirror-like sea. But soon he is conscious of someone swimming beside him. It is Irmi, a girl he has met at one of Ernst's friends'

parties back in Hamburg. They return to the beach and make
love before Irmi has to leave.

> *O vive lui! chaque fois*
> *Que chante le coq gaullois!*

An ambiguous couplet by Rimbaud, the young prodigy who
had slept with the much older *poète maudit* Paul Verlaine, is
running through his mind as he returns to the hotel for
breakfast.[53]

In strict literary-critical terms, Irmi seems a miraculous *dea ex
machina* in *The Temple*. Her appearance at Altamunde is too
heavily symbolic; a moral or at least 'normal' morning-after
corrective to the abnormal carnality of the night before.
Ultimately, however, whether or not she made so pat an arrival
is unimportant. What matters is that *she might have done*; for, as
we shall see, despite his vaunting ambition to be another Auden,
another Isherwood, the very fact that Spender could entertain or
fantasise over the idea of intercourse with her only underlines
the degree to which he was still fighting for a sexual identity of
his own.

━━━━━━

The Rhine walk was arranged for the first week of September
and, although we have only the accounts in *World Within World*
and *The Temple* to go on, to start with at least it seems to have
been considerably more successful than either the weekend at
Altamunde or the previous year's Wye tour with Marston.
Spender's companion, the Joachim Lenz of *World Within World*
and *The Temple*, was Erich's friend Herbert List, the nephew of
an eminent Great War *Wehrmacht* commander (who, as Field
Marshal Wilhelm List, was sacked by Hitler in 1942 after the
failure of a Nazi advance on the Caspian Sea).

Six years older than Spender, in 1929 Herbert was working in
his family firm of coffee merchants. Over the next decade,
however, he was to establish a reputation as a photographer,

particularly with his portraits of the young, sun-worshipping Germans of the pre-war years. ('On the Rhine, 1929' by Herbert List was used on the dust-jacket when *The Temple* was published in 1988.)

In sharp contrast to Erich Alport, Herbert was a hedonistic sophisticate with a starkly Modernist penthouse flat in Hamburg which overlooked the Alster and was furnished in up-to-the-minute Bauhaus style. Spender was mesmerised by him – by his dark hair, sallow complexion and almost Latin features, by his dark, attentive eyes and most of all by his sheer physicality. He swam every day, he played tennis, he skied, he even threw his arm around Spender's shoulders within minutes of meeting him. He seemed completely at ease with his sun-bronzed, muscular body in just the way Spender wished he was with his.[54]

More excitingly still, Herbert was as uncomplicated as Isherwood, Auden or any of their Berlin boys about sex and physical relationships. All he wanted to do was to *live* – and sun and air and water and making love didn't cost much at all, he said.[55]

Through a haze of absinthe at one of Joachim's parties, in *The Temple* Paul Schoner is simultaneously shocked and excited at the manner in which couples paired off in a thrilling 'modern' way and then rejoined their former partners, sometimes only minutes later. He shows his *naïveté*, too, when he discovers that even Irmi, the most innocent-looking girl in the room, has had an abortion.

But this was it! This was the Germany Spender had been looking for! Herbert had a casual but on-going relationship with a blond boy named Willi (Willy in *The Temple*) but even that did not prohibit his nocturnal cruising of the Sankt Pauli *Lokalen* with far more assiduity (and success) than Spender. He was at ease among the male prostitutes and rent-boys[56] – and indeed in *The Temple* it is Joachim who first introduces a rather drunk Paul Schoner to the 'low people' he so wants to meet. He takes him to a louche Hamburg bar called the Three Stars much frequented by transvestites where, among a scattering of respectable married couples, at long last Paul encounters a group of cloth-capped working-class boys. Attracted by the presence of the *Engländer*, of Willy, the monocled Ernst and the flashily dressed Joachim, three soon approach them, asking for *eine Zigarette* and cheekily taking four. Fritz, Paul is thrilled to discover, is a ship's stoker; Lothar works in a fairground. Another boy called Erich is unemployed and makes whatever living he can.[57] In the crowded, noisy *Keller* Joachim buys them drinks and plates of sausages and cold potato salad, all the while effortlessly maintaining his position as the centre of attention . . .

This vividly drawn scene is one of the most effective passages in *The Temple*. Through his account of Paul's terrified fascination, Spender catches something of his own astonishment at having finally arrived. There is too more than an echo of his amazement that Herbert List — that paragon, that *Übermensch* — had actually invited *him*, poor *unschuldige* Stephen, to come on a walking tour of the Rhine.

━━━━━

They met up at the railway station in Cologne (Köln) at the beginning of September 1929, and life at once reverted to the primal simplicity Spender had sampled in Hamburg on those few occasions when Erich was working and he could go to the *Schwimmbad* with Herbert and Willi. They swam in the River Rhine — whose strong currents were too much for Spender — and lazed on the beach and sunbathed; and Herbert flirted outrageously with every young man he met, a taste of what was to come.

After a few days they took the train south, travelling along the river, through Bonn and Koblenz, the hundred miles or so to the small town of Bingen. Despite what in *The Temple* comes over as a rather heavy-handed, and quite possibly retrospective, sense of impending doom,[58] Spender remained thrilled and intoxicated by the Rilkean presence and physicality of Herbert. He and his friends seemed to personify Germany — the Germany of the

Schwimmbad and bathing, Aryan arrogance and the pure, Second Reich *Wandervogel* ethos in which every Herbert, every Willi and every Fritz was nominally at least a fully Wagnerian Siegfried.

At Bingen, however, the idyll ended and, just like all Spender's previous forays into unknown or forbidden territory, the Rhine walk disintegrated into a nightmare of jealousy and frustration. Shortly after their arrival at the town the pair met up with a boy whom, in *The Temple*, Spender calls Heinrich. He had been born in a small village in Bavaria, but for the past two months had been 'wandering', carrying no more than a pair of lederhosen, a clean shirt, his shaving kit and a notebook in which he wrote poetry.

From the start Herbert was fascinated by Heinrich's Aryan perfection: even in Spender's descriptions he is almost too good to be true, with blond hair which incessantly flicked across his forehead and a faultless pale complexion. Superficially, Spender too found him attractive, but he was also immediately conscious of the skull beneath the skin and the fundamental gulf which stretched between him and this 'peasant' boy.[59] There was quite possibly an element of sour grapes about this, for from the moment they met, Herbert and Heinrich were mutually absorbed. Herbert in particular virtually forgot about the *unschuldige* Spender whom he had asked to accompany him. He insisted that Heinrich join them on the walk and abruptly announced that he and Spender would no longer be sharing a room at night; henceforth he would be sharing with Heinrich.

Overwhelmed by familiar feelings of anger, shame and self-pity,[60] Spender had to be persuaded to continue the trip. He was, he felt, suddenly *de trop* and 'a gooseberry'. Suddenly, everything had gone sour.

Increasingly, he implies in *The Temple*, he was discovering a less attractive side to Herbert's character, becoming aware of the cruel, stubborn and self-obsessed parts of his nature. He began to resent the way in which he continually spoke German with Heinrich (who could 'spik' only a few words of English), thus effectively excluding him from any real conversation.

Even Herbert's free, hedonistic way of life – the epitome of the 'Berlin spirit' which he had come to Germany to discover – was beginning to seem tawdry and superficial. Quite openly, he had told Spender that he could not see the point of writing poetry. Surely experiencing life as they were then doing was enough?[61]

No, no it wasn't. And ironically, as the three slowly made their way from village to village along the river – taking a week to cover the twenty or so miles between Bingen and Boppard – swimming every day and enjoying German wine and substantial meals at village inns every evening, Spender found himself drawn to Heinrich rather than Herbert. There was his undoubted physical beauty – he was as perfect as the naked gods of the swimming-pool in Hamburg[62] – but, more profoundly, despite the lack of education and sophistication, there was an innate seriousness which was much more to Spender's *real* taste than Herbert's callous matter-of-factness. He was a Communist and frustrated by 'that old patriotic stuff'. Like Spender, he found it all sentimental and old-fashioned. In *The Temple*, Joachim laughs at his political outbursts; Paul is moved . . .[63]

According to *The Temple*, again, Spender finally and not without some relief left Herbert and Heinrich at Boppard, which had originally been designated the half-way mark on the Rhine walk. (In *World Within World* the three youngsters, who are also described in the poem 'In 1929', part in Cologne.)[64] Herbert and Heinrich had decided to strike out westwards, following the Mosel into the heart of Rheinland-pfalz. Spender meanwhile retraced his steps and caught the night train for the long journey back to Cologne and on to Hamburg and Cuxhaven where the Felixstowe ferry was waiting.

He was back in London on 9 September.

———

The experience and memory of the *echt*, pre-Nazi Germany he first sampled in those few weeks in the late summer of 1929 colours and suffuses much of the poetry and prose which Spender wrote at this period. Raw and undigested, images of

Germany are far more central to his work than they are to Auden's or (with the special exception of the Isherwood of *Mr Norris Changes Trains* (1935) and *Goodbye to Berlin* (1939)) their contemporaries'. It is as if he felt compelled to record it all — but not, as Isherwood seems to have done, out of some prescient awareness of the impending '*Weimardämmerung*'. Rather, Spender's more self-conscious memorialising is exactly that: an implicit, self-conscious announcement that he had found what he was looking for. Despite the frustrations and humiliations of Hamburg, Altamunde and Bingen, the rude camaraderie of Germany was so much more to his taste than the costive, upper-middle-class niceness of Frognal and Oxford — or so he thought.

Typically, the Auden of the late twenties and early thirties subsumed *his* Germany of Berlin and boys — Goethe came later — into the greater, *abstract* landscape of what would become known as the Audenesque. It became part of a vague continent of fjords, uplands and passes, peopled by spies, riders and helmeted airmen; and only occasionally did its creator descend to the concrete, as in the opening lines of the rather bathetic minor poem 'On Sunday Walks':

> On Sunday walks
> Past the shut gates of works
> The conquerors come
> And are handsome.[65]

In direct contrast, the half-dozen or so of Spender's poems which were originally written in 1929 and 1930 and have survived in the 'Preludes' section of the *Collected Poems* are graphic postcards from a vanished world, snapshots of the prelapsarian days of Marlene Dietrich, Kurt Weill and *Die Dreigroschenoper* (1928). They are, deservedly, among Spender's best-known work. Quite as much as his later journalistic despatches from the Spanish Civil War, they are bulletins from a theatre of action — but much more so than has previously been recognised they also give an entrée into his own state of mind at this time.

Poems such as 'The Truly Great', 'Us', 'Helmut' and 'In 1929' have a muscle-bound and literally *muscular* vocabulary which is as distinct from Spender's later, more fluent style as it is from earlier attempts at the St Ebb's-and-limestone-Audenesque. In them, Spender adopts a veneer of cynical machismo,[66] suggesting that he is in his element. But ultimately it is all a front, all a bit of a performance. They are the poetic equivalent of Weill's astringent ballads, of Herbert List's strangely sexless photographs, the equally cold documentary films of Leni Riefenstahl and, come to that, the slightly later 'Social Realist' murals and *buon fresco* wall-paintings of Diego Rivera, examples of which survive in Detroit (1933) and elsewhere. (Interestingly, in *The Temple* Spender describes Lothar, the Hamburg fairground attendant, as looking like a poster of a Great War soldier.)[67]

Events take place in a landscape which is part Wagnerian, part Bauhaus; a clean but violent Germany which owes little or nothing to Bingen, the Rhine, the opulent Alport residence or even the sinister Europe of Auden's imagination. Instead, everything happens in an over-heated Hamburg – one poem is entitled 'Hamburg, 1929'[68] – in Sankt Pauli and prosaic and public locations in the industrial north.

The imagery is of masculine industry, action, modernity and progress. Fire, speed and thunder reach an apotheosis in descriptions of trains and the railway.[69] (Why? Because those trains brought him to that reincarnation of Wieland's smithy – or because they so effectively evacuated him when things got too hot?) These images are the natural predecessors of the slightly later poem 'The Express'[70], a confident cacophany of modernism whose startling success can be judged by a comparison with the second section of Auden's roughly contemporaneous 'Night Mail'. Spender has no time for Auden's uncharacteristic and rather sentimental romanticism – nor that of the G.P.O. publicity firm for which 'Night Mail' originally provided the commentary. His train has an abstract, almost mystical beauty.

Inevitably, the individuals who fill the foreground of these German poems also have a similarly mystical, god-like quality. The yearning homo-erotic overtones of such juvenilia as 'To J— H—' have gone. In poem after poem Spender now – rather unconvincingly – counts himself one of the privileged insiders. He writes directly for his young friends and his new young comrades. But, although all the poems are overtly physical, he still comes over as a curiously detached, clinical observer.[71] He slips into a rather hoarse vocative, but there is an unsatisfactory, voyeuristic edge to it, a smack of English upper-class smugness. Syntax splinters as if it is too narrow to confine this race of Lothars and Fritzs, this new breed of the Truly Great.

For all the disappointments and frustrations he had suffered, Germany – or more precisely the rather different Germanies represented by Herbert and Heinrich – had got into his blood. *Es war so wunder – wunderschön*. It was unlike anything he had experienced before; and like Paul Schoner in *The Temple* he wanted to get back as soon as possible.[73] At home in Frognal or, more particularly, in his lonely rooms at Univ in the spring and early summer of 1930, he could think of little else, certainly not cramming for the Finals which were looming at the end of Trinity Term.

By June he was being brought to book. The 'mad Socialist poet' was being confronted with the consequences of his actions. Eleven months earlier he had begun to keep a diary and in an opening paragraph had announced his intention to do no academic work during the 1929 summer vacation. Instead, he would concentrate on his own work, his own writing, his own life.[74] They were fine words, but neither trips to Hamburg nor the burgeoning portfolio of his own work cut much ice with his tutors.

Now, like so many students before him, Spender was no more than another begowned candidate sitting in the Examination Schools and doing his best to remember all he had bothered to learn of Politics, Philosophy and Economics. Sixty years later he looked back with uncharacteristic candour on this episode. No, he was no Isherwood, he said, nor had he ever really meant to be.

Accordingly there were no grand gestures, no blank verse

essays and no limericks in the examination rooms. There was none of Isherwood's confident, insolent rebellion. Instead, Spender recalled, he did his feeble best and wrote what he could; he was no more than a justified sinner.

In his Finals, he has since admitted, he 'ploughed' and did very badly.[75] That was putting it mildly. Hugh Corbett-Palmer admitted that he did 'badly' when he scraped a Third in History. Spender failed altogether and, despite much to-ing and fro-ing between Oxford, London and the continent until Easter 1931, eventually was to leave university without a degree.

———

Hedonism and Communism were only part of what Germany meant to Spender in 1929–30. More crucially, it was a district of the mind as much as a foreign country. The spirit of Germania had become his personal panacea; a solution to all the problems with which he had wrestled over the previous few years, and a poultice which would draw the poison from all his previous wounds.

Or so he thought – and quite how unrealistic this was is brought out in a letter he wrote to the ever patient Isherwood in the autumn of 1930. Only a page or two after he had announced that he had stopped being in love with Marston, he revealed that he would shortly be travelling to Berlin to meet a girl whom he was planning to marry. Spender hoped that Isherwood might smooth his path and go to see her – but not, under any circumstances, reveal his true intentions. She was very pleasant, very funny and only seventeen. She spoke English and had a brother who worked in the film industry and loved jazz. She was Jewish. Isherwood would like her. Her name was Gisa Soloweitschik.[76]

Spender had apparently met Gisa during an earlier under-graduate skiing holiday in Switzerland. However, this bald announcement of a possible marriage and one further suggestion that Isherwood should meet her[77] are the only references to her in his correspondence. Spender's notion that there might actually be a wedding seems to have been as quixotic as it was short-lived: although he mentions Gisa in *World Within World* it is as no more than a casual friend. Unsurprisingly perhaps, there is no hint of a romance between them or even of any unrequited feelings on his part.

Cooped up once more in Oxford, Spender seems to have been clutching at straws, both sexually and emotionally (and the letter's insistence that Isherwood must not tell Gisa of his plans only reinforces this view). It was apparently enough that Gisa lived in Berlin, had connections with jazz and even an entrée to UFA (at the time Germany's most prominent film production company) – although the fact that she was Jewish may also have had something to do with it.

Isherwood did eventually meet Gisa: somewhat apprehensively he used Spender's letter of introduction as a way of demonstrating *his* pro-Jewish sympathies to the other lodgers at the house in which he had a room, after a Nazi demonstration in October 1930.[78] They got on well – '*You like Mozart? Yes? Oh, I also! Vairy much!*' – and Spender's services as a go-between were soon dispensed with. Isherwood began calling at Gisa's home, allaying her mother's suspicions with large bunches of roses. Soon he had been introduced to the other members of her family, to Gisa's rather alarming father and in particular to her cousin Bernhard.

Rich and cultured, the Soloweitschiks were good copy and effective foils for his earthy landlady, the waddling, dressing-gowned Frl. Schroeder, in the diaries he was keeping at the time. Gisa, indeed, was to become the model for Natalia Landauer when he worked up those diaries into *Goodbye to Berlin*. In the story 'The Landauers' he describes her as

> . . . a schoolgirl of eighteen. She had dark fluffy hair; far too much of it – it made her face, with its sparkling eyes, appear too long and too narrow. She reminded me of a young fox.[79]

Ironically, there is no Spender-figure or go-between in 'The Landauers'.[80] As even Spender admits, in the story as in real life he was soon air-brushed out: within a matter of weeks

Isherwood had got to know Gisa better than he himself had managed to do in 'seven years'.[81] Strangely, however, Spender harboured no grudge at the way in which Isherwood had muscled in on the woman who was, after all, his putative fiancée. (Complicating matters even more, at precisely this time Isherwood — or at least the "I" of *Goodbye to Berlin* — was also half-seriously proclaiming that he and the English night-club singer he called Sally Bowles were 'going to be married, soon'.)

Spender had always maintained a rather naïve belief that all his friends should get on with and even *like* each other; but what in *World Within World* comes over as little short of his delight that Gisa and Isherwood were so close goes deeper than that. It was almost as if he was prepared to sacrifice his *droits de seigneur* in respect of Gisa in order to ensure the continuation of his own friendship with Isherwood. The Novelist certainly turned out to be more important to him than The Girl.

In all probability Spender had no concrete notion of what he was doing at the time; but in the following weeks and months and years it was Isherwood who became his greatest friend, his closest confidant and, on Spender's increasingly frequent visits to Germany, his near neighbour. Isherwood was, too, his best and most sympathetic critic[82] — good old Uncle Wiz had looked after his 'nephews' — and Spender relied upon him . . . until he found even more complete support in quite another quarter.

PART TWO

A Man
of the World

FOUR

Unter den Linden

Christopher Isherwood adapted better than just about every other British literary emigré to the bitter-sweet (and as time went on increasingly bitter) Berlin of the early 1930s. Unencumbered by anything but the smallest parcel of Party baggage, he became the most astute — or certainly the clearest-eyed — observer of the insidious rise of Hitler and the Nazis purely because he was in the thick of it all. (The card-carrying Communist novelist Edward Upward — the 'Allen Chalmers' of *World Within World* and Isherwood's early fiction — was there too; but his work, published under such titles as *No Home but the Struggle*, is suffocated by doctrinaire correctness.)

Isherwood noticed everything and was a part of everything. Not only did he live in damp attic rooms in working-class districts such as Hallesches Tor and Kottbusser Tor, both areas much frequented by Brownshirt S.A. (*Sturmabteilung*) thugs, he also day-tripped to the opulent homes of the city's doomed liberal-Jewish *haute bourgeoisie*, to Bernhard Soloweitschik's comfortable flat near the Tiergarten and the 'cubist flat-roofed steel- and-glass box' in the Grünewald at which he gave English lessons to Hippi Bernstein, his first regular pupil. He had a unique *carte blanche*, and used it to the full. His British passport and his almost protected status as the formidable Frl. Schroeder's 'Herr Issyvoo' gave him virtually ambassadorial status.

Thus, despite a later worry that the famous 'I am a camera' assertion at the beginning of his book *Goodbye to Berlin* made him seem no more than 'one of those eternal outsiders who watch the passing parade of life lukewarmbloodedly, with wistful impotence',[1] his view is very much an insider's. *Goodbye to Berlin* and the first part of *Christopher and His Kind* (which provides a hindsighted gloss on the novel and the Berlin of the thirties in general) are key documents in any understanding of the period.

Not the least reason for this is that, a full couple of decades before the term was coined, Isherwood was a born travel writer. From the very beginning, *Goodbye to Berlin* has an immediacy and honesty which is not present in Isherwood's earlier fiction:

> From my window, the deep solemn massive street. Cellar-shops where the lamps burn all day, under the shadow of top-heavy balconied façades, dirty plaster frontages embossed with scroll-work and heraldic devices. The whole district is like this: street leading into street of houses like shabby monumental safes crammed with the tarnished valuables and second-hand furniture of a bankrupt middle class.[2]

Isherwood loads his stories with topographical detail and local colour. A 'camera with its shutter open, quite passive, recording, not thinking', he scatters their pages with street names and descriptions of specific cafés, bars and restaurants — the Lady Windermere where Sally Bowles worked, the Troika, the Alexander Casino — and real people with just the same profligacy with which a tourist of considerably greater means would have showered their tables with marks and pfennigs.

There is a nervy disclaimer at the front of *Goodbye to Berlin* to the effect that 'readers are certainly not entitled to assume that [its] pages are purely autobiographical, or that its characters are libellously exact portraits of living persons'.[3] But its 'Berlin Diaries' — the first dating from August 1930, the second from the winter of 1932–3 — and its more obviously crafted stories are certainly exercises in *verismo*. If they don't tell the *whole* truth, they and Isherwood's previous novel *Mr Norris Changes Trains* (1933) preserve something, albeit a sanitised, asexual something, of life in Hallesches Tor, the cafés of Unter den Linden and the *plein air* boskiness of the Grünewald during the first half of the 1930s.

It would now be impossible (and tediously irrelevant even to try) to check their literal veracity. We have already seen that 'Herr Issyvoo' changed Gisa Soloweitschik's name to Natalia Landauer: can we therefore believe that the Nowaks, in whose cramped flat Isherwood temporarily rented a room, *really* lived in the Wassertorstrasse, or – for that matter – that they were even called Nowak? Happily, we are not put into the situation of having to do so – although ironically enough, the answer to the former question at least has been supplied by Isherwood himself. The family he always continued to call the Nowaks actually lived in Simeonstrasse, a road which led off the Wassertorstrasse in the Hallesches Tor district.

Fortunately for us, unlike Spender, in later life Isherwood drew a fairly distinct line between his fiction and his later, autobiographical work, even though most of the former continued to be closely based on events from his life. Thus, while it must be remembered that *Mr Norris Changes Trains* and *Goodbye to Berlin* are no more than novels – in 1977 Isherwood admitted that they 'leave out a great deal which I now want to remember; they also falsify events and alter dates for dramatic purposes'[4] – the very fact that the novels were closely based on assiduously kept diaries[5] means that *Goodbye to Berlin* in particular must be numbered among the earliest pieces of 'faction' to have been published.

For better or for worse, it is the definitive account of the way it felt to be a young, public-school-educated Englishman in the Berlin of the early 1930s. It does notice the rise of Hitler and the threat of Nazism, even if, for obvious reasons, it effectively though not entirely ignores the realities of the Berlin-meant-Boys side of things. There are, though, broad hints at the convenient, almost symbiotic, relationship which existed between the (comparatively) monied 'gentlemen' and the impoverished working-class German youths who, like Otto Nowak, were prepared to sleep with them in return for what are euphemistically described as 'gifts' – a couple of hundred marks for a new suit, a meal in a smart restaurant. (Looking back at *Goodbye to Berlin* in 1977, Isherwood noted that ' "Christopher Isherwood", the narrator of the novel [. . .] nearly gives himself away when he speaks of "the beautiful ripe lines of [Otto Nowak's] torso".[6]

Effectively, Isherwood hung on to his camera's early thirties negatives and then 'developed, carefully printed [and] fixed' them. It does not now matter that the whole business lasted a good six years, and that *Goodbye to Berlin* did not appear in print until 1939. It is enough that the pictures had been taken. However, in the light of all that came later – John van Druyten's stage-play *I Am a Camera*, based on *Goodbye to Berlin*, and *Cabaret*, the spectacularly successful but even more inaccurate stage musical and motion-picture spin-off – it is a pity that his snap of the Lady Windermere club was not taken with a slightly wider-angled lens. To the continuing chagrin of set-designers all around the world, this is all we get:

> The Lady Windermere (which now, I hear, no longer exists) was an arty 'informal' bar, just off the Tauentzeinstrasse, which the proprietor had evidently tried to make look as much as possible like Montparnasse. The walls were covered with sketches on menu-cards, caricatures and signed theatrical photographs – ('To the one and only Lady Windermere'. 'To Johnny, with all my heart'.) The Fan itself, four times life size, was displayed above the bar. There was a big piano on a platform in the middle of the room.[7]

In contrast, in the most unlikely situations, Isherwood can be as seductive and picaresque as any Hollywood director. *Goodbye to Berlin* marks his coming of age as a novelist. It has the same sureness of touch, the same eye for detail which characterises his 'mature' fiction, novels ranging from *Prater Violet* to much later works such as *A Single Man* and *A Meeting by the River*. There is something as romantically compelling as *La Bohème*, for instance, in his description of the squalor of the over-crowded Hallesches Tor flat of the Nowaks in which the young Otto is determined that his gentleman will come to live:

> 'Mother didn't like to ask you,' he told me, breathless. 'She was afraid you'd be annoyed . . . But I said that I was sure

you'd far rather be with us, where you can do just what you like and you know everything's clean, than in a strange house full of bugs . . . Do say yes, Christoph, please! It'll be such fun. You and I can sleep in the back room. You can have Lothar's bed – he won't mind. He can share the double-bed with Grete . . . And in the mornings you can stay in bed as long as ever you like. If you want, I'll bring your breakfast . . . You will come, won't you?'[8]

———

You will come, won't you? As Isherwood was to acknowledge, there are 'few surviving letters written at that time by Christopher and his friends to each other'.[9] But even the scattered and rather tatty fragments which have come down to us make it clear that by the beginning of 1930 even Stephen Spender had discovered – or, more accurately, been told – that Germany was more than a holiday. Isherwood wrote to him from Berlin on 6 February:

It's all so pleasant and I have utterly lost any sense of strangeness in being abroad. I even don't particularly care when I see England again. And when I read in my diary about my life at home, it's like people on the moon.[10]

It is doubtful whether this letter was written on the official letterhead (the present author has been unable to locate the original) but in February 1930 Isherwood's address in Berlin was in a street called In Den Zelten, near the Tiergarten park. The previous November, he had managed to rent a room in a building (once the home of the violinist Joseph Joachim) which was then occupied by some of the staff from Dr Magnus Hirschfeld's Institute for Sexual Science (*Institut für Sexual-Wissenschaft*). Isherwood's 'pleasure' was intensified by the fact that he had found a niche for himself in a *demi-monde* whose dramatis personae would sooner or later include the likes of 'good old, bad old' Gerald Hamilton, the engaging con-man and fixer who was later to be immortalised as Mr Norris; the anthropologist John Layard, who had so influenced Auden's thinking and writing; and the English night-club singer and would-be actress Jean Ross (Sally Bowles). Inevitably, there were, too, any number of Ottos – the could-be, may-be, should-be incarnations of the elusive German Boy, for the most part 'rank amateur' male prostitutes ('*Pupenjungen*'), he picked up at the Cosy Corner, the *bierkeller* in Zossenerstrasse whose address he could still remember more than fifty years later.[11]

Spender was beguiled and excited. Far more than even Auden, Isherwood was plumbing unsounded depths, reaching new uncharted heights. Living on what he could earn as a teacher of English, he was experiencing Germany in the raw, *life* in the raw – and Spender wanted a part of it. At the beginning of January 1931 he wrote to tell Isherwood that he would be joining him in Berlin within a few weeks. He had finally decided to make the break with London and Oxford and all they represented.[12]

Isherwood received this news with less than outright joy. For Spender, however, it presaged a new and significant stage in his development. For some unspecified reason, when he had finally been able to return to Germany in 1930 (on what was only his second visit) he had not gone to Berlin. Rather, he had chosen to return to Hamburg.

Erich Alport can hardly have been the lodestone which drew him back there. On the other hand, Spender's later explanation that he had specifically opted to make Hamburg his particular bailiwick because Auden and Isherwood had so successfully colonised Berlin[13] is both disingenuous and chronologically incorrect. By the summer of 1930 Isherwood had been in the German capital for little more than six months (he set out on 'what might even become an immigration' on 29 November 1929)[14] Auden too was hardly a Berliner at this period. Indeed, he was in Britain for most of 1930, in part because he was recuperating from an operation to repair a rectal fissure – 'the stigma of Sodom', he called it – but principally because that Easter he had accepted a teaching job in a boys' preparatory school.

Spender's own record of this second visit to Hamburg is characteristically vague. In *World Within World* he implies that he steered clear of the Alport mansion and all that it stood for, and even eschewed the Hotel Minerva. Instead, he roughed it and stayed in a boarding house.[15] Growing self-confidence also gave him the courage to revisit some of the port's *Lokalen* on his own.

For all his would-be independence, however, as his January 1931 letter suggests he was soon visiting Berlin more and more frequently – having chosen to interpret Isherwood's suggestion that it would be great fun if they were neighbours more literally than Isherwood perhaps intended.[16] And, in *World Within World*, he paints a picture of the two of them as bosom Berlin friends, united against the world.

Typically, he suggests, their days were spent in each other's company. Leaving his comparatively luxurious lodgings in Motzstrasse, Spender would walk down through streets of slums to the even more sordid Nollendorfstrasse – whither, at number 17, the rooming-house run by Frl. Meta Thurau (*Goodbye to Berlin*'s Frl. Schroeder), Isherwood had moved in December 1930 after leaving the Nowaks' and enduring a few weeks in lodgings at Admiralstrasse 38. (Interestingly, Isherwood described this latter move as 'westward, from working-class into middle-class Berlin'.)[17] Thence, the two would buy a cheap lunch before ambling over to a shop near the Bahnhof-am-Zoo to gorge themselves on sweets and toffees. On fine days they would then take the train out to the lakes and pine forests of the Grünewald; otherwise they would stroll through the Zoo or up and down the Unter den Linden . . .

This is a memoir of bachelor contentment, and *World Within World* only gilds its singular oddity by appending it almost post-coitally to an account of Spender's relationship with a working-class German boy whom he has identified only as 'Walter'. On the surface it is as if this long-delayed liaison with one of the so-sought-after 'low boys' had finally made Spender a man; at least the equal of Uncle Wiz and the libidinous Isherwood.

As even Spender recognised, however, the affair had serious and long-lasting repercussions. They stemmed directly from the moment when he decided to pick up the boy (whom in *World Within World* he rather ungraciously describes as a 'tramp').[18] In the short term the problems were predictable enough. Spender was, quite literally, an innocent abroad, ludicrously ill-prepared for the sordid, quotidian brutality of life among Germany's 'low-people'. Back at Oxford, as we have already seen, he had been living a life of Romantic purity as his attempts at sexual conquest collapsed in ignominious failure. (One putative inamorato completely misunderstood his advances and, at the vital moment, told Spender that he had been so impressed by his purity – for which we might read timidity – he had himself decided to give up masturbating and live a life of virginal purity!)[19] Frustrating though it must have been, it has to be said that this life suited him rather more than the erotic rough-and-tumble he was now encountering in Hamburg and at the Cosy Corner in Berlin.

John Lehmann was another of Isherwood's guests at that Zossenerstrasse *Bierkeller* at this period, and later gave a graphic description of the world into which Isherwood – he calls him William – was introducing Spender:

> One of the first things William did to further my education, was to take me on a tour of the homosexual bars and night-clubs. We started with one of the most popular non-smart *Lokals*, the 'Cosy Corner'. This *Lokal* was a sensational experience for me, a kind of emotional earthquake, and I think William was right to throw me in at the deep end. Things unimagined by me in all my previous fantasies went on there. The place was filled with attractive boys of any age between sixteen and twenty-one, some fair and curly-haired, some dark and often blue-eyed, and nearly all dressed in extremely short lederhosen which showed off their smooth and sun-burnt thighs to delectable advantage.
>
> [. . .] The lavatory had no cubicles. I was followed in by several boys, who, as if by chance, ranged themselves on either side of me and pulled out their cocks rather to show them off than to relieve nature as I was doing. I don't think a drop fell into the gutter from any of them; but many sly grins were cast in my direction. I returned to our bench, shaken by this

exhibition into a turbulence of anticipation. William said to me. 'Any you fancy?'[20]

Walter had a similar effect on Spender as the boys in the lavatory did on Lehmann. But by even Spender's account, Walter saw him coming and acted accordingly. He accepted the *Engländer*'s 'gifts' and by ever more transparent fabrications extracted even more. Asleep in a station waiting-room, he said once, he had been robbed of the money which Spender had given him to buy a ticket home. On another occasion he claimed he had lent the ticket money to a friend who needed it to pay for his mistress's abortion ... Months later, it took all Herbert List's skills as a stand-in Uncle Wiz before Spender could be persuaded to remove his *gemeine Leute* spectacles and write off Walter as a crook and a wastrel.

The boy was packed off home once again – this time Spender actually bought and presented him with the ticket – and Spender was left lonely and several hundred marks the poorer. He was, though, he thought, considerably wiser. Sex notwithstanding, through Walter he had gained a vivid, albeit sentimental, insight into the lives of the working classes and acquired the rudiments of a social conscience.[21] Thus he did not blame Walter for gulling him: rather, he came close to thanking him. In their relationship, Spender acknowledged, there had been moments, odd fleeting moments, when he had found the affection he was so desperately seeking.[22]

━━━━━━

Christopher Isherwood, with sixteen- or seventeen-year-old Otto Nowak still happily in tow, visited Spender in Hamburg that May. We can visualise the pair of them on their arrival: we only have to develop, carefully print and fix the images. *I am a camera* ... So –

Isherwood is smaller than – though not altogether unlike – the young Michael York who played Brian Roberts, the innocent, Englishman-abroad Isherwood-figure in Bob Fosse's 1972 film of *Cabaret*. He is correctly, almost punctiliously dressed. His shirt-cuffs are crisply starched, his hair neatly brushed and waving down over his forehead. In his face, however, at the corners of his eyes, around his mouth, there are tell-tale lines.[23]

Click!

Ten years Isherwood's junior, Otto is more earthy, less preoccupied with things; *mentem mortalia tangunt* means nothing to him. He is 'the exciting laughter of the crowd and the inviting shadow of the woods'.[24]

Click!

His face is 'like a ripe peach. His hair is fair and thick, growing low on his forehead. He has small sparkling eyes, full of naughtiness, and a wide, disarming grin, which is too innocent to be true. When he grins, two large dimples appear in his peach-bloom cheeks.'[25]

Click! click! – one for each!

It is nearly summer; after the dark, damp Hamburg winter the weather is turning warm and fine. Otto is 'a narcissist' and has been exercising with a chest-expander. Consequently, although he isn't conventionally handsome, he 'certainly has a superb pair of shoulders and chest for a boy of his age'. He is also inordinately proud of his 'sensual nostrils and lips' and of his skin, which is 'as smooth as silk'.

Click! . . . Albeit that they are seen through different eyes – that they were snapped, as it were, with different cameras – after more than sixty years these vivid images of Isherwood and Otto still have all the sunlit, soot-and-chalk clarity of black-and-white photographs. Just out of the picture, however, dark clouds are gathering . . .

Neither Isherwood nor Spender is exactly specific about what occurred in Hamburg that May, but it is clear that (for want of a better term) the lovers' visit was not a success. It is not difficult to imagine Spender's frustration and even jealousy at the apparent happiness and *completeness* of Isherwood and Otto; and indeed *Christopher and His Kind* seems to hint that the Hamburg débâcle – which marked the beginning of a radical change in the relationship between the two writers – may well have been caused by sexual tension. Isherwood certainly seems to have been suspicious that Spender was getting rather too friendly with Otto.

Psychologically speaking, such a scenario has a ring of truth about it. Isherwood and Otto arrived in Hamburg at precisely the time when Spender was finally convincing himself that he was not in love with Marston, and during a period when he was seemingly none too worried about the biblical and social strictures attached to the sanctity of 'thy neighbour's wife', however loosely that was interpreted. Only six months later, in the winter of 1930, when he was back at Oxford, Auden introduced him to *his* then boyfriend, Johnny Walker. The three went to the cinema together – and the following day Spender received a postcard from Auden: 'I hear you held Johnny's hand yesterday in the Super. Stephen, is this manners?'[26]

Whatever the facts of that incident (Spender later told Isherwood that it was quite untrue), it certainly seems to have been Spender who was chiefly to blame for the muted and then marked antagonism which came to characterise his relationship with Isherwood for the next couple of years. Although their individual accounts of the temporary suspension of friendship are subtly different, publicly at least they both ascribe it to Spender's gaucheness and his blatant hero-worshipping of Isherwood, which was then reaching extra-terrestrial heights. The sea captain has been recast as a polar explorer and Spender was at his most embarrassingly cloying, as is evinced by a reminiscence he sent to Isherwood more than forty years later reminding him of this period when, although poor himself, Isherwood had made heroic sacrifices to buy suits for Otto.[27]

World Within World explicitly admits all this, but is rather less frank than *Christopher and His Kind* about the extent of Spender's self-abasement and Isherwood's increasingly tetchy reaction to it. Indeed, while Spender could admit in 1951 that he was attracted to Isherwood's adventurous life, his complete independence and his interesting friends,[28] the later *Christopher and His Kind* – written, of course, with full access to *World Within World* – suggests that at this period Isherwood still regarded Spender as a half-hearted day-tripper dipping a timid toe into the thrilling, dangerous waters of Berlin.

It is certainly clear that Isherwood was getting tired of all the self-abasement and hero-worshipping. It is apparent too that matters started to get serious when Spender moved to Berlin on a semi-permanent basis and consciously began behaving as Isherwood's pupil, willy-nilly casting the erstwhile captain, admiral and polar explorer, as his 'mentor'. Not unnaturally, in private Isherwood began to rail against this unwanted new role:

> The pupil, striding along beside the brisk large-headed little figure of the mentor, keeps bending his beautiful scarlet face downward, lest he shall miss a word, laughing in anticipation as he does so. There are four and a half years between their ages and at least seven inches between their heights. The pupil already has a stoop, as all tall people must who are eager to hear what the rest of the world is saying. And *maybe the mentor, that little tormentor, actually lowers his voice at times, to make the pupil bend even lower.*[29]

As he saw it, Isherwood goes on, for all Spender's praise of his mentor's 'renunciation' of England and his 'heroic' poverty, his self-appointed disciple was little more than a dilettante, a well-heeled tourist 'doing' Berlin in exactly the same way that the likes of Nancy Cunard were at that time taking late-night taxi-rides from Mayfair and Belgravia to explore the pubs of Soho and London's 'bohemian' Fitzrovia.[30] 'Christopher let him have a glimpse of the rigours of Simeonstrasse, and he was suitably impressed,' he wrote.[31]

There is more than a little truth in all this. As we have seen, throughout 1930 and the early part of 1931 Spender *was* only an occasional visitor to Germany since, however much he may have resented it, his principal commitment remained with Oxford. With a modest but still useful private income of some £300 a year[32] (derived, it seems, at least in part from the continuing interest paid on Lily Spender's 'funds') he was also much better off than Isherwood, who survived on half that amount.[33] He did not need to teach. He could afford to shower Isherwood with 'books and other gifts' and embarrassing cash hand-outs which Isherwood sometimes paid back, and sometimes didn't.[34] He even dragged his mentor off to restaurants which served more palatable fare than the horse meat and lung soup on which Isherwood was then resignedly but contentedly living. '*Was ich habe gegessen ich habe gegessen*' — what I have eaten, I have eaten, he would say, making even Spender at least momentarily aware that by such little lapses he had betrayed his mentor.

Rather prissily, Spender later recalled that his (limited) consumption of such meals upset his stomach and rotted his teeth.[35] He was appalled that Isherwood was spending just sixty pfennigs on a meal and secretly delighted when he could slope off, on his own or in the better-heeled company of his brother Michael or the American composer Roger Sessions, and spend two or three times that sum on a decent meal in one of the pleasant restaurants on the Kurfürstendamm.[36]

A generous reading of *World Within World* suggests that Spender was at least dimly aware that he was a rather self-conscious 'slummer' during these early visits to Berlin. However, like *Christopher and His Kind*, the book is all but silent about the root-cause of the developing friction between Spender and Isherwood. Indeed, neither book puts forward anything which seems *serious* enough to have brought about a potentially permanent falling-out between the two men.

There is, however, one logical and indeed plausible reason for the abrupt rupturing of what had become one of the key relationships in Spender's (if not perhaps in Isherwood's) life. In a footnote to his limited edition of Spender's letters to Isherwood at this period, Lee Bartlett (who prepared the book with the co-operation of both Spender and Isherwood) explicitly states that 'Otto Nowak (in *Goodbye to Berlin*) was modelled on Walter'.[37] If it does not actually say as much, this is a strong hint that Walter and Otto (here we should perhaps remind ourselves that these are both pseudonyms) were actually the same person.

Ostensibly startling, even shocking, such a scenario does make sense: if the aloof and lofty Spender did make off with Isherwood's boyfriend it would certainly have proved an

effective catalyst for Isherwood's pent-up irritation and resent-
ment. If – not for the first time – we set aside Spender's
chronology in *World Within World* and allow Isherwood a
certain economy with the truth the facts certainly fit. Isher-
wood's rather enigmatic *Goodbye to Berlin* story 'On Ruegen
Island' also suddenly snaps into very much sharper focus.

We know from both *World Within World* and *Christopher
and His Kind*[38] that Spender and Isherwood, along with Otto –
and, for a period at least, W.H. Auden – did go to Ruegen (*Insel
Rügen*) in the summer of 1931. But even in *Christopher and His
Kind* ('The book I am now going to write will be as frank and
factual as I can make it.'[39]) Isherwood is unusually opaque
about what really happened; indeed, his glosses on the story
actually further muddy the waters.

In 'On Ruegen Island' he introduces us to a new character,
Peter Wilkinson, who is central to that story but never men-
tioned again. Although he is 'thin and dark [and] wears horn-
rimmed glasses' a protracted and largely irrelevant biographical
sketch of Peter suggests that he is principally based on Spender.

Peter is, for instance, one of four children (albeit that he is the
youngest and has two sisters). His elder brother is a 'scientist and
explorer' who reads papers to the Royal Geographical Society
about his work on the Great Barrier Reef. (After leaving Oxford
with a degree in engineering science, Spender's older brother
Michael had travelled to Greenland, the Himalayas and, among
other places, the Great Barrier Reef.)[40]

Furthermore, Peter's mother has 'petted and coddled him into
a funk', because he was 'delicate, as a boy'. Consequently,
Isherwood notes, he is still socially insecure – and, interestingly,
still 'flushing scarlet' in company. Peter is the only one of her
children to whom his mother had shown any affection. But then
'she got ill herself and soon afterwards died', leaving her
youngest son to the mercy of a father who 'with his diseased
kidney, his whisky, and his knowledge of "handling men", was
angry and confused and a bit pathetic'.

At Oxford, Peter 'always struck the wrong note'. However,
help was at hand: right on cue an uncle died and left him all his

money. Peter emerged into the world and, after a fumbled attempt at heterosexuality, pitched up at Sellin on Ruegen Island with Otto and an inheritance. It was 'not very much, but enough to live on, comfortably'.[41]

Confusingly, however, in *Christopher and His Kind*, Isherwood explicitly states that Peter was *not* a portrait of Spender and that the story was intended as 'an attempt to describe the relationship between Christopher and Otto as it may have appeared to a third party, Stephen Spender'.[42] There are, it has to be said, one or two features of Peter's background which are specifically drawn from Isherwood's rather than Spender's early life. It was Isherwood, for example, who inherited such money as he had from an uncle.[43] But even if we ignore the *roman à clef* elements, *Christopher and His Kind* still gives a vivid postcard account of events on Ruegen Island that summer:

> All in all, this Ruegen visit wasn't a success. Wystan soon returned to England. Christopher and Otto squabbled [. . .] On the last day, Christopher cut his toe on a sharp bit of tin while wading into the sea. The cut festered and he was a semi-cripple for several weeks after his return to Berlin.[44]

'Meanwhile, Stephen had been in Salzburg,' Isherwood goes on. He seems not to have left in a huff like Peter in *Goodbye to Berlin* ('I feel I've got to keep travelling until I'm clear of this bloody country.')[45] but to have kept to a pre-arranged plan to meet up with Isaiah Berlin, another of his Oxford contemporaries, at Salzburg in time for the start of the summer music festival. The two shared an enthusiasm for Beethoven's late string quartets and Mozart's operas. They heard Bruno Walter conducting *Don Giovanni*, and in Salzburg Berlin finally convinced Spender that this was ultimately more sublime than *Fidelio*.[46]

There is an inevitability about the fact that Spender felt much more at home with Isaiah Berlin than he had done with Isherwood. It is not just that they were both Oxford men. Rather, Spender's own recollections of this vacation trip (which laid the foundations for another life-long friendship) explicitly state that with Berlin he could see himself as an equal, something he could not do with Auden, who always reminded him of a schoolmaster.[47] Here we can justifiably read Isherwood for Auden and 'mentor' for 'schoolmaster' – and imagine Spender's delight at pitching up amidst the high culture and concert halls, the opera houses, chocolate-houses and expensive restaurants at Salzburg after his exposure to the spartan, if hedonistically healthy Ruegen regime.

For, as a later commentator has confirmed, even in 1931 Ruegen Island was well known as a centre of Aryan 'Naktkultur'. A mile or two off-shore in the warm, shallow Baltic Sea and no more than ten miles from end to end, the resort, with its sandy beaches, clap-boarded villages and forests of birch and fir trees, was little more than 'a place for enjoying sex in the sun with tanned German boys'. (Later, Hitler would use *Insel Rügen* as the code-name for his plans to aid the Nationalists in the Spanish Civil War, presumably aware of only the half of what passed as Aryan perfection on the island.)[48]

The 'tanned German boys' *double entendre* is probably accidental; although *Christopher and His Kind* makes it clear that, despite the proximity and sheer availability of Otto/Walter and any number of other bronzed and naked boys, Spender was not much involved in the Cosy Cornering side of things. As we might expect, he remained a lonely, self-obsessed outsider for much of his stay. But while Auden, who also had little time for the sun-sea-and-sex side of things, sat in his room and wrote during his brief visit – he was working on *The Orators*[49] – he announced his separateness rather differently.

Almost obsessively he began taking photographs. On one level this can be seen as his literally usurping Isherwood's *I Am a Camera* role. More profoundly, however, it is another symbol of Spender's own isolation. Only when he set the camera's time-release and then jumped in front of the lens was he ever *really* a part of things – and then, tellingly, only with his fellow Englishmen-abroad, Auden and Isherwood. Brazening things out far longer than necessary, Spender tacitly admitted all this four decades later when he reminded Isherwood how, with 'a masturbatory camera' he took a photograph 'US THREE'.[50]

This was the frequently reproduced snap – it really is no more[51] – in which Spender has 'an expression on his face which suggests an off-duty Jesus', while the much shorter Isherwood, as he himself noted, appears to be 'standing in a hole'.[52] There were many more pictures that holiday, and principally, inevitably, they were of Otto. Isherwood remembers Spender taking an endless number of photographs of him, 'some absurd, some animally beautiful'. There was 'Otto in a loincloth, strumming on a guitar and pretending to be an Hawaiian boy; Otto caught unconsciously taking the pose of a Michelangelo nude on the Sistine Chapel ceiling' . . .[53]

Click, click! . . . The pictures have faded now, or been lost altogether; sepia images of a vanished world . . . *photographs of boys, all taken with the camera tilted upwards, from beneath, so that they look like epic giants, in profile against enormous clouds.*[54]

The image of Spender taking them, however, a Leica or Voightlander between him and the real action, is a potent one. Nor is it an entirely inaccurate caricature, for the 1931 Ruegen Island holiday marked the end of his real involvement with Germany. He had written to Isherwood from Salzburg suggesting that he might move in with him at Frl. Thurau's flat in the Nollendorfstrasse when he returned to Berlin. But, understandably, Isherwood – still in pain from his inflamed and festering toe – had been less than keen:

> I think I could find you something cheaper two doors away. I think it is better if we don't all live right on top of each other, don't you? I believe that was partly the trouble at Ruegen.[55]

Spender, Isherwood recalls, took the hint: Isherwood was with Otto; he would have been quite definitely *de trop*. Thus, instead of going back to Berlin, Spender took the train to Hamburg and eventually arrived home in London.

And so, rather ignominiously, in the summer of 1931 his Berlin career effectively ended. He had been getting on Christopher's nerves and could see that he did not really belong

in the German capital. There were to be many further visits —
there was even another holiday on Ruegen Island the next
summer — but henceforth Spender's base was to be London. It
was rather more than two doors away from Isherwood, but it
was, as it would remain, his spiritual home.

His time with Walter and the experience he had gained living in
Hamburg and Berlin had nevertheless had a profound effect on
him. More so perhaps than it had even done to Isherwood,
Germany had atuned him to what was going on around him. In
Hamburg, in Berlin and now in London he responded to the
intangible mood in the streets rather than to the day-to-day
idiosyncrasies of the neighbours whom he (unlike Isherwood)
hardly knew. Thus it comes as no surprise to discover that the
real insidiousness of the rise of Nazism is better conveyed in
World Within World (and later volumes of Spender's such as
The Thirties and After) than it is in either *Goodbye to Berlin* or
Christopher and His Kind. Unhindered by Isherwood's studied
objectivity, Spender was able to come to his own conclusions,
and to ruminate at length in his Journals — Isherwood made do
with mere diaries — on what he saw happening around him and
on his own protracted but inexorable conversion to com-
munism.

He first heard of Adolf Hitler in 1929. Herbert List had
mentioned an hypnotic Austrian political orator who could hold
a crowd spellbound with 'nonsense'.[56] Two years later it was,
of course, far less easy to dismiss what Hitler said as nonsense. In
Berlin, as Isherwood observed, heads were already getting
broken. Even on Ruegen Island families were marking out their
places on the beach by planting fir-cones in the sand which spelt
out inscriptions such as *Waldesruh, Stahlhelm* and *Heil Hitler!*
There were other manifestations, too, of the way things were
going: 'I saw a child of about five years old, stark naked,
marching along all by himself with a swastika flag over his
shoulder and singing "*Deutschland über alles*" '.[57]

Spender saw such sights, but through a wide-angled lens rather than Isherwood's probing telephoto. At first he was just dimly aware that something was happening and that a feeling of doom hung over the streets of Berlin. They did not seem to belong to the people any more as foreign governments, money-lenders, industrialists, generals and would-be dictators squabbled over the Germany which he and Isherwood and so many others had once seen as the promised land.[58] Perhaps a new god was rising – perhaps, as the Nazis had it, in their simplistic parroting of Friedrich Nietzsche, he had just died.[59]

This bewilderment and equivocation did not last long, however; and Spender was soon galvanised into action. He and Isherwood went to see the films of Sergei Eisenstein and other committed Soviet directors – *Battleship Potemkin, The Mother, The Way Into Life* and *Ten Days That Shook the World* made particularly striking impressions – as soon as they opened in Berlin cinemas. They took trams to small, out-of-town picture-houses which showed the work of native German Left Wing film-makers. Overtly didactic though they were, these also seemed to offer a message of hope and an answer to the Jeremiahs who, like T.S. Eliot, were already prophesying an end to Civilisation As We Know It.[60]

So too, but on a more personal level, did Isherwood's school-friend Edward Upward (the Allen Chalmers of *Lions and Shadows*) with whom Spender became friendly at this period. Nervy and excitable, superficially Upward was little changed from the 'pale, small, silent' would-be poet, one year his senior, whom Isherwood had first met in the library at Repton School. With his dark hair and dark blue eyes, in 1931 he was still strikingly handsome,[61] although now more interested in prose. And against all the odds, by 1931 he was also a card-carrying Communist.

Upward had arrived in Berlin on the return leg of an official Intourist visit to Moscow. He talked of little but 'the Cause', thrilling and exhilarating both Spender and Isherwood (but more particularly Spender) by the very fact that *he* of all people – someone from their own class and background – could really be a Communist, as much as by his committed Marxist dialectic.

Resolutely heterosexual despite his close friendship with what would later be dubbed the 'Homintern', for all the championing he received from Isherwood and John Lehmann, Upward never really fulfilled his potential. (And how could he, Auden would ask, *a man who could never bring himself to sit down on a lavatory seat?*) Spender, however, was captivated by his personality and wholly won-over by his ideas. Upward seemed to have an answer for everything. A newly flourishing German nationalism – *just look at the Nazis!* – was being aided and abetted by Western capitalism, he said. It all amounted to a vendetta against Soviet socialism and could only lead to an annihilating pan-European war. Unless . . .

Unless . . . unless . . . In his heart at least, Spender was converted. Surely, he believed, he could now see a way forward from the lazy liberalism of his youth. If only the conflict between those whom he chose (or learnt) to see as the bourgeoisie and the proletariat could be ended, then all would be well and all manner of things would be well. For his own part, he decided after some reflection that he was quite prepared to make the material sacrifices necessary to bring this utopia about; they would be worth it if 'socialism "happened" '.

There is no reason to doubt the sincerity of this argument – it is essentially the same as that rehearsed by any number of his contemporaries on the intellectual Left in the early 1930s – but, typically, Spender was unable to take it to its logical conclusion. *Fain I would climb, but fear I should fall* . . . Rather presciently, he saw that actually signing up and becoming a member of the Communist Party, or even publicly espousing communism as a concept, *de facto* went against his liberal concepts of freedom and truth. He was, he recognised, an outsider – and in his head rather than his heart he could not conceive of himself as a member of a classless society any more than he could really see a place for himself in Isherwood's classlessly promiscuous Berlin.

Consequently, he hedged. (When he did finally join the Communist Party in February 1937 it was, as we shall see, for fundamentally different reasons.) He said all the right things, parroted the slogans and tried his best to assimilate the dialect of the new tribe.

This is reflected in his published work from this period. His poem 'Perhaps' is one of several experiments which failed: as W.B. Yeats had already written, 'The best lack all conviction, while the worst are full of passionate intensity'.[62] It boasts a vocabulary every bit as urgent as Isherwood's historic present tense and one which easily outdoes the telegraphese of the Audenesque. There are motorcycles, aeroplanes, cars, trains, headlines and maps; but there is also a distinctly leaden thud. The newsreel details seem merely pasted on. It is not great poetry.

In the summer of 1931, however, Spender was not in the business of writing poetry. Concommitant with his being a fellow-traveller there was, he felt, the implication that he should at least try to provide ideologically correct texts. He was not alone in any of this. Like him, like Upward, many of the young writers of the thirties had also decided that it was their duty to write forthright, commited poetry and prose in which 'analytic intellect' would replace daffodils and old-fashioned bourgeois inspiration.[63] This was to be their sacrifice for the Cause. Humbly though, Spender later accepted that, ironically, it did little to promote them into Shelley's poet-legislator class. It just left them preaching to the converted, writing for each other or for the sixth-formers at their old schools.[64]

Running parallel with this 'public' pseudo-communism there was a more private spring to Spender's sudden politicisation. His relationship with Walter had given him an insight into pro-letarian reality unlike anything which he had previously known. *If only his parents had not kept him from those children who were rough!* He picked at this scab of class-based guilt with a guilty compulsion. Luckily, in the thirties no one was looking to poets for an intelligent, Oxford-educated man's considered response to *Mein Kampf* (which Spender read out of appalled curiosity) or even *Das Kapital*. It did not matter that a poem like 'Unemployed'[65] rang horribly hollow. Nor, for that matter, did many of his first readers pause to ask what *real* experience Spender had had of an elementary school classroom or, for that matter, a slum. To his essentially London-based readership, composed as it principally was of the metropolitan literati, the publication of 'An Elementary School Classroom in a Slum'[66] merely confirmed that the young, handsome Stephen Spender was one of the coming men, the ideal guest at luncheon parties and good value for weekends in the country.

And, in their own phrase, many of the leading society hostesses of the day were not slow in 'taking him up' on the strength of his convictions. He was, after all, amusing.

FIVE

A Charmed Life

Having at last severed his connections with Oxford University, early in 1931 Stephen Spender had finally become a free agent. After fifteen frustrating years in which he had had no option but to bend to the will of preparatory school masters, the whims of his father, the dictates of Hilda Schuster and the dogmatism of the University College dons, he was at last able to do as he liked. Ironically, however, this amounted to little more than joining the family firm.

A few years previously, a long-lasting family feud had developed when the young John Betjeman announced that he was not interested in succeeding his father as the head of G. Betjemann [sic] & Sons Ltd, the cabinet-making business which had been founded by John's great-grandfather as long ago as 1820. In direct contrast, Spender was determined to continue into a third generation the fifty-year-old literary traditions of his family. His grandmother Lily had started the ball rolling, various great-uncles and then Harold and J.A. had kept it in motion: now, although there is no evidence of any overt dynastic pretension, Spender was preparing to run with it.

He was just twenty-two years of age and had published little more than a couple of reviews and essays; but, rapidly and with remarkable assiduity, he assumed the role of Man of Letters. Perhaps he was *too* assiduous – T. S. Eliot gently pointed out that Spender's review of his *The Use of Poetry and the Use of Criticism* (1933) was rather over-serious and made no allowance for irony[1] – but it hardly mattered. Soon, people – university friends, editors, publishers, society hostesses; *really, the right sort of people* – were taking at least as much notice of

the *Wunderkind* Stephen as they and their likes had ever taken of
Harold or even the revered J.A.

Eliot himself, this time in his role as prim publisher, had
already begun to make encouraging noises about Spender's
poetry from his desk at the offices of Faber & Faber. Two or
three streets away at the Hogarth Press, Virginia Woolf was also
(rather reluctantly) reading the manuscript of what can only
have been an early draft of *The Temple*.

In 1931 Michael Roberts had accepted 'Oh young men oh
young comrades' and a handful of Spender's other poems for
inclusion in what would become one of the most influential – if
idiosyncratic – anthologies of the decade, *New Signatures:
Poems by Several Hands*, which was published early the
following year. (Fellow contributors included W. H. Auden,
Cecil Day-Lewis, John Lehmann, Julian Bell, William Plomer
and William Empson.) A few months later the 1932 anthology
of *Oxford Poetry* appeared with a fond dedication to Auden,
Day-Lewis and Spender.

It was all good publicity, as was the appearance in July 1932
of Virginia Woolf's mischievously polemical pamphlet *A Letter
to a Young Poet*. Ignoring the fact that it was John Lehmann
who had originally put her up to writing it[2] and that it was the
Hogarth Press – then run by Woolf herself and her husband
Leonard, with Lehmann as their newly installed 'manager' –
which had originally published the *New Signatures* volume, the
essay is a traditionalist's assault on the 'dead' work of Auden,
Lehmann, Day-Lewis and Spender in particular. Pondering why
'modern poets should write as if they had neither ears nor eyes,
neither soles to their feet nor palms to their hands, but only
honest enterprising book-fed brains [and] uni-sexual bodies',
Woolf added for good measure that Spender's work (which she
had only just discovered) was 'unintelligible', to her ears and
eyes at least.[3]

Things got even better when, a few months later, the Hogarth
Press published a spirited *Letter to Mrs Virginia Woolf*. This too
seems to have been something of an in-house job. Even before
beginning her own Letter, Woolf had written to Lehmann that

he 'must reply, "To an old novelist" [. . .] The whole subject is crying out for letters – flocks, volleys of them, from every side.'⁴ In the event, however, it was not Lehmann but Peter Quennell, an Oxford contemporary of Auden and Spender, who leapt to his friends' defence. Writing, like Woolf, about an anonymous amalgam-poet, he excused the fact that the contemporary bard might seem 'dull' by reference to the world in which he was forced to live: 'the prodigious melodrama of modern Europe casts its shadows in some form on to his mind'. And then, in a passage which seems particularly apposite to Spender and his childhood, he went on:

> Remember [. . .] the placid pre-war universe – how tranquil and how olympian it must have been! Was the pound really worth twenty shillings, and were there parties every night and hansom cabs? Did noblemen not write for the Sunday Press? –he can recall barely five or six summers; then the War to End Wars and so good-bye.⁵

And is there honey still for tea? . . . Quennell was almost audibly championing the comradely, friendly young poets over Wilfred Owen, Edmund Blunden, Robert Bridges and the rest of the so recently feted Georgians. At the Hogarth Press and elsewhere, battle-lines were being drawn. All seemed set for nothing less than a clash of generations, with Leonard and Virginia Woolf ('the Wolves') and what was left of Bloomsbury manning the barricades of privilege and decorum on which Auden, Day- Lewis, Spender and the rest were relentlessly advancing, flaunting 'uni-sexuality' and waving red flags . . .

This is obviously a vastly over-simplified caricature – consider the position of T. S. Eliot, temperamentally a 'Bloomsberry', but also the champion of modernists such as Ezra Pound and James Joyce and later the editor and publisher of many of the Auden group. (There was also the fifty-year-old Wyndham Lewis, stuck out in No Man's Land and dyspeptically blasting and bombadiering in all directions.) To the likes of Peter Quennell and Michael Roberts, however, it was the way things *should* have been.

But to Day-Lewis and Spender, particularly Spender, those things were rather more complicated. Even the sudden flurry of publicity was not entirely to their taste. When all was said and done, its chief effect had been to make them no more than virtually anonymous 'Thirties Poets', rank-and-file squaddies in what, after the publication of *New Country*, Roberts's 1933 follow-up to *New Signatures*, was already publicly referred to as 'the Auden Group'.

Each is still best remembered as a 'Thirties Poet', of course. Like Plomer, Bell, Empson, Louis MacNeice, A. S. J. Tessimond and many more of Roberts's protégés, in the reader's mind neither has ever risen much beyond N.C.O. level in Auden's new model army. However, this enduring – and undoubtedly convenient – bracketing of Day-Lewis, Spender, MacNeice and even Isherwood with Auden is and always was misleading. It ignores what can only be described as the very real rivalry which existed at the time between a group of strikingly different writers, each of whom was very keen to make his own particular mark.

In their separate studies of 'the Auden Group' and the other writers of the 1930s Valentine Cunningham and Samuel Hynes properly stress this separateness (even if the publishers of the paperback editions of both books have seen fit to perpetuate the myth by using on their covers group shots of Auden, Isherwood and Spender). But, then as now, the individuality of the various members of the Auden Group was recognised only by the most perceptive critics. Geoffrey Grigson showed rare perspicacity when he asked in 1933: 'How, as an artist, is Auden united with Day-Lewis, Day-Lewis with Spender, Spender with Upward?'[6]

How indeed! Understandably, the Other Ranks of the Audenesque felt frustrated, if not exactly threatened, by the growing pre-eminence of their 'leader'. He was assuredly a Hero, a word which resounds through his and their poetry of the period. In all senses of the word he was also an inspiration – *Look west, Wystan, lone flier, birdman, my bully boy! [. . .] Gain altitude, Auden, then let the base beware!*[7] – but his 'followers' had their own positions to consider, their own careers to make. Thus in September 1932 Day-Lewis, then unwillingly teaching at Cheltenham College in order to support his wife and young family, was writing candidly and cold-bloodedly to Grigson:

> I see from the *Bookman* that you have now arranged us in the correct order – 1, Auden; 2, Day-Lewis – but I shall chase him home, you can rely on that, and I think we'll make the pace pretty hot between us. I hope you will like *The Magic Mountain* book when it comes out; I am stealing some of Auden's thunder for it, but I don't believe either of us will be the worse for that [. . .] By the way, Auden's (and my) frequent use of school imagery is due more to our profession than to lingering adolescence. And I don't think Empson is a stayer – I doubt if he'll do much more, though what he has done is good. [Robert] Graves, I feel, does himself down by perpetually writing about how difficult it is to write poetry just now. My final order – another professional weakness! – is 1, Auden; 2, Day-Lewis; 3, Spender.[8]

Spender too was jockeying for position and, for all his personal affection for Auden, also attempting to assert his own individuality at this time. He wrote to John Lehmann from Berlin, probably in 1931, patiently explaining that although there was a so-called Auden gang, they were not really a group at all. They worked separately and he did not even know some of its supposed members.[9]

This amounted to the opening shot in what would become a life-long battle for self-preservation. As late as 1978 he was still asserting rather tetchily (and incorrectly) that the first time that Auden, Day-Lewis and Spender were in a room together was in 1948, at a conference in Venice.[10] (He did have a point; it seems that there was no occasion on which the three were *ever* all together in a room with both Isherwood and MacNeice.) But by 1978 Auden was dead, and Spender had long since made his mark.

Back in 1931 his only real asset was the ostensibly unlikely talent for self-advertisement which he had discovered at U.C.S. and deployed to such good effect at University College, Oxford. He might not have been a properly published poet (like Auden) but he knew that *socially* he still held a good hand of cards. Now he threw them defiantly on to the table – and right at the top was the ultimate ace.

He was a full-time Man of Letters, better placed than Auden, Day-Lewis or any of the others to parade the colours of youthful modernism. He could still depend on his allowance of some £300 a year – at that time almost double the annual salary of a teacher or middle-ranking clerk – from the family 'funds'. He was not distracted by the necessity of earning a living; literature was his full-time 'career'. What was more, he was doing as best he could to live the life of a rather penny-plain Acton or straight-laced Brian Howard.

Unlike contemporaries including John Betjeman, Bernard Spencer, Evelyn Waugh and Michael Roberts as well as Day-Lewis and Auden himself, after coming down from Oxford he had not needed to join the stream of Oxbridge graduates with poor – or non-existent – degrees who had no option but to register with agencies such as Truman and Knightly or Gabbitas-Thring for appointments as personal tutors or teachers in the more obscure public schools and colleges – what Isherwood called 'that last refuge of the unsuccessful literary man'.[11] Auden too later wrote about the seeming inevitability of young writers having to supplement their income by 'teaching English in a boarding school': 'For budding authors it's become the rule./To many an unknown genius postmen bring/Typed notices from Rabbitarse and String'.[12]

Instead, Spender was able to enjoy a more leisured life and even travel extensively in Europe. He finally got himself to Paris. The *poste restante* addresses at the top of his surviving letters from this period reveal that he also went to Barcelona and, in the spring of 1933, enjoyed a protracted holiday in Italy. Berlin and Ruegen Island – that Berlin-on-Sea – also retained their appeal. He made several further visits to the city, calling on friends including Isherwood and William Plomer, and (this time accompanied by his brother Humphrey, then a student at the Architectural Association School of Architecture) spent part of the summer of 1932 back at Ruegen.

If we are to believe *World Within World*, he was actually in Berlin for about half of every year between 1930 and 1933.[13] However, on the best available evidence this seems to be something of a wistful exaggeration. It would probably have been more accurate if Spender had written than he was *abroad* for about half of every year during this period, and in London – or at least in England – for the remainder.[14] For, despite all his increasingly compulsive foreign travelling, it was Hampstead and not Hallesches Tor which remained his base throughout much of the thirties.

After his rather ignominious return from Oxford in the early spring of 1931 he temporarily reinstalled himself at Frognal. But soon, like many another unattached man in his early twenties, he graduated to a succession of rented flats. Fending for himself in these unheated,[15] unservanted 'digs' marked a sort of rite of passage and gave him a new freedom – but it is noticeable that many of them (like the family house into which he was to move much later) were also in the affluent, 'artistic' postal districts of London North West and almost umbilically close to his childhood home.

Both personally and professionally there were good reasons for his social recidivism. Throughout his early life Spender had always manifested signs of a personal and intellectual élitism. Mainly because of the influence of his parents, as a child he had learnt to keep himself apart, reading Milton and Wordsworth and communing with his caterpillars. At Oxford he had distanced himself from the Univ hearties and (just like his father before him) sought out the luminaries, whatever their year, wherever their college: Wystan Auden, Dick Crossman, Isaiah Berlin . . . Nor had his reputation been harmed by his association with the Oxford University English Society. For all the ribbing he had received in *The Gower*, as the dinner-suited secretary of the society he had at least got the ear of some of the greatest literary names of the day.

Now he was attempting to take his place among them. He was coming to realise that he was more at home in the tea-time salons and editors' offices of literary London than he was in cheap Hamburg hotels or among the rough-and-tumble of Isherwood's Berlin – and, more importantly, that this was where he would encounter his sort of people: Mr Norris paled in comparison with Mrs Woolf.

Making a name in London had after all been implicit in his actions since he began submitting work to the *Spectator* and other magazines in 1929. Consequently, he did not hesitate to use his Oxford contacts to further this metropolitan advance. He seems to have held in reserve his acquaintanceship with the members of the old guard such as J.C. Squire, Edmund Blunden and Walter de la Mare whom he had met during his secretaryship of the English Society. On the other hand, he was quick to capitalise on the student friendships he had made during his time at Oxford. John Lehmann, for instance, records that it was 'through my sister Rosamund' – an undergraduate contemporary of Spender's – that he came to know his fellow-writer.[16]

For Spender, however, Lehmann was more than the brother of a university acquaintance. If, like many of his fellow students, he had once found Rosamund one of the most beautiful women of her generation,[17] professionally he found John even more attractive in 1931 and 1932. Good-looking, with what Christopher Isherwood called 'extremely becoming, prematurely grey hair', Lehmann was both homosexual and impeccably well-connected (another of his sisters was the actress Beatrice Lehmann). Even more pertinently, because of the position he was then taking up at the Woolfs' Hogarth Press, he was also a sympathetic conduit through which Spender's name – and to a lesser extent those of Isherwood and the rest of the gang – could be brought to the attention of those at the heart of the literary establishment. Inevitably, it was John Lehmann who had persuaded Virginia Woolf to consider reading *The Temple* in the summer of 1931

Given the uneasy pupil-mentor relationship that existed between Spender and Isherwood, it is rather surprising that

Isherwood was the first to benefit from this new friendship. By the spring of 1931 he had completed a second novel. Jonathan Cape had been delighted to publish his first, *All the Conspirators*; but the firm was now regretting that it was unable to accept the new book, a typically unmemorable second novel which was ironically entitled *The Memorial*. So were many other publishers. Even Curtis Brown, the prestigious firm of London literary agents, had been unable to 'place' it.

It was at this point that Spender arrived on the scene, and in *Christopher and His Kind* Isherwood pays tribute to the trouble he took in pushing *The Memorial* in Lehmann's direction. (His persistence paid off; largely through Spender's and Lehmann's good offices, *The Memorial* was published by the Hogarth Press in February 1932.) It is difficult, however, to discern the true motives which lay behind Spender's sudden solicitude. That he believed in the novel – and in Isherwood as 'The Novelist' – is beyond doubt; but it is also possible to see a further element of self-promotion in his actions. To some extent he seems to have been acting as a self-appointed London agent or ambassador for the gang. In the letter to Lehmann mentioned above he certainly appears to be presenting himself as their spokesman. They were kindred spirits, he explained. Whatever any of them did, wherever any of them went, was likely to influence the others.

Ironically, and even more interestingly, however, it was Spender's very success as a London 'fixer' which brought Isherwood's simmering resentment at his dual, 'touristy' life to a head.

Isherwood came to London in the autumn of 1932, buoyed up by the mixed but generally favourable reviews which *The Memorial* had received and full of his ideas for a new novel about Berlin.[18] (This was, of course, his putative epic *The Lost*, which later became *Goodbye to Berlin*.) He naturally linked up with Spender and was dragged by him into what, for Isherwood, was a comparatively new world of publishers, editors and literary parties, the metropolitan *beau monde* which Spender was rapidly making his own. He hated it – and hated the Spender who had so willingly allowed himself to become a part of it, not least by telling embarrassing stories about his friend Christopher Isherwood and what he got up to in Berlin . . .

The inevitable confrontation took place towards the end of Isherwood's stay. A few bitter, wounding letters were exchanged. Frustratingly, these have apparently not survived. However, something of their tone can be appreciated from Spender's recollections of one of Isherwood's which said, in effect, that if Spender returned to Berlin Isherwood would not do so; that Spender was unbearably indiscreet and only out for publicity.[19] Isherwood confirms all this in *Christopher and His Kind* (even quoting Spender's account of the incident) and adds telling details of his own. Behind his impatience with Spender's toe-dipping dilettantism the previous year there had been at least a suspicion that Spender would 'scoop him by writing Berlin stories of his own and rushing them into print!'

His patience finally snapped during a party at William Plomer's home, Isherwood recalls, when Spender suggested that the two should actually make a clean break and go their separate ways: 'If we're going to part, at least let's part like men.' Even as he spoke, to Spender it must have seemed like Marston all over again.

Isherwood's reply was crushing but true. With a 'bitchy smile', he merely told Spender: 'Stephen, we *aren't* men'.[20]

To some extent this showdown cleared the air. It was mutually agreed that Spender would not return to Berlin; that Germany would henceforth be Isherwood's province, and London Spender's. A truce was negotiated; but thenceforth the friendship, though enduring, developed along different and more casual lines.

━━━━━

A virtual stranger in London that summer, Isherwood can be forgiven for feeling something of an outsider. Even by 1932, the Stephen Spender he had got to know on his visits to Oxford and during Spender's tentative forays to Germany was a very different figure from the newly confident young Man of Letters whom he was now encountering. Five years his junior, by dint of sheer effort and grim persistence his erstwhile 'pupil' was already making a mark which, on a social level at least, easily surpassed W.H. Auden's literary eminence. As early as October 1931 the massively popular (and homosexual) novelist Hugh Walpole was asking Virginia Woolf to 'give my love to Stephen Spender whom I think one of the nicest and handsomest of men'.

Perspicaciously – and wholly characteristically – Walpole's letter then goes on to enquire whether Woolf knows 'why in *New Writing* does [Spender] talk of the 'English Idle Rentier Class' – where *is* it these days? And why are the young Rentier class so much more Communist than the young working class?'[21]

In retrospect, we can reconstruct much of the young Spender's ineluctable rise from such independent sources as Walpole and Woolf. Along with Auden, he was, for instance, seemingly one of the targets in Percy Wyndham Lewis's *The Apes of God*, a bitter, rebarbative tirade agaisnt the new London literati. Indeed, the novel, which was first published in 1931, features *two* characters who seem to have something of Spender in them. The fashionable Daniel Boleyn, a nineteen-year-old who has written just one poem, is one. However, Valentine Cunningham has also made out a plausible case for Siegfried Victor, 'a massive young man' who has a 'handsome nobly proportioned head', largely on the strength of the fact that he is closely associated with the splendidly named Hedgepinshot Mandeville Pickwort, 'a small bleached colourless blond' who bears a striking resemblance to Auden. Between them, the pair edit a periodical called *Verse of the Under-Thirties*.[22]

Lewis is, however, a notoriously unreliable witness. Born in 1882, he first made his name before the Great War, but never quite won the eminence he thought he deserved. Chronologically if not temperamentally one of the lupine old guard, he spent much of the thirties castigating what he discerned as a new generation of epicine 'youthies' and denigrating the manner in which his amoral contemporaries were, in his eyes, quite literally sucking up to them. If it can be said to have one, the central image of *The Apes of God* might well be that of the awful moment when: 'The aged drink-puffed lips pressed the baby-red and the breath of old carouse and the aridness of cigarettes blew round the astute juvenile nostrils.'

Poor Lewis. Some index of his standing at this time is provided by a list of his non-fiction writings of the period. As well as *The Apes of God*, in 1931 he also produced *The Diabolical Principle and the Dithyrambic Spectator*, and a eulogy merely entitled *Hitler*. The next year saw the appearance of a book called *The Doom of Youth*, while as late as 1939 he still found a publisher (George Allen & Unwin) for an essay entitled 'The Jews: Are They Human?'

It is no wonder that the name Lewis, P. Wyndham does not occur in the index to *World Within World*. He was, understandably, no friend of Spender's. On the other hand, we should remember that Lewis's sheer fecundity at this period made him a potent force on the literary scene. Thus it should not come as too much of a surprise to find Spender reviewing his *One-Way Song*, a volume of poems first published in 1933, in unexpectedly generous terms. Yes, the book's tendency is fascist and anti-democratic, he says; yes, Lewis is still 'the Enemy' – but it remained possible to respect him.[23]

These are weasel words – what must Isherwood have thought? – but vividly illustrative, if not exactly characteristic, of Spender's efforts to 'get on' and be 'taken up' by the old guard. (A few years later he complained to Virginia Woolf that Lewis was 'furious' at another review in which Spender had used the word 'malicious', stressing that he had always been an admirer of Lewis and his work.)[24]

In the event, Spender succeeded in scaling the heights far more quickly and easily than even he could have hoped. By the end of 1931 his growing reputation and bashful, blushing good looks had caught the attention (or maybe just appealed to the frustrated maternal instincts) of some of the greatest hostesses of the day. At Lady Colefax's dinner table, first at Argyll House in the King's Road, Chelsea, then in her much smaller home in Lord North Street, Westminster, he became acquainted with the

Stephen Spender
A studio portrait of the poet, seemingly taken in the late 1930s.

Alfred Spender
'J.A.', the eminent editor of the *Westminster Gazette*, remained tight-lipped about his nephew's literary career. 'A remarkable self-possessed young man', was his only comment after meeting W.H. Auden.

No.10 Frognal, Hampstead
Now divided into flats, the imposing red-brick house was Spender's London home during his school and Oxford days.

Christopher Isherwood
The Novelist strikes a thoughtful pose for Humphrey Spender
in this photograph taken in Berlin in 1931.

upferberg
old
WIEN
BERLIN
LIBELLE
VERA SCHUH
Juwelen
Ankauf
Verkauf
er Kindl
VERA AMERICAN SHOE
U

The Berlin of the Thirties
The two faces of the pre-war German capital.
Isherwood's *Goodbye to Berlin* celebrates both the
sophistication of the city which so captivated
Auden and Spender, and the sinister rise of Nazism.

W.H. Auden, right, and
Christopher Isherwood
A publicity shot taken in
1938 as they left
London to collaborate
on a book about China.

Virginia Woolf
Sometimes 'snide',
Spender felt, Virginia
Woolf nevertheless took
a great interest in the
careers of the Auden
Gang. Spender was a
particular favourite in
the years before her
death in 1941.

T.S. Eliot
Poet, playwright and publisher T.S. Eliot, who described Spender's work as 'as definite step forward in English poetry', pictured on the set of his play *The Family Reunion* in 1939.

John Lehmann
Well-connected and mesmerically attractive, John Lehmann became one of the *eminences grises* of London literary life during and after the time he spent working for the Hogwarth Press.

Inez Spender Sir William Coldstream's portrait captures the quick intelligence of Inez Pearn, whom Spender married in December 1936. The painting was completed after around 40 sittings.

Cyril Connolly A photograph taken long after Connolly's days as editor of *Horizon* graphically depicts his appeal as a host and *bon viveur*.

Fire service Spender (standing, left), director of education at the No.34 Fire Force in London, lectures to a group of fire officers in the last months of World War Two.

W.H. Auden, Cecil Day-Lewis and Spender, 1949 Probably the only photograph of (left to right) Auden, Day-Lewis and Spender together. It was taken by Natasha Spender during the 1949 P.E.N. conference in Venice.

No.2 Lansdowne Terrace In 1939 Spender's ground-floor flat at No.2 Lansdowne Terrace became the editorial office of *Horizon* and a regular port of call for authors such as Dylan Thomas and Julian Maclaren-Ross seeking work during the war-time austerity.

Spender and Natasha Spender and his second wife, the pianist Natasha Litvin. This photograph was in all probability taken during the 1949 International P.E.N. conference in Venice.

Stephen Spender
A previously unreproduced sketch of Spender made by the cartoonist David Low, probably in the late 1940s.

The Cultural Arbiter I
Spender poses for an illustration in a post-war newspaper article entitled 'Young Poets of Democracy'. Note the photograph of Isherwood propped against the wall above his head.

The Cultural Arbiter II Spender photographed in June 1951 with his fellow-poet Kathleen Raine for a newspaper article which asked 'Are Poets Really Necessary?'

likes of H.G. Wells, T.S. Eliot, Somerset Maugham, Nancy Mitford, Edith Sitwell and Cyril Connolly.[25]

Soon, too, he was an even more familiar figure in the eclectic Gower Street Thursday afternoon *salons* of Lady Ottoline Morrell, the wife of the Labour Member of Parliament, Philip Morrell. Indeed, *World Within World* devotes no less than four pages to an account of them and the glorious dottiness of Lady Ottoline herself. They make hilarious reading with their account of 'Lady Ott' parading around Bloomsbury with a shepherdess's crook, attached to which were a couple of yapping pekinese dogs.[26]

One of the last great aristocratic eccentrics, Lady Ottoline seems to have been devoted to Spender. It was at Gower Street – and not always during her formal 'Thursdays' – that she arranged for him to meet both W.B. Yeats and Aldous Huxley. In October 1933 she noted in a letter to a friend that

> The best of the *young* men is Stephen Spender. They are quite nice & charming his Poems, but nothing to Shout or Trumpet about. The trouble is that they (the young) have too little experience, & no philosophy or Spiritual vision to inspire or stimulate them.[27]

That last sentence is, however, only partly true. By October 1933, in large measure because Faber & Faber had published his *Poems* the previous January, Spender was getting a great deal of experience. At a time when – as Samuel Hynes usefully reminds us – Oswald Mosley and his British Union of Fascists were rallying in London and Oxford and hunger marches were setting out for Hyde Park, everyone wanted to know the good-looking young Socialist. *World Within World* relates how he was suddenly swept up into a sophisticated, Bloomsbury-and-country-house world of weekends and books and polite conversation. Staying with Rosamund Lehmann and her husband Wogan Philipps at Ipsden House in the Chilterns or with Harold Nicolson and Vita Sackville-West at the Long Barn in Kent was just like a deliciously prolonged luncheon or the infinite extension of one of Ottoline Morrell's intimate tea parties. It was all so different from his own bed-sitter mundanities and, for all his radicalism, Spender frankly revelled in the urbanity of it all: houses which had libraries and modern pictures on the walls, good food, fine wine and entertaining gossip.[28]

Indeed, it is impossible to conclude other than that sudden celebrity and the concommitant and equally sudden welter of invitations to lunches, dinners, teas and weekends in the country went to his head. Certainly his work began to suffer. Whole days went by in which he did nothing at all apart from toddling out to lunch parties. They went on until at least half-past three, and that left just three hours to fag all the way home, change and start out for the evening dinner parties. He was so bad at saying no to anything.[29]

Behind the literary discussions and endless gossip, however, the strains were beginning to show. As Isherwood had noticed, Spender was finding it difficult to, as it were, keep one foot in Berlin and the other in Bloomsbury. In a way which is disturbingly reminiscent of his treatment of Isherwood, he seems even to have repaid Ottoline Morrell's genuine affection by caricaturing her undoubted eccentricities to those of his friends who had not been favoured by her interest. Like D.H. Lawrence, who based the character of Hermione Critch in *Women in Love* on her ('her hair looped in slack, slovenly strands over her rather beautiful ears, which were not quite clean. Neither was her neck perfectly clean') he appears to have been very ready to laugh at and lampoon Ottoline behind her back. Robert Gathorne-Hardy points this out rather tartly in his introduction to an edition of her own early memoirs:

> Mr Stephen Spender has not only confused the portrait of Ottoline, but even the very nature of her house. He speaks [in *World Within World*] of seeing the walls hung with pictures by Sickert and A.E. Now the Morrells had sold the last of their Sickerts more than a quarter of a century before he visited their house; and they had never at any time owned a painting by A.E. Such errors in a man devoted to the arts diminishes our confidence in his other records of the Morrell household. Must it not be that, dazzled by the picture drawn distortedly

for him by eminent friends, he had failed to descry the true nature of his hostess?[30]

For better or for worse, Lady Colefax's contemporary accounts of Spender's visits to Lord North Street have not survived, if indeed they ever existed in written form. Even among Ottoline Morrell's surviving correspondence there is only one other reference to Spender – this, however, hits what in the circumstances seems a thoroughly justified note of exasperation. Replying to a letter from a friend in New Zealand on Christmas Eve 1937 ('It is extraordinary to read in your Letter that it is *Summer* with you!') the by then elderly *grande dame* came as close as she ever did to setting down what she finally thought about Spender and the 'youthies':

> I am glad you have the 'urge' to come to Europe – I am only afraid you may be disappointed. *I get* disappointed with the young writers, Stephen Spender, & Auden etc. I don't know Auden, but he has written an article in *The Listener* on 'Gossip' that so *enrages* me. I should like to see him to scold him about it! Not that he would care twopence what I think. He is much too conceited & school boyish to care what an old fashioned Lady like me thinks of Life. He and Stephen are gabies![31]

There is one further archive of material directly relevant to the way in which Spender was perceived at this period. Ever since she had first been persuaded by John Lehmann to cast an editorial eye over the original draft of *The Temple*, Virginia Woolf had taken a keen interest in its young author. No matter that she eventually decided against publishing the novel – 'Scrap it! Scrap it and write something completely different,' she said[32] – she saw something in Spender himself. Modern poetry was increasingly coming 'beneath the scrutiny of my aged eyes', she told Lehmann, and by October 1932 – she had inveigled a far from unwilling Spender into her own far from inconsiderable social circle. At first he remained on the outer fringes; Woolf continued to regard him, Plomer and many of the other young homosexual and/or socialist writers of the 1930s as 'niminy piminies [. . .] whose minds are refrigerators, and souls blank paper'.[33] But Spender was also 'charming', and something of a curiosity.

Consequently, he was bidden for dinner with Leonard and Virginia at No. 52 Tavistock Square in October 1932. Lest he expected a grand evening like those he might have become accustomed to *chez* Colefax or an intimately Morrellian tête-à-tête, however, Woolf's curt invitation promised little more than a well-cooked[34] casserole and, no doubt, cocoa *à la Bloomsbury*: 'Would you dine with us on Tuesday (11th) at 8? Don't change of course – I expect we shall be alone.'[35]

Contemporary records suggest that she and Leonard were more alone than they planned that evening: Spender seems first to have met Virginia a couple of days later, and for afternoon tea rather than dinner.[36] Whenever, he still made a forcible impression on the novelist who was then more than usually preoccupied. She had written 60,000 words of a novel then called *The Pargiters* (published as *The Years* in 1937) in just nine weeks and completed an abnormally large volume of reviewing. A couple of weeks after the tea party she noted in her diary:

> He is a rattle headed bolt eyed young man, raw boned, loose jointed who thinks himself the greatest poet of all time. I daresay he is – it's not a subject that interests me enormously at the moment.[37]

For his own part, Spender found Woolf (born, like Wyndham Lewis, in 1882, and thus around fifty when he first got to know her) equally unsettling. It was not just that she smoked cheroots at a time when 'society' ladies hardly dared smoke at all. Her whole demeanour was little short of alarming. Before dinner parties in the Tavistock Square house she and Leonard shared with the Hogarth Press offices, she was nervous and sometimes even distraught as she poured out the drinks. But later her talk, about literature, politics and – that Bloomsbury staple – her friends was entrancing. Virginia, Spender discovered (in *World Within World* he always calls her Virginia) also had an insatiable 'social curiosity'.[38] As her works, and not least her letters and diaries, have subsequently revealed she had a morbid fascination with the minutiae which differentiated upper-, middle- and lower-class behaviour.

It was in all probability her 'social curiosity' which motivated Woolf's initial cultivation of Spender and the affection which she showed him during the remaining nine years of her life (she committed suicide in March 1941). In addition to her un-doubted class-consciousness, she had an ambivalent interest in homosexuality and the lives of those of her male friends who were homosexually inclined (and never more so than at this time, since homosexuality was one of the underlying themes of *The Pargiters*). She commonly called them by what were even then pejorative terms – 'Bugger Boys', 'sods', 'queers'. But she was also personally devoted to E. M. Forster, John Maynard Keynes, Lytton Strachey (who had died in January 1932, but once half-heartedly proposed to her) and the many other homosexuals who had comprised the supporting cast of the pre-1914 Bloomsbury Group. More latterly, of course, she had taken John Lehmann under her wing.

In particular she was fascinated by their interaction with women (and by implication, with herself). It was a subject she wanted to try and explore in *The Pargiters*. She wrote to her nephew Quentin Bell in January 1934: 'how far can one say openly what is the relation of a woman and a sod? In French, yes; but in Mr [John] Galsworthy's English, no.'[39]

Right from the start then, Spender was something of an unwitting guinea-pig. But Woolf could never quite pigeon-hole him, and as late as December 1933 she was still addressing him with a cautious formality: 'Could you dine with us on Tuesday 19th at 8? – without changing of course. I hope you may be able to.'[40]

This time Spender could – although for some reason the dinner seems to have been postponed until the 20th. Another of

Woolf's letters to Quentin Bell takes up the story (like Ottoline Morrell's, her personal correspondence displays a curious contemporary reluctance to use the apostrophe):

> Stephen Spender and Miss Lynd — I can't name her, for being Irish her parents have christened her some faery Celtic name — dined here last night. She is dusky, twilit, silent, secretive. He on the other hand talks incessantly and will pan out in years to become a prodigious bore. But he's a nice poetic youth; big nosed, bright eyed, like a giant thrush. The worst of being a poet is one must be a genius; and so he cant talk long without bringing in the abilities and disabilities of great poets; Yeats has praised him; I see being young is hellish. One wants to cut a figure. He is writing about Henry James and has tea alone with Ottoline and is married to a Sergeant in the Guards. They have set up a new quarter in Maida Vale; I propose to call them the Lilies of the Valley. Theres William Plomer, with his policemen; then Stephen, then Auden and Joe Ackerly, [*sic*] all lodged in Maida Vale, and wearing different coloured Lilies. Their great sorrow at the moment is Siegfried Sassoon's defection; he's gone and married a woman . . .[41]

Virginia Woolf's typically waspish reference to Spender's being 'married to a Sergeant in the Guards' and note that, by the end of 1933, he was living in the unfashionable West London district of Maida Vale may well say as much about her as they do about him, but they also serve to highlight a fundamental change in Spender's circumstances.

At some time in 1932 he had left the house in Frognal and made his London base two miles south in a flat at No. 43 Boundary Road, Maida Vale (his first extant letter to Isherwood mentioning this address is dated 10 January 1933).[42] The flat was little more than a bed-sitting room;[43] it cost him '£13 extra' (a quarter?),[44] but he determinedly made the best of things. Everything was so much closer to hand when you lived in one room, he rather redundantly explained to the Isherwood who had spent most of the past three years living in hotels and boarding-houses.

The fact that it was in Maida Vale and not, say, Bloomsbury or Hampstead was also important to Spender. As Woolf's comments about 'a new quarter' and 'the Lilies of the Valley' suggest, it put him very conveniently *in medias res*. At this time it really did seem that the rather upper-class, genteel, bottom-pinching amorality of Bloomsbury would soon be upstaged by the more prurient, proletarian gropings of a wholly new literary tribe. And the uneasy tone of Woolf's letter, as well as an allusion in *World Within World* to what appears to have been a running joke or quarrel between Spender and Woolf about how the new, predominantly homosexual 'Maida Vale group' would come to supplant the elderly Bloomsbury Group,[45] suggests that this was more than a purely literary argument.

William Plomer christened them the Canal School of English Literature (a reference to the proximity of Maida Vale, also known as Little Venice, to the Regent's Canal), but the rift, such as it was, went deeper than a mere difference of opinions over names and ages. As Woolf could not have failed to notice, the raffish literary and homosexual community in Maida Vale had already embraced and welcomed such surviving Bloomsberries as Forster and Keynes's erstwhile lover Sebastian Sprott, even if it was Plomer, J.R. ('Joe') Ackerley, and – fleetingly – W.H. Auden who set the tone. At every level, its very existence was forcing her to confront the relationship between 'a woman and a sod'.

Spender too must have felt some of this tension. As we have already seen, he had found himself immediately at home among the vast vestiges of Bloomsbury. By all accounts he seems to have put on his best bib and tucker and been an exemplary guest; he liked 'Virginia' – but his work, his politics and even his sexual tastes conformed exactly to the more 'modern' mores of the 'Maida Vale Group'.

Like Oscar Wilde half a century earlier ('The working class is with me – to a boy!') the Little Venice bugger boys were principally attracted to 'rough trade': to short, anonymous couplings with young, predominantly heterosexual and prefer-ably uniformed working-class men. Plomer was not alone in his taste for policemen. Forster had a long-lasting relationship with another, Bob Buckingham. The notoriously promiscuous Ackerley (who, after his appointment as literary editor of *The Listener* in 1935, became something of a patron saint to the group) enjoyed, *inter alia*, a similar affair with a bobby called Harry Daley. Although he was never a real member of the group – preferring more salubrious surroundings 'up West' – John Lehmann too favoured the company of the young guardsmen and sailors he picked up in pubs around Victoria.

Not entirely coincidentally, Maida Vale had become a pale, poor London palliative for the Cosy Corner atmosphere which Spender, Plomer and Lehmann had all sampled in Berlin. And it is hardly too much to say that, well before he settled down and 'married' the man whom Woolf inaccurately (but wholly characteristically) called his 'Sergeant in the Guards', Spender had seen in him something of the spirit of the Fritzs and Lothars whom *The Temple*'s Paul Schoner had so delightedly encoun-tered at the Three Stars.

Tony Hyndman (who is referred to as Jimmy Younger in both *World Within World* and *Christopher and His Kind*) had indeed spent three years in the Army, but at the time Spender met him he was just another unemployed man, lounging at corners of the street and greeting friends with a shrugged shoulder[46] in the bleak aftermath of the Great Depression. He was, however, satisfactorily working class and only the latest in a series of young would-be Lothars with whom Spender had been trying to form a permanent relationship.

He had already enjoyed and then ended what seems to have been a rather half-hearted fling with a boy called Georg, whom he met in Berlin (and in whom Isherwood later seems to have taken some interest),[47] and then in November 1932 he had optimistically travelled to southern Spain, half hoping that he would be able to live there permanently with another German boy, this time a beautiful but neurotic twenty-two-year-old called Hellmut whom Harold Nicolson and Edward Sackville-West had discovered.

Hellmut was then in service, but Spender quickly persuaded him to give all that up and live with him. He could cook and clean while Spender wrote, and the new domestic stability would be good for his nervy condition.[48] Even though Hellmut refused his new employer's less professional advances, for a few weeks at least this new friendship seemed to presage something of the true, fulfilling 'Marston' relationship that Spender had been seeking for so long. Hellmut, he said, filled his life ten times as much as Georg had ever done.[49] And in a fragment of a journal which he kept as this time (the '1932 Journal', now in the Bancroft Library at the University of California at Berkeley) the characteristic leitmotiv is one of extreme, even excessive, concern for Hellmut's happiness. There is, however, the draft of a hubristic (and not unnaturally unpublished) poem extolling the delights of true love.[50]

The pair visited Gibraltar, Algeciras, Tarragona and finally Malaga looking for a house to rent. But Spender disliked Malaga and its beggars and undernourished children.[51] Before they had even arrived at the city proper, however, they were involved in an incident which must have had peculiar resonances. Just as they were coming into a town square, children started throwing stones at them. Helmutt rapidly took command of the situation; but Spender was shocked and alarmed.[52] It was those rough children again . . .

Inconveniently, Spanish food disagreed with Hellmut (who apparently had a stomach ulcer), so he and Spender were forced to retreat to the relative civilisation of Barcelona. There at least Spender could enjoy cinemas and concerts and get access to books, while Hellmut could eat properly, make friends in the city's German community and pursue his ultimate ambition of acting with the German theatre company.

They bought a cooker and installed themselves in a room with an adjoining kitchen where they catered for themselves, carefully abjuring anything cooked in oil because of Hellmut's ulcer. Much to Spender's pleasure, it was all very domestic. Hellmut was living up to expectations, keeping house and dealing with everything very well, he reported to Isherwood in December.[53]

Ominously however, the same letter noted that they were both running out of money. (It may be coincidence, but only a few months previously Spender had watched Georg laboriously copying his signature in an attempt to forge a cheque.) They were dipping into Hellmut's savings in order to survive; and, despite all Hellmut's home-making, Spender was still unable to do any substantial work.

Inevitably, this quixotic Iberian idyll collapsed within weeks. In a letter to Isherwood begun on 5 January 1933 Spender admitted that it seemed to be failing, and then broke off. Two days later he took up his pen again and (in the very next sentence) admitted that it had failed. Quite why remains unclear. The letter is as obscure as it is full of self-pleading. It is certain, however, that Spender's plan to 'cure' Hellmut had not been helped by the unexpected arrivals of his brother Humphrey and an alcoholic American called Kirk who had apparently been rather unceremoniously dumped on them by his physician or analyst, a Dr Möring.

Kirk made an ill-advised pass at Humphrey and wrote him an eight-page love letter; Spender threatened to report him to the U.S. Consulate – and eventually Hellmut packed his bags and decamped from what even Spender was calling the 'insanity' of it all to Basel, Switzerland. (He then travelled on to Berlin where he bitterly criticised Spender's ambivalent attempts to 'cure' him, much to the discomfiture of Isherwood and others.) The idyll had degenerated into nothing less than a fiasco, with Spender left to cope with Kirk, who reminded him of a character out of the pages of William Faulkner. On 10 January he noted that Kirk had been drunk for a week. he had consumed anything he could get his hands on, and that included most of a can of fuel they used for lighting stoves and even his own hair oil.[54]

Finally, with the assistance of Dr Möring, Kirk was packed off to Ibiza 'to die' and – his own life once again seemingly in ruins – Spender licked his wounds for a few days in Paris before returning to England. He had spent too much money, become infested by a tapeworm, and another putative relationship had disintegrated. But once again he determinedly put the best face on things when he wrote to Isherwood a few days after his arrival in London, where there was only winter and the cold flat in Boundary Road. If he could only find a reliable partner his new life would be fine, he said.[55] For the next six months at least.

About the only thing that he had been able to salvage from the Barcelona débâcle was Faber & Faber's advance copy of his soon-to-be published *Poems*.

———

Poems duly appeared in the bookshops on 19 July 1933 (a planned dedication to Isherwood having been hastily deleted at the height of their quarrel), and it was the book's *succès d'estime* rather than any real commercial profit which indirectly led to Spender's appointment of Tony Hyndman as his first real partner.

Right from the start, Faber & Faber had pulled out all the stops to 'puff' *Poems*. Much to Spender's embarrassment, the jacket blurb (in all probability written by T.S. Eliot) proclaimed that 'If Auden is the satirist of this poetical renaissance, Spender is its lyric poet'. That, Spender felt, might have hurt Auden's feelings. On the other hand, even Spender cannot have been too upset by the rather hyperbolic claim that 'technically, these poems appear to make a definite step forward in English poetry'. Good old Tom!

Other friends too were rallying round to support the book. Plomer, Michael Roberts and Herbert Read all let it be known in advance that their reviews would be favourable,[56] and in general they were as good as their word. What if the anonymous – and tardy – review in *The Times Literary Supplement* bemoaned Spender's 'unpoetic leaning'?[57] In the *Adelphi* Read had already noticed how in his work (and, though Read may not have known it, in his life too) 'Mr Spender is conscious of his social heritage of chaos and despair'.[58]

Suddenly, although perhaps not with Byronic suddenness, Spender had awoken to find himself famous. In addition to Read, William Plomer had predictably come up trumps in *The*

Referee and Michael Roberts had done his bit in *The Listener*.
Spender had become literary London's bench-mark of 'social
consciousness' (Read). *Everyone* had noticed what the *TLS*
eventually called his 'love and pity towards the hungry, the
unemployed and the oppressed' — but no one bothered to
mention his parallel love for Bloomsbury society, country-house
weekends and the bitchy back-stabbing of the literary world.

SIX

The Ballad of Sexual Confusion

A squeeze-box and some mournful woodwinds: on the bare boards, under the harsh white light, a man and a woman sing of the power and frustration of love. '*Ballade von der sexuellen Hörigkeit*' ('The Ballad of Sexual Bondage') is the emotional heart of Kurt Weill and Bertolt Brecht's masterpiece, *Die Dreigroschenoper* (*The Threepenny Opera*).

The jangly tunes — 'harmonies so artfully twisted that the wrong chords and progressions sound right again', one critic has written — command attention like insistent background music to the jerky, nervy movie-thriller that was the late twenties and the early thirties. Even Brecht's artful *faux-naïf* script somehow echoes the urgency of a newsreel commentator. His sloganeering and moral outrage still come through almost unscathed in Hugh MacDiarmid's rather tame English translation:

> That's why he keeps well clear of women's claws.
> By day he thinks he can escape the danger
> Before the night falls he lies with a stranger.

If the milieu of the late 1940s was summed up by the plangent zither theme and the stark black and whites of Carol Reed's 1949 film *The Third Man* (set in post-war Vienna), twenty years earlier Brecht made no attempt to conceal the fact that his 'beggar's opera' was also conceived as a state-of-the-nation work. Ostensibly an updated version of John Gay's phenomenally successful 1728 *Beggar's Opera*, it specifically pointed up the lubricious, Hogarthian similarities between Gay's London and the Berlin — or for that matter the London — of the late

1920s. And, almost three-quarters of a century on, it is only now becoming clear just how vividly and accurately this tale of moral corruption and sexual exploitation caught the mood of the times, the *Zeitgeist* which lingered for so long in what Auden would later call the 'low dishonest' thirties.

It was only in 1991, for instance, that the artless, verbatim recollections of a working-class homosexual man identified as 'John' appeared in print, alongside those of other gay men whose lives had been shaped in the days before the decriminalising of adult male homosexual acts in 1967.

Born on Tyneside in 1917, John arrived in London in 1932, and his reminiscences paint a graphic picture of the class-based gay scene in the capital in the years leading up to the outbreak of the Second World War. It was the period when homosexual acts could still lead to imprisonment. (In 1895 Oscar Wilde had been sentenced to two years' hard labour under the terms of the Criminal Law Amendment Act of 1885 which remained on the statute book until 1967.) It was the period when 'One used to say, are you "so"? Or he's *comme ça* if you were higher up, or TBH [to be had]'; a time when, before the inflationary arrival of American G.I.s who demanded $10 for sex, boys like John could be had for about £1 a night – or less:

> During the thirties the whole of the queer world was divided into castes, right. There were the boys on the game, there were the boys who weren't on the game but who were amenable (pick someone up, and go and have dinner with them, go to bed with them), and there were the 'kept' boys. And then, of course, there were the 'steamers' or punters themselves. That's the old-fashioned term for them. I first heard it when I was about thirteen and somebody said, oh he's a steamer, he'll give you half a crown, you see. They tended to be older and better off and, of course, in high society.
>
> You weren't just taken out because you were pretty, you were taken out because you were a pretty face in the first place, but you weren't taken out the second time because you were just a pretty face. What a lot of people do is, they find a boy they like and then they try to remodel him. Which is stupid.[1]

━━━━━━

Wholly coincidentally, John's frank analysis gives an approximate worm's-eye-view of the relationship which developed between Stephen Spender and Tony Hyndman in the first half of the 1930s. Almost uniquely, it describes the nether end of a world which had only previously been examined through the other end of the telescope – with the loftier, more literary perpectives common to a great many biographies and autobiographies (Tom Driberg's *Ruling Passions* is perhaps the most notorious of these, although James Kirkup's *A Poet Could Not but Be Gay* runs it close) as well as a fair number of more or less autobiographical novels. John Lehmann's almost wholly-autobiographical *In the Purely Pagan Sense* (1976), for instance, tells in graphic detal how an Eton-educated 'steamer' pursues and purchases the affections of 'amenable' young men in Berlin, Vienna, London and, for that matter, anywhere else he happens to be throughout this period.

Like Tony, in the early 1930s the young John found himself in a class-based relationship: 'After I met my lover, he took me everywhere with him. I was never kept in the background. He wore me like a badge. He was one who had a penchant for the working class. I used to do the housework, until eventually I had someone come in . . .'[2] Tony himself apparently left no record of the tortured, increasingly tormented years during which he and Spender were together – but Spender's own accounts (even the discreet version which he presents in *World Within World*) are graphic enough to imply that John could almost have been speaking for Tony at this period. As Virginia Woolf had noticed, Spender did wear Tony like a badge; and as we have noticed, Spender certainly had a penchant for the working class . . .

━━━━━━

Exactly when and where Spender first met Tony Hyndman remain unclear, although it is not impossible that Spender initially encountered him while 'cruising' the amusement arcades near Marble Arch or in the Haymarket where he was passing many of his evenings.[3] Tony is first mentioned in Spender's surviving letters to Isherwood in September 1933, but the familiarity of the reference suggest that by then Isherwood had already met him.[4]

All that can be said with certainty is that, buoyed up by his sudden celebrity, Spender soon invited Tony to move into the flat with him; that Tony accepted, and was soon being paraded around London as Spender's 'secretary'. The euphemism fooled nobody, as Virginia Woolf's letter makes clear. Even Tony and Spender himself were in no doubts about what they were doing. And the dynamics of the relationship were to trouble and haunt them both for many years.

Tony felt increasingly trapped and suffocated, while Spender was locked into the seeming inevitability of it all. Published and talked about though he now was, he could see that he did not need a secretary.[5] Nor, now that he was struggling to earn a mere £3 a week[6] by hack reviewing and essay writing (as well as cobbling together the study of Henry James[7] for which Jonathan Cape had given him a down-payment of £25 and the promise of another £25 on completion) could he actually *afford* a secretary, least of all one who lived in.

But at the same time he realised that in his relationship with Tony he had finally found what he had been looking for during the previous six years. Second only to his new worries about money, his letters to Isherwood reveal how emotionally lonely and confused he was at this period, and how much he was now investing in Tony.[8]

Tony Hyndman suited him down to the ground. He had been born at Tiger Bay, near the docks in Cardiff, where his father ran a hotel. He had run away from home when he was eighteen, Spender boasted (although it has to be said that this was not a particularly dramatic move at a time when elementary education ceased at the age of fourteen). He had come to London and drifted from one temporary job to another before joining the Army. Now discharged, he was, in all senses of the word, on the streets.

Spender had first encountered him at a time when – in what we must assumed was the aftermath of the Hellmut fiasco – he too was down on his uppers, emotionally at least. He did not want to live alone, but still could not consider getting married. He was desperate for someone, *anyone*, with whom he could share his life, and even considering advertising for a companion in the lonely-hearts column of a newspaper. Tony was good-looking, friendly and seemed to have a certain native wit. He fitted the bill exactly; but there is still a chilling Maida Vale matter-of-factness about the way Spender later described in just one sentence how he met Tony, asked him to work for him and invited him to move into the Boundary Road flat.[9]

Tony accepted, and to begin with things went well enough. Spender got on with his writing (a second, expanded edition of *Poems* and his long poem *Vienna* were both published in 1934; his inflated study of Henry James, *The Destructive Element* appeared in 1935). Just as Hellmut had done, Tony cooked and cleaned. Between them they redecorated the Boundary Road flat, threw parties and went out to others. There was a real affection in their relationship, one mark of which is the fact that in 1936 Spender dedicated a volume of short stories *The Burning Cactus* 'To W.H. AUDEN and T.A.R. HYNDMAN' – but one has to wonder whether even Tony really appreciated the full mythic significance of that.

As well as Tony's pleasant good looks, there was also that beguiling class difference between them. Unceremoniously, Tony 'would call Stephen "yer silly thing!" and tell him "don't be so daft!" ', Isherwood recalled. But more disturbingly, Isherwood also noticed how much Tony enjoyed a quarrel: 'He was full of fun and the love of argument – left-wing political or just argument for its own sake. He used the jargon of a left-wing intellectual.'[10] (Together with his own description of Tony as 'attractive; curly red-brown hair, sparkling yellow-brown eyes, big smiling teeth', this may, however, have been something of a *post hoc* assessment. Much later, Isherwood has admitted, he had 'a duet' with Tony.)[11]

Despite this ominous streak of independent-mindedness,

Spender stubbornly clung to his belief that Tony was 'right' for him. If he wasn't exactly in love with the boy from Tiger Bay, he was certainly in love with his working-class background. When Tony talked about his childhood, Spender said, it was more like poetry than anything his fellow poets could come up with. Everything about him was reminiscent of elements of his 'rough children' childhood[12] and, of course, of the old days of Hamburg, the Three Stars, Fritz and Lothar.

In all fairness it should be added that many of Spender's friends were also charmed by Tony and warmed to his 'intuitive and emotional' intelligence and beguiling openness. Somehow the uneducated ex-soldier could recognise and understand what Spender and even Auden were writing about. He showed a surprising appreciation of architecture and the visual arts and, although he never produced anything longer than a letter, he wrote intelligently and with a moving simplicity.

For his own part, it is inconceivable that Tony Hyndman did not enter into the relationship with Spender with his eyes wide open. Spender might not have been a 'steamer' in the real sense —in comparison with the likes of Lehmann and Driberg he was an innocent – but he was honest, genuine and everything Tony thought he had been looking for. Tony actually told Isherwood that meeting Spender was 'when the curtain went up, for me.'

However, a brief glance at the relevant pages in *World Within World* is sufficient to show that, for all Spender's and Tony's hopes, the day-to-day reality of living together soon proved to be no West End romance. As his later actions will reveal, Spender was and always remained as genuinely attached to Tony as Tony was to him; but the 'marriage' to which Virginia Woolf had alluded soon degenerated into melodrama and loosely plotted farce – although perhaps a bare-boards and white-light Brechtian parable would be the more suitable theatrical metaphor.

In large measure, it was inevitable that it should have done so. Just like Isherwood was with the Heinz whom he (foolishly as it turned out) once described as his *Hausdiener*, or domestic servant, Spender was incapable of establishing a real rapport with Tony. Not only were their backgrounds so dissimilar, the absurdity of their domestic situation caused further complications. They were ostensibly living on equal terms – but with Tony still playing what both knew was the superfluous and inevitably demeaning role of 'secretary'. Spender found it difficult to force him to do even the minimal work which needed doing; while Tony, the ex-guardsman, understandably skived (as he would probably have put it) as much as he could and exploited the all too apparent ambivalence of this new 'officer'.[13]

Soon the arguments started. Spender began quietly fuming that, apart from the cooking, Tony did little or nothing around the flat. His impatience only increased when he realised that there was actually nothing he *could* do. There really was no need for his 'secretary' to type manuscripts he could just as easily type for himself; nor, despite his published-author status, were there elaborate luncheons for Tony to plan or incessantly ringing telephones for him to answer.

Tony was also chafing at the bit. In terms strikingly reminiscent of John's, he early on complained to Spender that he was being taken over, that Spender behaved as if he owned him.[14] Intriguingly too, he also longed to meet Heinz,[15] no doubt to compare notes. (The unnatural closeness between Isherwood and Heinz was beginning to have equally corrosive effects on their relationship at this time. Ironically, it was Spender's German sister-in-law Erica, the newly married wife of his elder brother Michael, who first alerted Isherwood to that. 'When I see the two of you walking down the street together, buttoned up in your overcoats, I think: My God, they must bore each other to death, how can they *bear* it?' she said to him.)[16]

———

It was probably as much an attempt to appease Tony and paper over the insidiously widening cracks between them as it was a recurrence of his own wanderlust which led Spender to begin taking Tony on increasingly protracted foreign trips at this period. In the spring of 1933 what seems to have been the first of these brought them to northern Italy. They visited Venice and Florence, and spent some time doing little more than swimming and sun-bathing at Lévanto, a small port on the Ligurian Sea between Rapallo and La Spezia. Even there, however, occasional moments of tension had to be defused or deferred. One day Tony announced that he was unhappy and wanted to get away – from Italy, from Spender, from everything. Spender hedged, agonising over whether he should let him, thus forcing Tony to stand on his own two feet. Somehow, however, things were once again smoothed over, and between them the two contrived to ensure that the rest of the holiday passed off without incident.[17]

'Slowly the poison the whole blood stream fills,' wrote Spender's near contemporary William Empson in his poem 'Missing Dates'. It goes on: 'It is not the effort nor the failure tires./The waste remains, the waste remains and kills'. The whole poem (and also Empson's sly, joshing 'Just a Smack at Auden') can be taken as a cynical gloss on the boys-or-work predicament in which Spender, Isherwood, Auden and the rest found themselves at this period. There are surely few other interpretations which can be placed on a phrase such as 'the exchange rills/Of young dog blood gave but a month's desires'. Indeed, the poem ends explicitly enough:

> It is the poems you have lost, the ills
> From missing dates, at which the heart expires.
> Slowly the poison the whole blood stream fills.
> The waste remains, the waste remains and kills.

Coincidentally or not – and Empson was certainly no fan of the boy-culture of the gang – there was a lot of truth in that. Poems *were* lost; as we have seen, Spender was enduring periods in which he could do little or no work, principally because the 'waste' was already beginning to build up to a toxic level in his mind. As early as September 1933 he was rather ambiguously hinting at this in a letter to Isherwood.[18]

He and Tony were soon on the move again, as much to get

away from themselves as for any other reason. During 1934 and 1935 they visited Greece, Austria, Belgium, Spain and Portugal as well as making two trips to a village called Mlini near Dubrovnik in Yugoslavia. Understandably, few letters or other souvenirs of this compulsive wandering have survived, and it is difficult if not impossible to reconstruct a precise itinerary. About the only records are those contained in the impressionistic account of this period of his life which Spender gives in *World Within World*. There are certainly substantial *lacunae* in his correspondence with Isherwood. Gaps of one or two months – and in 1934 more than nine – are not uncommon and Spender is frequently forced to confess that he never got round to writing a promised letter or to make his peace with phrases such as 'I'm sorry not to have written for so long.'

However, certain themes obtrude in those letters which he did get around to writing, and they cast a characteristically sharper light on the way things were than does *World Within World*'s cautious probity. Spender was still fond of Tony and still usually enjoying both his company and the vicarious pleasure of sharing his discovery of new places and new experiences. And, temporarily at least, during trips on Mediterranean ferries or Greek buses something of the old Tony and their old love seemed to be there. In Vienna in the summer of 1934, Spender noted, Tony was happy and at ease. Unlike Venice, which he hated, he could come to terms with the city. Curiously, its baroque architecture had interested and amused him.[19]

This suddenly sanguine note might, however, have had more to do with Spender's own resurgence at this period. Never one to let a contact die, in July 1934 he wrote agitatedly to Virginia Woolf that he was composing a long poem (600–800 lines, he hoped) which was going to be the best thing he had ever done. He was writing a play and his Henry James book was nearly finished, too.[20]

Vienna, the poem to which he had referred, was published later that year, and along with the play – in all probability a first draft of *Trial of a Judge*, subtitled a 'Tragic Statement in Five Acts' – it marks what would come to be seen as the beginning of a new chapter in Spender's moral and political stance. That also prefigured a marked change in his personal life; but for the moment Spender remained trapped in the there and then. Emotionally he was still tied to Tony as much as Isherwood was to Heinz; however, the artificiality of the bond within and between the two couples was beginning to show.

In December 1935 they all met up in Antwerp and took cabins on a Brazilian ship bound for Rio de Janeiro. They were travelling only as far as Lisbon, en route to the nearby village of Sintra where they intended to spend the winter working. But even though the cottage had five bedrooms, the three-month sojourn and even the seven-day voyage out imposed strains of their own.

Isherwood remembered the latter 'in terms of opera, with the four of them relating to each other as quartets, trios or duets [. . .] The trio was between Stephen, Christopher and Jimmy. It now seems to me that it was performed for Jimmy's benefit, to make him feel that Stephen and Christopher regarded him as one of themselves. They didn't altogether, and Jimmy must have been aware that they didn't.'[21] (In *Christopher and His Kind* Isherwood followed *World Within World* and referred to Tony as Jimmy Younger.) Tony consoled himself with Heinz – this was apparently their first encounter – while Spender and Isherwood tip-toed among the eggshells: 'There was no duet between Spender and Heinz or between Christopher and Jimmy, perhaps because both Stephen and Christopher were afraid of being drawn into relationships which might have made them disloyal to each other.'

Happily for us, however, the group's 'conscious effort to enjoy itself' led Spender and Isherwood to collaborate on a daily journal of their self-imposed exile in Sintra.[22] Behind the frequent, rather forced jocularity and The Novelist's snap-shot portraits of the local inhabitants, it gives a revealing insight into the day-to-day life of the ménage and the comings and goings of their guests – Humphrey Spender stayed from time to time, Auden arrived the day after Spender and Tony left in mid-March, an ailing E.M. Forster sent his apologies.

With only momentary breaks while he paused for a 'spirit portrait', Spender quickly settled down to work. By the beginning of 1936 he was writing a new book (to be published as *Forward from Liberalism* in 1937) and tinkering once more with *Trial of a Judge*. Apart from his contributions to the journal itself, Isherwood, on the other hand, was finding it difficult to write anything at all. It was a classic case of writer's block. He had published novels, even written the screenplay for Berthold Viertel's film *Little Friend* (in a bizarre collaboration with Margaret Kennedy, author of the phenomenally successful novel *The Constant Nymph*). But now, not only was the very idea of *The Lost* disintegrating in his hands, a story provisionally entitled *Paul is Alone* was also proving stubbornly difficult to complete.

Below the salt – and it is difficult to escape the conclusion that, in spite of themselves, Spender and Isherwood still subconsciously saw them there – Tony and Heinz generally made themselves useful. Tony kept the household accounts and organised the servants as well as continuing with his nominal duties as Spender's secretary, while Heinz was doing the gardening and looking after the animals. As well as Teddy, his un-house-trained mongrel puppy, the quartet had acquired six hens, a rooster and some rabbits.[23]

But inevitably, Isherwood's memories and the journal's veiled references to domestic discord rather vitiate the group's pretence of creating something approaching a New Age Walden up in the 'mist and thin rain' of Sintra. Tony found that giving orders to the cook and maid conflicted with his left-wing political convictions. He and Spender were upset by what they thought was Heinz's ill-treatment of his dog. (He used to bite it whenever it bit him.) Isherwood loyally stood by Heinz . . .

Poor Isherwood. He frequently found himself a somewhat beleaguered figure. He was certainly 'the least contented member of the group', but he tried to keep his grouches and grumbles to a minimum. Rather than disrupt an already fragile status quo he scribbled his real thoughts into a separate, private diary he was keeping:

Stephen and [Tony] have honestly done their best to get along
with Heinz, who certainly can be maddening when he sulks.
Although sharing the expenses for the animals, they now
hardly dare look at them, for fear of precipitating another
row.

It's all very friendly and we are perfectly pleasant about it,
but of course we all know that our attempt at living here
together has been a complete flop.[24]

On 15 December 1935, as they crossed the Bay of Biscay on the
way to Lisbon, Isherwood noted in the group's daily journal that
he, Spender, Tony and Heinz had all had their palms read by one
of their fellow-passengers, a fat Irish-German woman who had a
marked fondness for Tony. She had announced that

Stephen is self-willed, violently pursues his ideas and changes
them frequently, listens to advice and has a nature of gold.
Heinz is conceited, ambitious and will succeed. [Tony] is
Welsh — and therefore conceited — strong-willed and mad on
girls. And I — ah, I am the kind of boy Madame has adored all
her life: wherever I travel, whatever I do, I'll always remain
real hundred per cent English — just a shy, modest, charming
boy.[25]

As its tone suggests, this was one of the journal entries
which Isherwood remembers 'were written in a tone of ship-
board humour and were meant to be read alone at once, before
they could go stale'.[26] It is certainly not difficult to imagine the
tensions which already existed within the group being at least
momentarily released by guffaws and giggles at Isherwood's
good-natured dissection of their individual characters in the
passage quoted above. For, whether or not they emanated from
the palmist, with the possible exception of Isherwood's com-
ments about himself, all his observations contained elements of
truth.

This is especially true of those he made about Spender. As
Isherwood, Tony and in all probability even Heinz would have

been aware that December, over the past few months the violent pursuit of his own ideas had led Spender to a radical change of mind. In sharp (and for Isherwood and Tony no doubt painful) contrast to his previous assertion that he could not consider marrying, the gradual disintegration of his relationship with Tony had led him to realise that if he was going to live with anyone it could not be with a man. Furthermore, he had actually begun to think about women – and to look for them.[27]

The seeds of this revelation had been sown in the spring of the previous year, during Spender and Tony's first trip to Yugoslavia. They were still arguing along old familiar lines – '*You have helped me at the price of taking away all possibility of my having any self-respect*' . . . '*Your complete independence on me, your lack of any life of your own, your indolence, sap my work*'. Back in London there had been a particularly violent oh-yes-it-can, oh-no-it-can't quarrel about whether roast chicken could be bought in tins.[28] Now, in Mlini on the Adriatic coast, matters were not helped by the fact that Tony had developed an inflamed appendix. And they were only exacerbated by the unexpected arrival of a woman named Muriel Gardiner at the *pension* in which they were staying.

When he first met her, Muriel (the 'Elizabeth' of *World Within World*) reminded Spender of his mother.[29] She seemed to have the same dark hair, dark eyes and clear complexion, the same look of having suffered which, if he could not quite remember them himself, he was at least familiar with from photographs of Violet. Muriel was on holiday with her three-year-old daughter and the child's nurse. She was then twenty-nine and, as Spender soon found out, the twice married and twice separated daughter of a wealthy Chicago meat-baron. She had read English Romantic literature at Oxford University and was currently studying medicine and psychology in Vienna.

Right from their very first meeting, Spender was fascinated by her. When he should have been working on Henry James, he just sat watching her. Her eyes, her face, her hair bewitched him. She was like a Leonardo da Vinci drawing of Leda[30] – and he felt himself suddenly and unexpectedly cast in the role of the swan.

There was 'a curtain of wonder' cutting him off from her in those first few days, but he already knew that at some time in the future he was going to draw it aside.[31]

His chance came sooner than he could have hoped or expected. Tony's appendix was getting no better and he and Spender were forced to take the ferry to Dubrovnik and consult a doctor. The doctor unequivocally recommended its removal, an appendisectomy. That meant a stay in hospital followed by a period of convalescence. But where? Yugoslavia did not seem the best place.

It was then that Spender remembered that Muriel – Mrs Gardiner – had uttered the usual polite pleasantries before her departure from Mlini, *If ever you're in* . . . She had a flat in the centre of Vienna and a secluded cottage, the Blockhaus, in the Wiener Wald forest about an hour's drive from the city. She would be glad to put them up, any time. Not only that, she was sure that, if Tony really did need an operation, through her connections in the Vienna medical world she could fix things up.

When Spender contacted her, she was as good as her word. While hospital arrangements were made, she settled Spender and Tony into her dark, oak-panelled flat in Vienna and insisted that they spent their weekends at the cottage. Six months later Spender was writing rather guiltily to Isherwood that he and Tony were reduced to relying on Muriel's generosity. They weren't taking advantage of her; there was simply no other way of remaining in Vienna.[32]

This was only half the story. Originally, Spender had seen Muriel as an intermittent but increasingly powerful presence. He had watched with admiration as she effortlessly managed to be by turns a student, a mother and a housewife. But soon, he had blurted out that he was attracted by her – and Muriel had added the additional role of 'lover' to her repertoire.

As Spender realised, this new turn in his life could hardly have come at a worse time. In 1934 he had just made his reputation in London; he had new books scheduled for publication there later that year – and yet he was way out of things in Vienna, where he couldn't even depend on the post.[33] What was more, he was sleeping with Muriel at the very time when Tony was in hospital and needed him most. *Is this manners, Stephen? . . .*

He was racked by guilt. Tony needed him; he needed Tony; he was still very fond of him and, for all their arguments, Tony still provided the enduring companionship which he had been seeking for so long. But now there was Muriel. He tore himself away from her to visit Tony in hospital – and immediately fell back in love with Tony. He took Tony off to convalesce in a mountain village – and soon found himself desperately missing Muriel.[34]

Creditably, Muriel gave him all the space he needed. A combination of her American upbringing and her interest in psychiatry, perhaps, gave her a clear and unsentimental view of life.[35] Her two marriages had failed – no matter, she'd go on until she found one which succeeded.[36] Now, fully aware that Spender might be quite literally unable to choose between her and Tony – and accept all the ramifications which such a choice would entail – she stood in the background and let Spender sort things out for himself.[37]

Spender was indeed temperamentally incapable of making such a decision, and once again he hedged, and attempted to split his life between Tony and Muriel – or as he put it in *World Within World*, between London and Vienna.[38] Certainly there were separations from Tony and, ironically, occasions when Tony actually lived up to his notional role as secretary: writing to Isherwood from Vienna in September 1934, Spender reassured him that Tony would be sending him, from London, a copy of the second edition of *Poems*, in which the dedication to Isherwood had been reinstated.[39]

Everything boiled over in an agonised letter which Spender wrote to Geoffrey Grigson at this time. Ostensibly, he was trying to apologise to Grigson for what seems to have been an injudiciously phrased review he had written; but, perhaps for no other reason that that Grigson was *not* Isherwood, he went on to unburden himself about everything which was then worrying him. He was writing to a (virtual) stranger, abasing himself and at the same time indulging in a bout of special pleading of the very highest order.

This letter (now in the Berg Collection at the New York Public Library) is merely dated 'July 6', but Spender's opening account of his work in progress strongly suggests that it was written in July 1934. It contains what amounts to the most searingly honest assessment of his own character that Spender ever wrote. He admits that he *had* gone out and assiduously courted publicity, even though he actually disliked being in the spotlight and being forced to live up to a false image. Hence, he was now planning to remain living abroad, where he could just get on with his work. That was all that was important. With luck, too, he would be able to sort out his personal life and decide once and for all whether he was homosexual or whether he was going to settle down and get married, the option he really preferred.[40]

It seems, however, that for a while at least Spender really believed he could incorporate both Muriel *and* Tony into his life. Nothing had changed, he assured Isherwood in a sudden stream of letters;[41] indeed, though he preferred sleeping with Muriel, her presence had actually improved his relationship with Tony. As if that was not enough, Tony himself was roped into what was in all probability something like a knowing conspiracy. At the end of one letter – signed 'Stephen and Tony' – he added a touching postscript of his own:

> Hope you are well, Dear. Try and hop over to London some time. Congratulations on 'Little Friend'. I have seen it twice and think it is a beautiful film. Best love to you both.[42]

Spender also laid elaborate plans for Isherwood to meet Muriel – she was just the sort of woman they had hoped to meet in Berlin, he told him in the Vienna letter we have already noticed – but he didn't see how it could be arranged. They always seemed to be in different countries. Now, he, Muriel and Tony were planning to go off, *à trois*, to Albania for a holiday. Then, *à deux*, he and Tony were thinking of retiring to a country cottage . . .

Poor Tony. A full six months after he added that rather pathetic postscript, in March 1935, he was still having to fit in with Spender's preoccupation with Muriel. On 7 March Spender wrote to tell Isherwood that he and Tony were about to set off for Austria to stay with Muriel in Vienna and then, once more *à trois*, adjourn for a holiday among the Austrian lakes.[43] With what now reads as little more than brazen insensitivity, he then went on to suggest that Isherwood and Heinz could meet up with the three of them in Austria, or possibly Yugoslavia, at some time during that summer.

Not unnaturally, Isherwood – who was then more concerned with the fact that Heinz was about to be conscripted into the German army – felt compelled to say no. So how would it be if I (and presumably Tony and Muriel) meet up with you in September on the way home? Spender wrote back in June, when the three had established themselves for a second summer at the Pension Mlini. He was pleading for acceptance, still convinced that all his friends would like one another. But it was too late; at about the time he and Tony had set off for Vienna, Isherwood and Heinz were already draft-dodging in Denmark and Belgium.

I could come home via Amsterdam, or wherever you are, Spender persisted (rather illogically) in another rather oleaginous letter. He had enjoyed Auden and Isherwood's recently published verse play *The Dog Beneath the Skin* he wrote – but then spoilt the note of magnanimity by adding that Isherwood should buy the *London Mercury* ('price 1/–'), in the current edition of which Spender (erroneously) believed one of his own stories was being published.[44]

━━━━━━

In *Christopher and His Kind* Isherwood maintains an ominous silence about Spender's relationship with Muriel. In *World Within World* even Spender paints a modest, domestic, almost casual picture of his life with her – even though, after more than fifteen years, just writing about this first stab at real domesticity still made him feel that he was living in a poem. But in 'The Dead Island', a short story which he wrote in the latter half of 1935[45] (and published in *The Burning Cactus* the following year) he seems to have probed its emotional depths in greater, almost excessive detail.

The story is set in a hotel and concerns the relationship between a thrice married woman with a wealthy background and a younger, possibly homosexual, man who arrives at the hotel after having undergone some kind of alcohol-induced crisis. His analyst, Dr Giuseppe Rooth is an unseen third figure who, by letter, fills in essential information about his patient.

Quite rightly, Lee Bartlett suggests that Spender drew on his time with Hellmut – and in particular the intrusion of the alcoholic Kirk and the enigmatic Dr Möring – for 'material for his short story "The Dead Islands" [sic]'.[46] In 'The Finish', the first of a couple of pseudo-Brechtian codas to 'The Dead Island', the man is indeed, like Kirk, reduced to drinking methylated spirits and hair oil. This, however, is a character point. At a deeper level the story seems far more firmly anchored to the actuality of Spender's encounter with Muriel at Mlini.

The circumstantial detail certainly bears this out. The hotel in which the man and the woman meet, for instance, is in a small town overlooking the Adriatic and within easy reach of a walled coastal city which bears a clear resemblance to Dubrovnik. Such direct parallels should not be pushed too far, however. Not only are both protagonists left unnamed, the man is specifically described as a short chorus-boy with curly black hair, although he does have a poet's smile. Similarly, there is no suggestion that the woman has a child. But we must remember that this is fiction rather than autobiography – even 'poetic' autobiography of the *World Within World* kind. Such clues as it offers therefore yield themselves only to the closest reading of the nodding, winking subtext.

Thus, in the light of Spender's unequal relationship with Tony, it is significant that the woman muses that she has turned the man, her lover, into little more than a pet.[47] And it is worth noting too that, after they have made love for the first (and only) time, she tells him she knew all along that this was the first time he had been in bed with a woman.[48] And so on. The man has been through a trying period in his life and now blurts out that he loves the woman . . .

In the story the couple part. He goes off to the eponymous Dead Island and from there to Egypt and his death, rather like Kirk. She returns to Vienna and divorces her husband, changed and somehow enlivened by her encounter with the man. Evidently then, this is a complex, convoluted work in which author and characters sometimes collide and sometimes coalesce. It is even tempting to argue that Dr Rooth can be seen as standing for Auden and the whole 'psychological' circus which had made Spender believe himself to be homosexual. Meanings slide.

In real life things were just as complex. Largely, it seems, through his relationship with Muriel and the coincidence of her living in Vienna, at this time Spender abruptly emerged from the solipsistic world in which he had been immersed since he went up to Oxford. Suddenly, just like the man in 'The Dead Island', over no more than a few weeks he discovered his place in the scheme of things.

Inspired by Muriel and her tales of Austrian socialists, he broke out of the shuttered, private, self-pitying world of his own emotions and, rather than sailing off to die, began to confront public and political realities as he had never done before. Almost overnight, his work and his every action came to embody this political rebirth. He felt bound to make a statement, to minute his liberal opposition to the rise of right-wing iconoclasm. This tension between what, *pace* T.S. Eliot, we might call the Destruction of Tradition and the Individual Talent would continue to inform his writing for the next half century.

In 1990 he was still talking about 'Po-etry' and pronouncing the word with a very audible capital p – a Horatio struggling to hold the bridge against a terrifying nightmare world in which standards were numinous and any notion of correctness was at best relative.[49] This, however, is only part of the story. For whereas Eliot retreated further into the prim redoubt of Anglo-Catholicism every time the barbarians so much as looked at the door, Spender's reaction was quite the opposite. Like many of his generation, he girded up his loins for a hand-to-hand fight, imbued with an unshakable belief in himself and the rightness of The Cause.[50]

It is no accident that 1935 saw the first publication of poems such as 'The Exiles' and 'An Elementary School Classroom in a Slum' where the latter, with its crude imagery of starving, rat-eyed children cynically denied the azure elysium of sun and golden sands, acts as a sort of party-line corrective to the bucolic, wistful 'Rough'/'My parents'.[51] *Vienna* and, when it finally appeared, *The Destructive Element* confirmed Spender in this new role of literary commando, the *'little liberal'*, the *Po-et*, the lonely sniper pitched against the massed and massive forces of a big bad world.

We had already seen how outside events – First World War bombs at Sheringham, Nazi gatherings in Berlin, knots of the unemployed on London street corners – had influenced his early work. Now, as he was ineluctably swept up into 'the struggle', it was suddenly Spender *contra alium*. Almost in spite of himself he became a neo-Shelley crying – like Auden – that 'We must love one another or die';[52] a Jeremiah excoriating the Fascist, Nazi here-and-now in favour of a call-collect future. Once again though, Auden was doing it better:

To-morrow for the young and the poets exploding like bombs,
The walks by the lake, the weeks of perfect communion;
To-morrow the bicycle races
Through the suburbs on summer evenings. But to-day the
    struggle.[53]

Auden could afford to hold himself apart; and indeed his work is still often criticised for its 'clinical' detachment. But by his very nature Spender was incapable of making such a division. And in both *Vienna* (heavily influenced by Auden's *The Orators*) and *The Destructive Element* he sought to fuse the private and the public, to unite political and moral concerns. If *The Destructive*

Element (which had expanded from the original study of Henry James to take in the work of Eliot, Yeats and D.H. Lawrence as well as writers from Spender's own generation) was about writers who found themselves cast as Hamlets adrift in a world to which they could not relate,[54] then so too was *Vienna*.

Like some angry canvas by Goya or Delacroix, the poem was originally intended as a reflection on the forceful suppression of Austria's anti-fascist Social Democratic party by the 'pocket chancellor' Engelbert Dollfuss on 12 February 1934. But, huddled in a corner of the crowded picture, there are also the figures of Spender and Muriel. For, although he took no part in fighting –he was not even in Vienna on the fateful day when shells rained down on its working-class suburbs– Spender found himself drawn into the maelstrom by Muriel's decision not only to join the Socialists but also to give them as much money as she could afford. What was more, she allowed her flat to be used by one particular 'cell' of six guerrillas who paraded under such pseudonyms as Jo, Anna, Poldi and Karl[55] – and who were led, it is not irrelevant to note, by her then fiancé, Franz.

Thus, as well as expressing Spender's indignation at the events taking place outside his (or rather Muriel's) window, *Vienna* also specifically tried to depict their effect on another tortured and tormented love relationship. Spender realised that his love for Muriel and what amounted to civil war were hardly the same; but he insisted that they were related, since private love and affection could not survive in a world so notably devoid of those qualities.[56] Pointedly, *Vienna* was dedicated to Muriel.

———

Back in London, Spender and Tony found a new flat at 25 Randolph Crescent, Maida Vale. It is likely that this was in the house at which a friend later recalled that the linoleum was worn and there was 'that broken strut in the bannister, and the slightly musty smell'. But Spender's first-floor flat was 'cheerful and gay'. His books lined the walls of the sitting-room, his papers covered the Finnish dining-table and there were striped curtains at the tall Georgian windows.[57]

It was here that Spender excitedly awaited the publication of *Vienna*, still convinced that, as he had told Virginia Woolf, it was the best thing he had ever written. (So convinced, indeed, that he even began adapting it for the stage. It was a quixotic scheme which seems to have been inspired by Auden and Isherwood's verse play *The Dog Beneath the Skin* and possibly by Eliot's succes with *Murder in the Cathedral*, first staged in 1935. Equally, it may have been prompted by the trouble Spender was still having with *Trial of a Judge*.)

When the reviews appeared in November 1934, however, the critics were almost unanimous in their disapproval, and its fashionable young author had to endure a first and quite unexpected taste of obloquy. 'Mr Spender has published a bad poem "Vienna",' Geoffrey Grigson noted; while the *Spectator* commented that Spender was 'in a sense too involved in his material'. The *Times Literary Supplement* cavilled because 'we are led, on the whole, not only to pity for those Socialists, but also to a view of the poet himself in the act of being pitiful'. Admitting that 'the theme is there, and the emotions are there', the *Nation* went on to lament that 'the two do not coalesce in a way that would give an ordered intensity to the whole'.[58] Privately, Virginia Woolf too expressed reservations about what she called the 'Epic' in a letter to Spender that was typically frank: 'youve not got the elements yet rightly mixed [. . .] That hints at the reason why I felt it jerked broken incomplete.'[59]

Spender's disappointment was such that he even asked T.S. Eliot whether Faber could withdraw the book.[60] However, he has subsequently admitted that the critics were quite right; with its mixture of prose and poetry and urgent, italicised, rather Brechtian questions, *Vienna* was a failure.[61]

In the light of Spender's words, Samuel Hynes's later evisceration of the poem and its author is perhaps unnecessarily severe. Nevertheless his conclusion that *Vienna* (or at the very least its final section, 'Analysis and Statement') is a 'psycho-sexual' drama certainly holds true. So too does his characterisation of 'the first-person speaking voice of the poem'. According to Hynes he is

> an isolated, ineffectual, emotionally sterile young man who thinks of love for a woman as admirable and fertile, but cannot feel it, and who is drawn to the beauty of boys, but is troubled by those feelings.[62]

Ironically, however, it was Spender who had the last laugh. Indirectly, Dollfuss and his lieutenants Starhemberg and Fey *did* affect his life. The public, political theatre *did* impinge on his own psycho-sexual drama. Muriel, Franz, Dollfuss and Vienna had together awakened in him a latent anger which over the next eighteen months expressed itself in an attempt to re-establish priorities. *To-day the struggle . . .*

Fascinatingly, this period in Spender's life has been detailed in his friend T. C. Worsley's 'fictionalised memoir', *Fellow Travellers*. Although this was not published until 1971, it was drafted in the late 1930s and is very clearly based on contemporary letters, diaries and notes. 'Events and happenings, though they actually occurred, have been rearranged and reattributed,' Worsley warns in a prefatory note; but, as he goes on to explain, Spender was always very much in his mind as the basis of one of the major characters:

> Martin Murray, the well-known young novelist, was then just thirty, but already on the strength of four books he had established himself as the representative figure of his generation. He was for us what someone like John Osborne was a few years ago to the young of the Fifties.
>
> He – or someone like him – was to have been one of the main characters, and one of the threads of the novel was to have been his relationship with Harry Watson, an engaging young man who had been 'bought out' of the Scots Guards and was living in a rather uneasy domesticity with Martin at the time [the book begins].[63]

Though it must be treated with some caution, because of its very close correlation to verifiable facts Worsley's narrative, artfully constructed out of a series of 'files', letters and authorial notes, thus provides a valuable inside account of the private feelings and motivations of Spender and his friends at a time when they were being publicly feted in a manner not seen before or since.

Significantly, it was at exactly this period that Spender completed and published his 'imaginary autobiography' *Forward from Liberalism*. An impatient, even intemperate, piece of neo-J.A.-ism which eclectically and unquestioningly mixed 'historical analysis and political ratiocination',[64] it was not a good book but – such was the mood of the times – it was selected by Victor Gollancz to be one of his Left Book Club's Books of the Month in 1937. That, Spender hoped, would mean sales of an extra 25,000 copies and some reasonable royalty cheques[65] – even if the connection with the Left Book Club would also cast him as a spear-carrier in what the painter C.R.W. Nevinson (an arch-enemy of the Bloomsberries) referred to as 'the stage army of the good'. He would, he realised, have to turn up at political meetings, write propagandist articles for little or nothing and lend his name to innumerable worthy causes.[66] He accepted it all with alacrity.

Significantly too, Spender was also attempting to clean the Augean stables of his personal life. He bade a final farewell to Vienna, Muriel and Franz in the summer of 1936 and made a semi-permanent return to London, Tony and the Randolph Crescent flat. It was, however, an unsatisfactory home-coming. Both he and Tony had come to realise that there was no future in their relationship. As much as six months previously, in November 1935, Spender had already hinted to Isherwood that he was on the point of giving up the flat and happy at the prospect of going his own separate way.[67] Now, as Tony veered ever more strongly towards communism, thought about joining the Communist Party itself and wondered whether he should even go off to fight in Abyssinia; as Isherwood jeered at his new-found belief in the 'superiority' of heterosexuality over 'buggery';[68] as the bad reviews continued to come in, he had been forced to conclude that, once again, his life was nothing but failure.[69]

Soon he and Tony separated, albeit on amicable terms, and Spender started doing everything he could to get himself out of the complaisant liberal rut along which he seemed to be travelling. Freed from the financial burden of supporting Tony and buoyed up by the unexpected royalties from Gollancz, he found another flat, this time a much smaller studio at Queen's Mansions in Brook Green, Hammersmith, and unashamedly furnished it in a modern, Bauhaus style which echoed Herbert List's riverside apartment in Hamburg. There were copper-bowled lamps and neon lights, along with bentwood tables and chairs. According to Louis MacNeice the flat also had 'a colour scheme out of *Vogue*, a huge vulcanite writing-desk and over the fireplace an abstract picture by Wyndham Lewis'.[70]

It looked resolutely and rather uncomfortably modern, with Swedish plain wood furniture, lights reflected from the ceiling, chairs that looked like inverted mushrooms, and semi-abstract pictures on the walls. All this was sufficiently unusual at this time to give the journalists and gossip-writers just the right revolutionary image with which to start their paragraphs.[71]

Meanwhile, finally released from his exiguous secretarial commitments, Tony also moved into a new flat of his own, across the river in Battersea, and temporarily joined the staff of the magazine *Left Review* . . .

———

By this time the plight of the Austrian Socialists had been driven off the front pages of the newspapers by the outbreak of the Spanish Civil War in July 1936. Dollfuss had been forgotten and – second only to Hitler – General Francisco Franco, the self-proclaimed Spanish *Caudillo*, had emerged as the new *bête noir* of the intellectual Left. Support groups for the anti-Franco, anti-fascist Spanish Republicans had been established in Britain; and George Orwell, Tom Wintringham, John Cornford, Julian Bell and 2,758 other Britons were actually going off to fight in the International Brigade.

Spender thought about doing so too – but, possibly remem-

bering his lack-lustre days as a lance-corporal in the University
College School Officer Training Corps, quickly decided against
it.[72] He would be better employed as a propagandist on the
home front, he argued. He and Tony had, after all, spent a
couple of weeks in Barcelona in the spring of 1936, just as things
were getting hot.

They had indeed; but Spender's letters suggest that this trip to
Spain was made simply because Spain was 'abroad'. Beyond a
bland announcement that 'the politics are very interesting', there
is certainly no sense of commitment or burning indignation in
what he wrote to Isherwood and Auden at this time. His letters
say little more than that Spender had decided he liked Barcelona
very much, that he had dined with the British Consul and had
met a generous convivial Spaniard called Maria Manent who
was introducing him to the poetry of Lorca.[73]

It hardly mattered. Back in London, the newly politicised
Spender, the newly commissioned officer in that stage army of
the good, the controversial young author of *Forward from
Liberalism* soon heard his telephone ringing. Would he speak to
the Birmingham University Socialist Society? Would he support
the Spanish Republicans at a *Sunday Times* book exhibition?
Would he give a talk at St Pancras Town Hall? Would he,
perhaps, even care to consider a lecture tour of America?

Yes, yes, yes! No more an expert on Spain than the Nicolsons,
the Woolfs, John Lehmann, Lehmann's brother-in-law Wogan
Philipps or any of the rest of the intellectual Left who had visited
the country, at the end of October 1936 he resolved to turn no
invitation down for six months[74] – not even the one which
arrived from Harry Pollitt.

Pollitt, the secretary of the British Communist Party, had read
Forward from Liberalism and written to Spender suggesting that
he should join the Party and lend his weight to its campaign in
favour of the Republicans.

Well . . . Ideological compromises were made. Both men
recognised that, unlike Pollitt – or, for that matter, Tony –
Spender was hardly a working-class revolutionary for whom
black was black and red was red. They agreed to differ, for

instance, over the independence of Stalin's show trials. Pollitt also sat and listened when Spender argued that, although the tone of *Forward from Liberalism* had been overtly anti-fascist, Spender himself was not wholly, totally pro-communist. In return, Spender finally agreed to forget about Stalin – and, after a lot of soul-searching, he filled in the forms and joined the Party to do his bit.

Joining the Communist Party was something different. It was the spiritual equivalent of changing one's religion. It was an act of Faith. The Party, like the Catholics, demanded absolute obedience. If you joined the Party, you had to renounce the freedom of thinking for yourself. You thought what you were told to think. The Party, like the Pope, was infallible. So it was an Act of Renunciation as well as an Act of Faith, and in return for what you gave up, you received Absolute Certainty.[75]

Not unnaturally, Pollitt regarded Spender as a star catch, and rapidly capitalised on his name. He arranged for him to write an article for the Party paper, the *Daily Worker*, almost before he had received a membership card from his local Communist 'cell' in Hammersmith. Within a few days Pollitt had also arranged for him to fly out to Spain as the paper's new investigative reporter.

It was a role for which Spender was ludicrously ill-equipped – as ill-equipped, indeed, as the luckless nature writer William Boot who, in Evelyn Waugh's novel *Scoop* (1938) is dispatched by Lord Copper's newspaper *The Daily Beast* to cover a civil war in Africa. He had no clue about how to discover the fate of the crew of a Russian ship which had been sunk in the Mediterranean by the pro-Franco Italians, the task to which he was assigned. He knew no one and spoke only faltering Spanish. Inevitably, this hastily arranged return to Spain – and a number of subsequent visits – soon disintegrated into farce.

So too did Spender's spectacularly brief career in the Communist Party. In his original article in the *Daily Worker*, which was bluntly entitled 'I Join the Communist Party', he had gone all out for political correctness. The piece contained repeated references to 'Comrade Campbell' and almost obsessively toed the anti-fascist Party line. Castigations of 'the capitalist press' and 'a gigantic plot against the Soviet Government' were only equalled by its declaration that the Spanish Civil War was 'the class war played out on an international scale', a battle which pitted 'international imperialism against the democratic will of at least 80 per cent of the Spanish people'.[76] Ironically, however, even that had not been good enough.

Spender recently wrote that he was now thoroughly ashamed of the abject tone he adopted in the article;[77] but in February 1937 it was not abject enough and signally failed to convince the Party die-hards. No one from the communists' Hammersmith 'cell' contacted him, and soon he gave up carrying his Party card. His flirtation with the Communist party was as ineffective as it was inglorious. Looking back on it in 1992, he recalled that he had joined and left the Party within a month.[78]

Even such a brief affiliation was, however, to have long-lasting repercussions on the complicatedly entwined strands of his personal and professional lives. It led to his being unexpectedly offered a job as the head of English broadcasting for the anti-fascist (UGT) radio station in Valencia. Back in Britain, it also gave him extra credibility as a guest speaker at Spanish Aid Committee meetings.

━━━━━

It was at one of these, in Oxford, that he first met Inez. Marie Agnes Pearn, always known as Inez, had a pretty, almost beautiful face and fair hair which contemporary photographs show she wore cut rather shorter than was normal for the time.[79] She was twenty-two, five years younger than Spender — *this rather unsophisticated Oxford girl a bit below his intellectual station*[80] — and forthright almost to the point of rudeness. She lived in London, near the Thames in Pimlico. She was in Oxford because she was then studying the work of the Spanish poet Góngora (Don Luis de Góngora y Argote), a near contemporary of Shakespeare. She had come to hear Spender speak because she too was a member of the Spanish Aid Committee and had indeed spent the summer of 1936 working in Spain, albeit as governess of the young children of 'rich Spanish reactionaries'.[81]

Like many of his friends, including Wogan Philipps and the artist William Coldstream, Spender was fascinated by her – although there seems to have been something peculiarly cold about their subsequent romance. In *Fellow Travellers* Cuthbert Worsley has Martin (Spender) comparing his relationship with Judy, an Oxford student, to a past fling with Elvira, a Viennese woman writer with whom he and Harry (Tony) had stayed 'just outside Dubrovnik':

> I wanted to prove to myself that my affair with Elvira was not, on similar lines, merely the search for a mother-figure, that I could equally find a young girl attractive enough to go to bed with. I certainly assured myself on that point so that the experiment from my point of view was an unqualified success.[82]

Impulsively, Spender invited Inez to the flat-warming party he was planning for his friends in Hammersmith. Impulsively too – although she had disliked the flat and especially hated its modern lighting – on the day after the party he took her to lunch at the Café Royal and asked her to marry him. 'Yes,' said Inez. Hurriedly, Spender then wrote to Isherwood explaining that he was in love with Inez and, as far as he could tell, she was with him. Tony, he admitted, could not understand what was going on. Half the time he was angry; half the time he was just upset – however, everything would calm down as soon as he was settled into his new flat, got used to his new job and found himself a new lover.[83]

Quite what Isherwood thought about all this has gone unrecorded. However, Worsley saw through all the persiflage. Communism, heterosexuality . . . they were no more than the accoutrements of the new Stephen Spender, his Martin Murray – and pretty tiresome 'heavy stuff' too:

> You know what he's like in that mood, totally taken up with the great public drama of whether Martin Murray likes

women. *How* Martin Murray likes women. *Why* Martin Murray
likes women. Why our generation ought to be bi-sexual! The bi-
sexual ideal and modern Communism! Forward from
Homosexuality! Outward from the single sex! And all that![84]

Spender, though, was certain that marrying Inez was going
to make all the difference in the world: he was tired of the sordid
round of 'affairs', and a number of factors meant that he *needed*
to make what he called 'an absolute final step'.[85] Exactly what
these were even he did not seem to know, and as his wedding day
approached he was manically veering from being ecstatically
happy to being very worried about what he was embarking
upon.

When he married Inez at Hammersmith Register Office on 15
December 1936 he was still very conscious of the fact that he had
known her for less than a month.

At the ceremony, Spender signed the register – seemingly on
the strength of his *Daily Worker* columns, he gave his occupa-
tion as 'journalist' – and, in the unavoidable absence of Michael
and Humphrey, his grandmother Hilda Schuster acted as his
witness. Later, Mrs Schuster hosted a reception at her flat during
which Spender's uncle J.A. met W.H. Auden: 'A remarkably
self-possessed young man', was his only comment. Ostenta-
tiously, Spender withdrew from the festivities in order to correct
some proofs and then returned to demonstrate his new political
sympathies by distributing the wedding presents among his
'pauper' friends.[86]

———

Not for the first time, it was Virginia Woolf who really had the
measure of what Spender was doing, and of the extent of the
personal confusion which lay behind it. She may not have
known – as Spender certainly did – that W.H. Auden had
married Erika Mann, the daughter of the German novelist
Thomas Mann, in June 1935 without having previously met her.
(It was part of a scheme, pandered by Isherwood, to secure

British citizenship for Erika.) On the other hand, she and Leonard were fond of Spender – 'a beautiful if too convention-ally poetic young man' – and seemed to have spent most of an afternoon and evening in February 1937 interrogating him in a typically Bloomsbury-ish way about his motives. Virginia noted in her diary:

> Stephen Spender came to tea & dinner the other day [. . .] great enthusiasm, now tempered, & rather metalled because, having married, his friend, the male, joined the F[oreign] Legion, is fighting in Spain; Inez, who is political in the Oxford way only, sits at Brussels studying Spanish MSS. Stephen finds this intolerable. To stabilise himself; because he dreaded the old Brindled Tom puss life of William [Plomer], safe by the fireside. Now [he] is torn two ways: so Inez sits there, in order, should he be killed in Spain – but he's only broadcasting – she may have her job to fall back on. A curious interpretation of marriage: [I] told him not to fight. He said it was the easiest thing to do. I said give up speaking – he said But it brought in money. He argued that we cannot let the Fascists overrun Spain: then it'll be France; then us. We must fight. L[eonard] said he thought things had now gone so far it did not matter. Fighting did no good. S. said the C[ommunist] P[arty] which he had that day joined, wanted him to be killed, in order that there might be another Byron. He has a child's vanity about himself.[87]

Cruel and (in Spender's own description of the tone of Woolf's diaries and letters) somewhat 'snide' though this is, it still has a ring of truth about it. And Mrs Woolf was hardly alone in finding Spender's marriage 'curious'. We have already seen something of Cuthbert Worsley's reaction. Much later, John Lehmann was to resurrect what must have been the mood of the streets:

> Billy and I exchanged many reminiscences of Vienna, capping each other's stories and delighting Charlie who evidently envied our time in Austria very much. He had read Stephen Spender's poem about the February workers' rising, [i.e.

Vienna] and questioned me closely about the facts that had inspired the poem. And then: was Spender queer? Were the other young writers of his circle queer? He had heard so many rumours. Of course I, who had only hearsay to go on, and liking the exactitude above the pleasures of myth-making, could only tell him: read his poems, read *their* poems, and make up your mind for yourself. 'Anyway, he's married, you know,' I added. 'Doesn't mean a thing!' said Charlie gaily, his eyes sparkling.[88]

SEVEN

On the Front Line

In *Forward from Liberalism* Stephen Spender tried to stand back and assess the world in which he and his kind found themselves in the mid-thirties. Less confidently, he then went on to sketch the sort of world in which he thought they *should* be living. The book was concerned with the Big Themes and Real Life – in direct contrast, perhaps, to the interminable and impenetrable public-school 'Mortmere' fantasies which underlay Auden and Isherwood's verse dramas. But for all that, and for all its contemporary popularity, in critical terms *Forward From Liberalism* was as big a failure as *Vienna* had been. It was too personal, too involved and too contrived. Even Harry Pollitt called it 'completely wrong'. More woundingly, the *Left Review* commented that it 'signally lacks' any 'historical perspective'.[1]

Reading it today, even in the context of the plethora of leftist, anti-fascist literature, both factual and fictional, which was published in Britain during the 1930s – everything from Ralph Fox's unambiguously titled two-volume study of *The Class Struggle in Britain in the Epoch of Imperialism* (1932–4) to Walter Greenwood's novel *Love on the Dole* (1933) – one is constantly left wondering whom Spender is trying to convince. He erects a Kafka-esque – or Audenesque – background of capitalist, totalitarian state (the adjectives are virtually synonymous) replete with propagandising newspapers, down-trodden workers and cynically staged show trials. But centre-stage he places a lonely, vulnerable and strangely familiar individual who has to confront the big issues. He has to be true to himself. Existentially, he has to commit himself, to come down off the fence: *We must love one another or die . . .*

Ultimately, of course, this was exactly what Spender himself was incapable of doing. At school he had never been a 'team man'. At Oxford he had been a self-conscious loner. Now he was finding it equally difficult to follow the doctrinaire Communist Party line in which like a wavering communicant he so fervently wanted to believe.

As we have already seen, he accepted Harry Pollitt's shilling and went to Spain on behalf of the *Daily Worker* in the first weeks of 1937. But even this seems to have been done out of the most divided of motives. Not only was he going as little more than a voyeur, he was sick at the thought that Tony (who had followed his lead and finally become a Communist) and several other of his friends including Giles Romilly, the nephew of Winston Churchill, had actually joined the International Brigade and gone off to fight.[2]

To-day the struggle . . . It was all beginning to seem a bit of a joke. Was he no more than part of what Cyril Connolly was calling an 'English band of psychological revolutionaries, people who adopt left-wing formulas because they hate their fathers or were unhappy at their public schools or insulted at the Customs or lectured about sex'?[3]

On all the available evidence, probably not. Indeed Spender's private writings at this time suggest that he was stung by Connolly's words.[4] Even they, however, tell only half the story, for the *Daily Worker* escapade was undertaken more out of his feelings for Tony than any real ideological fervour. Spender was already blaming himself for the break-up of the relationship and convincing himself that, if they had still been together, Tony would not have gone to Spain at all. Only a fortnight after his marriage to Inez, he confided to Isherwood that he still loved Tony and missed him terribly.[5]

―――――

Spender left for Spain in the very first days of 1937 on a tight schedule. Quite apart from the *Daily Worker* deadlines, he was booked to give a talk to the Left Book Club in London on 19

January before taking Inez to Brussels to meet Isherwood the following day.[6] Out of an excess of conscience he stipulated that he should receive not more than his expenses for the trip, but asked that Cuthbert Worsley be allowed to accompany him.[7] Both requests were acceded to (although we only have Spender's word on the latter point. In his memoir *Fellow Travellers* Worsley makes no mention of the trip but gives a detailed account of Spender's *next* trip to Spain. It is possible, then, that *World Within World* is at fault here.)

According to *World Within World*, the pair flew to Marseilles (probably the first time Spender ever travelled by air) where they had arranged an overnight stay. The next day they continued their journey, flying on to Barcelona and, eventually, Alicante. There, well-steeped in propaganda about a 'ravaged Spain', Spender was rather disappointed – but, because of his fears for Tony's safety, also somewhat relieved – to find no signs of war at all. Neither, unsurprisingly, could he or Worsley find any real clue about the fate of the crew of the Russian ship, the *Comsomol*. Aimlessly and almost randomly, they pottered about, eventually travelling hundreds of miles along the Mediterranean coast in search of any hard information they could take back to the *Daily Worker*.

They got as far as Gibraltar, some four hundred miles from Alicante, and tried to push on another seventy-five miles to Cadiz, where they had been led to believe (correctly, as it turned out) that the Russian sailors were interned. Pro-Franco Nationalists prevented that trip, but could do nothing to stop them pursuing their 'enquiries' in North Africa. Accordingly, they took the first available ferry to Tangier, where Spender dutifully interviewed the Republican representative and scribbled a quick, uninspired piece for the *Left Review*.[8] Those chores over, they went on, as little more than tourists, to visit Oran, Casablanca and even Marrakesh, a good three hundred miles from the southern shores of the Mediterranean.

Wherever they went, however, in Spain, Algeria or Morocco, Spender's thoughts were more concentrated on Tony than the plight of the Russian sailors. In Marrakesh he broke down in tears at the sight of a donkey whose face obscurely reminded him of Tony's.[9] This was, admittedly, an exception; more commonly the Tony–Spain connection was forged by Spender's realisation that he was on the fringe of an actual war zone. The contrasts and contradictions he found – so much starker than those he had seen in pre-Hitler Berlin, so much more *real* now that the bullets had started flying – served to reinforce what he did not then recognise as his own deep ambivalence.

On the one hand he was the politically correct Left Wing fellow-traveller. He identified with the struggles of the working classes in Barcelona, castigated the pro-Franco attitudes of the British ruling class in Gibraltar and ridiculed the aristocratic posturing of the British members of a fox hunt he encountered at Calpe, a small, Nationalist-held coastal town some miles north-east of Alicante.[10] On the other he was still racked by guilt and the idea that Tony would never have become embroiled in the chaos if he had taken better care of him – a feeling which was only reinforced when Tony's sister let it be known that she blamed Spender for her brother's sudden decision to join the International Brigade.[11]

Wholly typically, then, Spender returned to London and Inez in the middle of January as dazed and confused about the primacy of personal feelings over public responsibilities as he had been when he'd set down to write *Forward from Liberalism* or, for that matter, *Vienna*. Only one thing was certain: Inez or no Inez, he had to get back to Spain as soon as possible. Spain was the crucible.

———

As we have seen, the opportunity was not long in coming. The arrival of the invitation to head the English section of the Socialist Broadcasting Station in Valencia could not have been better timed. Within a few weeks Spender was back in Barcelona where he had arranged to meet Wogan Philipps who was driving an ambulance unit down to the town of Albacete and had offered to give him a lift. Once again, he travelled via France and, before his rendezvous with Philipps, he spent a day in the small town of Port Bou which sits virtually astride the Franco-Spanish border. Later, he was to use memories of that day when, literally and metaphorically, personally and publically, he sat in the middle of crossfire for what was to become one of his finest poems.

Reticent but revealing, 'Port Bou'[12] is more fluent, more honest and more successful than any of Spender's earlier poems in its sketch-portrait of a man coming to terms with himself, or at least with his problems.

And these problems were now coming in battalions. Tony was depressed, frightened and completely disillusioned with the reality of war. Having come through the Battle of Jarmara (12 February 1937) he had written to Spender from Albacete saying, in essence, You forced me into this, now you've got to get me out.[13] In *Fellow Travellers*, Worsley graphically recreates the urgency of all this in a series of letters from Harry to Martin. They are seemingly based on those of Tony's from which Spender quotes in *World Within World*:

> *What are we to do, Martin? Things are pretty bad. We've decided we won't obey silly orders we don't agree with and see what happens* [. . .]
>   *Do write to me, Martin, and do try to get someone* with real authority *sent out to report on the situation. Otherwise I don't know what may happen.*
>   *Can't anything be done for us? I feel we're rotting out here. Rotting and forgotten. Does anyone at home remember us? Parcels would be a help. Chocolate, things like that. The food is terrible and getting worse.* There are rumours today of our being sent forward. *But what use should we be? We're ill-trained, ill-disciplined, rebellious rabble.*
> DO SOMETHING.[14]

Do something . . . But what? Spender had no influence in Spain – and, besides, he was committed to doing his bit for the Republican radio station in Valencia, around a hundred miles from Albacete – and even getting to Valencia was proving difficult enough.

There had been an element of farce about the journey from the moment Spender met up with Philipps in Barcelona and discovered that one of the two co-drivers who were also making the trip was a 'cellist from the palm court orchestra at the Lyons Corner House in Tottenham Court Road. Making matters worse was the fact that a couple of Spanish militiamen who had been assigned to guide the Englishmen to Valencia insisted on taking a meandering inland route instead of the obvious coastal road. Disconcertingly, this took them some fifty miles inland, very close to the front line and Nationalist-controlled territory,[15] although Spender was also acutely aware that each mile they travelled indirectly brought him closer to Tony.

We drove to the base at the bottom of the famous hill that Harry described in his letter and, as you climb up into the reserve trenches, already the spent bullets are flicking past one, making one duck humiliatingly at every other step. I didn't find it hard to imagine the horror and confusion Harry described when the enemy broke through. What I can't possibly imagine, what is totally unimaginable to me, is to be stuck there, bound as these men are to living in this danger day after day, night after night. I simply couldn't do it.[16]

By the end of the first day the ambulance had finally bumped its way back on to the coastal road and reached Tortosa, barely half way to Valencia. Tortosa was practically deserted, however, since many of its inhabitants had decamped to the hills for the night to escape a predicted air-raid. Woken by their return early the following morning, Spender, Philipps and the party doggedly pressed on. But when they finally arrived at Valencia a further shock was waiting. Spender presented himself to Señor Thomas at the UGT radio station, only to discover that it had already ceased broadcasting. For all that he was once again prepared to work for nothing, there was no job for him to do – nothing except try and extricate Tony from the mess he had got himself into.

Thus, Spender quickly re-established contact with Philipps and hitched another lift, this time to Albacete. There, by scouring the cafés and bars popular with the International

Brigade, he finally tracked Tony down. He was well and sun-
tanned but still fed up. Why had he ever decided to come to Spain
in the first place? he asked. He wasn't prepared to die for the
Republicans. Ultimately, he was a pacifist. Spender had to help
him.[17] *Do something!*

Well . . . It wasn't quite as easy as that. Quite rightly, Spender
pointed out that Tony had entered into a commitment when he
joined the International Brigade. Quite rightly, too, he was
irritated at having to sort things out. *He might show some*
awareness of the spot he's put us in, and some slight remorse for
having landed himself in this mess. But when I saw him this
evening there wasn't a sign of it. On the contrary, he was in the
most exasperating and argumentative mood.[18]

'*I expect you think I've let you down. You always have been*
on the look-out for that, haven't you, ever since we've been
together?'[19]

Another row was brewing. Tony could not just walk away
now, Spender told him patiently. And even if he did, through the
perceived influence of his 'writer-friend' – assuming he had any –
what would that do for the morale of other, similarly disaffected
members of the Brigade? Still, Spender promised, he would do
what he could.

He did. He pulled every string and knocked on every door he
could think of in a desperate one-man campaign to get Tony
transferred from front-line fighting to something safe, some-
thing desk-bound. *I pressed the point that he might really be ill,*
he might have a stomach ulcer, for instance.[20] It was not an easy
task since the 'Comrade officers' of the International Brigade
were as unimpressed by Spender as they were by Tony, and
cynically aware of what lay behind Spender's concern.

'*What exactly is your interest in this Comrade, Comrade*
Murray?'

'*He was my secretary in England.*'

'*And was he only your secretary? [. . .] I think I know exactly*
why you don't recognise the worthlessness of this particular
Comrade.' *The smear was obvious and I decided to attack.*

'*I'm not here for what you call propaganda work, Comrade.*

*For I just don't believe in propaganda. I'm here to find out the
truth and write it, when I get back, as truthfully as I can.
Remember that, Comrade.'*

'As a Socialist, Comrade, it is your business to find out the
useful *truth and write that.*'[21]

It took all Spender's *Daily Worker* credibility to achieve it, but
the English 'political commissars' finally agreed, and Tony was
given a non-combatant role.[22]

As if to atone for this piece of blatant special pleading,
Spender also used his stay in Albacete to visit the front line. After
a 150-mile north-westerly drive he arrived in a valley near
Madrid in the company of an Indian writer and an eighteen-
year-old boy he identifies only as 'M—'. The experience affected
him deeply. Seeing corpses rotting beneath olive trees and being
forced to stoop because his six-feet-three-inch stature would
make him an obvious target in the shallow trenches[23] finally
brought home the reality of the war he had made his own but
stubbornly refused to take any part in:

> *Our guides were touchingly careful to make us keep our heads
> down, as if, because we were visitors, we were more important
> than the mere cannon-fodder who remained there day in and
> day out. We fired a few rounds from a machine-gun and I
> aimed to miss. Who was I to intrude on this private affair
> between the two armies who were both more like each other
> than I was to either?*[24]

The sense of dislocation that this brush with reality evoked
is apparent in the clutch of poems which resulted from Spender's
brief but memorable trip to the front. (In the *Collected Poems* a
whole section is entitled 'Spain'.) They are not *committed* or
overtly propagandist works; rather, they are lyric postcards, the
private thoughts of an outsider as unfamiliar with dead soldiers
as he was with the olive trees which feature so prominently in
poems such as 'A Stopwatch and an Ordnance Map', 'The
Coward' and the more famous 'Ultima Ratio Regum', the poem
which contains the bathetic image of a dead soldier who should
have been kissed rather than shot.[25]

Several of the other 'Spain' poems continue the solipsistic theme. Both 'Thoughts During an Air Raid' and 'The Room above the Square'[26] have the poet alone, detached from the action and bleakly contemplating his lot. *We must love one another or die* ... How difficult the commitment implied in those words seemed now! Two further poems are little more than literary exercises, translations or reworkings of poems by the contemporary Spanish poets Garcia Lorca ('Adam') and Manuel Altolaguirre ('My Brother Luis').

Perhaps then, we should not be surprised that, having done his bit in the trenches, as February became March Spender moved on – to Madrid itself and the then relatively safe and convivial surroundings of the Casa de la Cultura. Despite the numbing cold, at the Casa *los intellectuales* were able to fight their war of words and sleep under velvet bed-covers rather than olive trees. There were butlers and servants, but no coffee – so they made do with rough brandy for breakfast.

In the room the women come and go/Talking of Michelangelo, Eliot had written. Now it was El Greco: two previously unknown paintings had been discovered in palaces hastily abandoned by wealthy Nationalist families. The Casa's art historians could talk of nothing else. It was a surreal, pseudo-military environment – the front line of the intellectual high command – and one with which Spender was to get increasingly familiar.

For the moment, however, his time was limited. After only a few days at the Casa he had to return home. But he had got no further than Albacete when a further problem confronted him: he learnt from contacts in the International Brigade that Tony had deserted and after a week or so been recaptured and imprisoned. 'A disgusting thing happened last week,' Harry writes to Martin in Worsley's *Fellow Travellers*: 'I was given two days in the cells. Yes, they've got their cells now just like any capitalist army. Wooden bench. Bucket in corner. Foul smell all day. Only one meal – beans in water.'[27]

Do something ... Once again Tony's plight occupied Spender's mind. What could he do? What *should* he do?

On reflection he decided that there was nothing he reasonably could or even should do – *The agony of this war! Of all wars, I suppose*[28] – and, not without misgivings, he pushed on to Valencia, trying to banish Tony's problems from his mind. *IN A WAR THERE'S NO ROOM FOR AMATEURS.*[29]

Everything caught up with him, however, when he reached the city. In the bar of the Victoria Hotel he was accosted by a British Foreign Office official. Did he know a man named Tony Hyndman, a member of the International Brigade? Yes, said Spender. *Yes!* Did he also realise that Tony was in big trouble and that, because he had enlisted in the International Brigade, the British government was technically unable to help him? They couldn't even guarantee to prevent his being shot as a deserter.

In his defence, Spender could only plead that Tony did have a stomach ulcer, he was a sick man.[30] Non-committally, the man from the Foreign Office said he would see what he could do. There wasn't much. There wasn't much anyone could do; even Manuel Altolaguirre and his friend Hidalgo de Cisneros, head of the Republican Air Force, could only put Spender in contact with the Spanish Foreign Minister, Señor Del Vayo.

But at least that started a few hares, and once more Spender returned to Albacete. Predictably, however, neither his intervention nor Spender's renewed lobbying of British officials was of very much avail. Spender was told that Tony was in jail and there he was going to remain – whatever his 'friend' said, whoever his 'friend' was . . .

Wholly coincidentally, Tony was finally released and expatriated shortly afterwards, for medical reasons.

———

Back in Valencia once more, Spender continued to fight a predominantly literary war. It was a new kind of battle which was symbolically inaugurated when Altolaguirre presented him with all eleven volumes of a late-eighteenth-century edition of the works of Shakespeare. The first was inscribed '*A mi querido camarada Spender con profonda gratitud por su visita a España*'.

Like many of the foreign journalists covering the conflict, his base camp was the Victoria Hotel, and it was there that he ran into Ernest Hemingway, who was also covering the Republican campaign. To begin with, the two very different writers talked about Stendhal's *La Chartreuse de Parme*, but soon conversation turned to more serious matters, like work. Hemingway had little time for Spender's style of journalism, and thought him lily-livered and squeamish.[31] Spender, on the other hand, saw in Hemingway the image of everything he was not:

How much easier it would be if only I had the undivided passion of H . . . M . . . an American war correspondent with whom I spent most of yesterday. He is tremendously and rightly honoured among the war correspondents, both for his unfaltering devotion to the Republican cause and his courage in getting nearer and sooner to the fighting fronts than anyone else [. . .] Acclimatised as he is now to the atmosphere of war, he accepts [the Republicans'] deaths as gratefully as he does their deeds: he glories in both. To him there is only one side, ours; only one activity, fighting; and his dispatches, always in the heroic mould, have done a great deal for the Cause in America, and are widely quoted and re-published here. It shames me to listen to him.[32]

These encounters, with Altolaguirre and Hemingway, set the tone of the rest of Spender's involvement with Spain and, indirectly, of the rest of his life. Living up to all those early comparisons with Shelley, he began to see the poet, the writer, as the real legislator or moral force in the world. He was not alone in this, of course, but he came to embody the view far more than Auden or any of the other 'committed' writers of the period. Quite how far this was the case is brought out in Hugh Kingsmill and Malcolm Muggeridge's *1938: A Preview of Next Year's News*, which was published by Eyre & Spottiswoode later in 1937. The entry for 20 June reads:

Mr Stephen Spender and Spain

At a literary luncheon in the Holborn Restaurant yesterday,

the guest of honour, Mr Stephen Spender, gave readings from poems written while on active service in Spain. Proposing a vote of thanks, Miss Maude Royden said that whatever their political views might be, they must all surely recognise in the poems they had just listened to the most poignant expression, since Rupert Brooke, of youth going gallantly into battle. Certain lines of those they had just heard would, she knew, for ever linger in her memory:

> If I die in Spain
> I do not die in Spain
> I die in the future
> And shall live again
> When the future has overtaken the past.

━━━━

Not least among the motives which provoked this squib was the fact that, shortly after his return from Valencia, Spender paid a third visit to Spain, once more on active service of a particularly literary kind. In the summer of 1937 he had been invited to take part in a Writers' Congress in Madrid. He accepted enthusiastically and later published an account of the proceedings – and his own exploits – in John Lehmann's magazine *New Writing*.

On this trip too, however, farce was never very far away. In London, Spender had been refused a visa and was forced to travel to Madrid (once again via France and Port Bou) on a forged passport provided by the French writer André Malraux. Malraux hustled him through customs checks, somehow managing to explain that this tall blond 'Spaniard' with the unlikely name of Ramos Ramos was really a Spaniard. It was a pure linguistic coincidence, he said, that his friend spoke a northern dialect which seemed so similar to English.[33]

Feted and fawned upon, Malraux, Spender and 'the world's writers' ambled down from Barcelona – to Valencia and eventually Madrid – in chauffeur-driven Rolls Royces and considerable style. The champagne flowed, there were dinners, receptions and parties; and the fact that they were in a country which was tearing itself apart hardly impinged on the delegates, as Spender recalled on *World Within World* and implicitly recognised in his report of the congress, 'Spain Invites the World's Writers'.[34] Insulated in his car with the other members of the British delegation (which was led by Ralph Bates and also included Sylvia Townsend Warner, Claud Cockburn and the poet Edgell Rickword) Spender creditably enough felt himself useless. He was disappointed and embarrassed that he was not once asked to speak at plenary sessions of the congress and, if only symbolically, demonstrated his working-class solidarity by opting to sit next to the Spanish drivers in the cars the delegation was assigned.

André Malraux, for whom the phrase '*Il faut agir*' – a French equivalent of Auden's 'To-day the struggle' – had become something of a personal maxim, was the undoubted star of the Congress.[35] His style of life, which was mainly comprised of a constant round of travel and political involvement, deeply influenced Spender, who compared him with T.E. Lawrence.[36] In a bombed and strafed Madrid the majority of the delegates (Spender included) failed to understand *everything* he said, but it sounded right; in that most political and emotional of wars Malraux seemed to be doing something on both fronts.

After his return to London in mid-July 1937 Spender resolved to do something similar. Despite his less than vocal presence at the Congress and his lack of any real combat experience, he was recognised as one of Britain's most eminent and well-informed authorities on what was then merely referred to as 'Spain'[37] and he rapidly allied himself with Nancy Cunard's bizarre campaign to persuade the whole British public to join in and do something.

Nancy, a wealthy socialite and the daughter of Lady Emerald Cunard, had first visited Spain in the autumn of 1936 as a freelance journalist and immediately become, like Spender, a passionate champion of the Republican cause. (She is seemingly the original on which the character Lady Nellie is based in Worsley's *Fellow Travellers*.) She edited and hand-printed a series of leaflets entiteld '*Les Poètes du Monde Défendent le Peuple Espagnol*' ('Poets of the World Defend the Spanish People') and sold them in London and Paris to raise funds for the

Republicans. Each contained poems in French and Spanish as well as English. The majority have been long and deservedly forgotten, but Auden's 'Spain' – inspired by a single tour of duty as a stretcher-bearer in January 1937 – was first published in the fifth issue, in April 1937.

Even this, however, was not enough for Nancy, and in the early summer of 1937 she hit on the idea of contacting all the British writers she could think of, asking for their views on the Spanish question with a view to publishing their replies. She was confident that they would be predominantly pro-Republican and that their eminence would lend further weight to her fund-raising activities.

But to lend sufficient weight to her own letter she first had to persuade some prominent figures to act as co-signatories. It is illustrative both of his own position at this time and of the international politico-intellectual circles in which he was beginning to move that Spender was among these. He had met Nancy Cunard in Spain, and was flattered and delighted to be approached. He signed up and his name duly appeared at the bottom of Nancy's broadsheet along with those of Louis Aragon, W.H. Auden, José Bergamïn, Jean Richard Bloch, Brian Howard, Heinrich Mann, Ivor Montagu, Ramón Sender, Tristan Tzara and Nancy herself.

Above them, printed in red and black, the text was loosely phrased in a kind of verse. It still says much about the mood of the times – and (together with her slim volume *Sublunaries*, first published in 1923) about Nancy Cunard's slender talent for poetry [38]:

THE QUESTION
To the Writers and Poets of England, Scotland, Ireland and Wales

It is clear to many of us throughout the whole world
that now, as certainly never before, we are deter-
mined or compelled to take sides. The equivocal
attitude, the Ivory Tower, the paradoxical, the ironic
detachment, will no longer do.

We have seen murder and destruction by Fascism in
Italy, in Germany – the organisation there of social
injustice and cultural death – and how revived, imperial
Rome, abetted by international treachery, has con-
quered her place in the Abyssinian sun. The dark
millions in the colonies are unavenged.

To-day, the struggle is in Spain. Tomorrow
it may be in other countries – our own.
But there are some who, despite the martyrdom of
Durango and Guernica, the enduring agony of Madrid,
of Bilbao, and Germany's shelling of Almeria, are
still in doubt, or who aver that it is possible that
Fascism may be what it claims it is:
'the saviour of civilisation'.

This is the question we are asking you:
Are you for, or against, the legal Government
and the People of Republican Spain?
Are you for, or against, Franco and Fascism?
For it is impossible any longer to take no side.

Writers and poets, we wish to print your answers. We
wish the world to know what you, writers and poets,
who are among the most sensitive instruments of a
nation, feel.

148 writers responded to the questionnaire. 126 – includ-
ing Spender – were explicitly pro-Republican. Samuel Beckett
responded with a mere three words: 'Up the Republic!' In her
own response Nancy Cunard cried that it 'is as unthinkable for
any honest intellectual to be pro-Fascist as it is degenerate to be
for Franco', while Auden explained that he supported the
Republican cause 'because its defeat by the forces of inter-
national fascism would be a major disaster for Europe'. But
there were some surprising – and equally notable – dissenters.
T.S. Eliot, H.G. Wells, Vita Sackville-West and Ezra Pound
refused to commit themselves. Typically, Evelyn Waugh was less
than cooperative ('If I were a Spaniard, I should be fighting for
General Franco'). George Bernard Shaw also played his cards

very close to his chest until the very last moment – and then replied: 'Spain must choose for itself: it is not really our business.'

Interestingly, Nancy found it surprisingly difficult to involve publishers in her pet project. Several, including Victor Gollancz, turned it down, and it only appeared at all when the *Left Review* issued it as a six-penny pamphlet in November 1937. Wrapped around the cover was a strip of pink paper saying: 'YOUR FAVOURITE AUTHORS TAKE SIDES – ON FASCISM, ON THE SPANISH WAR. THIS DOCUMENT REVEALS THE MINDS OF LEADING BRITISH AUTHORS TODAY. NEVER BEFORE HAVE SO MANY IMPORTANT PRONOUNCE-MENTS BEEN ASSEMBLED WITHIN A *6d* BOOKLET. IT IS CAUSING A SENSATION!'[39]

Spender must have been cheered by that.

———

Long before the pamphlet appeared, he had finally returned to England and, although he was still undertaking fund-raising events, put Spain *qua* Spain behind him. Once again, personal problems were making demands on his time. There was *Trial of a Judge* to think about. There were worries about his physical health. There were renewed money problems. And there was Inez.

Since their wedding the previous winter, Spender and Inez had been apart for as long as they had been together because, immured in her research, Inez had never accompanied him to Spain. Now Spender determined to make amends. Conse-quently, the two moved out of London to spend the summer together at a cottage in the village of Mersham, near Ashford in Kent.[40] (It was there that, during a weekend visit, Auden wrote his ballad, 'Miss Gee'.) Later they gave up the Queen's Mansions flat altogether and took another one, this time at Lansdowne Terrace on the fringe of Bloomsbury. However, that quickly became little more than a London base, for very shortly they moved again, to Lavenham, near Bury St Edmunds in Suffolk.

There they shared the Great House, a seventeenth-century manor house with Georgian additions, which Spender bought with his brother Humphrey and his wife Margaret ('Lolly') who, like her husband, had originally trained as an architect.

At Lavenham – and on occasional visits to Paris – in part because of the quiet, practical support of Margaret, with whom Spender was especially close, the marriage actually seemed to blossom. Spender would sit out in the house's courtyard, under the fig tree, or wander the gentle Suffolk countryside and once again try to convince himself that all would be well and, in his personal life at least, all manner of things would be well.[41] They were, for a time; but Spender was soon unable to ignore Inez's hints that she was getting fed up with him.[42]

In what was either another symbolic expression of his attempts at expiation or a last-ditch scheme to save the marriage, at around this time he arranged for portraits to be painted of Inez and himself. W.H. Auden had introduced him to the artist William Coldstream with whom he had worked the previous year in the G.P.O. Film Unit. Keen to see Coldstream establish himself, both Auden and Isherwood had already commissioned him to paint their portraits (sadly, both are now seemingly lost). Auden had also commissioned a painting of his mother: the 'Mrs Auden' which now hangs in the Stoke-on-Trent Museum and Art Gallery. Not to be outdone, Spender also approached Coldstream. He was already a practised sitter; quite apart from the innumerable photographs which Humphrey had taken over the previous decade, at around this time he had also been painted by Wyndham Lewis (the completed portrait is also now in Stoke-on-Trent).

Coldstream accepted the commissions and began work on the Spender portrait (currently in a private collection) in the late spring of 1937, shortly after his subject's return from Spain. A meticulous artist who demanded many sittings, he completed it later that year after twenty sessions, and Spender was so pleased with it that he urged his new friend to begin work on the portrait of Inez as soon as he could. However, by the summer of 1937 Auden's proselytising was beginning to pay off, and the negotiations were complicated and protracted. Not only were there problems about when and where the painting could be undertaken, Coldstream was also starting to command fees which Spender feared he might be unable to afford.

Letters went backwards and forwards. Spender sent Coldstream a downpayment of ten pounds.[43] Coldstream replied that 'I would rather not keep it unless there is a fairly definite prospect of your wanting the painting done & Inez having the time before the end of the year.'[44] Back in London, a week later Spender put his cards on the table. He and Inez *did* want the portrait but would not be able to pay anything like five hundred pounds for it. That was the sort of fee Spender estimated that Coldstream would be able to command by the time it was finished.[45] The money Spender had received from Victor Gollancz for *Forward from Liberalism* had only just got them out of debt . . .

Eventually an agreement was reached. Inez would visit the Fitzroy Street studio which Coldstream then occupied for the sittings and Spender would make payments as and when he could. Everyone was apparently satisfied, and after no less than forty sittings and some five months the portrait was completed. It was worth waiting for. More finished than 'Mrs Auden' or the portrait of Spender, it is one of Coldstream's finest works of this period, in which Inez's charm and intelligence are clearly apparent. It is impossible to discover how much Spender finally paid for the picture – but in 1939, after the break-up of his marriage with Inez, it was offered for sale at the Artists International Association exhibition and knocked down for just £105. It is now part of the Tate Gallery collection.

Parallel with all this was the fact that Spender had realised that he was ill. As early as January 1937 he had mentioned in a letter to Isherwood that he had colitis and was passing blood.[46] Now matters had got worse and at the beginning of September he went into a nursing home for an operation.[47] He told friends that this was for appendicitis,[48] and there are no grounds for disbelieving this.

Following his discharge from the nursing home he went with

Inez to convalesce at Salcombe in Devon, where he had often been as a child,[49] and his thoughts turned once again to *Trial of a Judge*. It was still proving stubborn and intractable – he had only completed four acts of the projected five-act tragedy[50] – but now there did seem a chance that the play might finally reach the stage.

It is surely significant that Spender always conceived of his play as 'a tragedy' – Auden and Isherwood wanted theirs, *The Dog Beneath the Skin* (1935; 1936), *The Ascent of F6* (1936; 1937) and *On the Frontier* (1948; 1938),[51] to be seen as melodramas – for *Trial of a Judge* was yet another 'committed' work. It was one more of his attempts to show that the public mood of a time in which 'Spain' had suddenly jostled 'Austria' out of the headlines (and was itself about to be marginalised by the new imperatives of 'Munich') and his own private *angst* were implicitly connected.

'Only connect, the prose and the passion,' E.M. Forster had written in *Howards End*, first published a quarter of a century earlier. Now a very different writer was sympathising with Spender's predicament. In 1938 George Orwell wrote to him complaining that, much against his will, he was having to devote a great deal of a memoir of his time in the International Brigade, *Homage to Catalonia* to 'controversial' (ie political) themes:

> I hate writing that kind of stuff and am much more interested
> in my own experiences, but unfortunately in this bloody
> period we are living in one's only experiences *are* being mixed
> up in controversies, intrigues, etc. I sometimes feel as if I
> hadn't been properly alive since about the beginning of 1937.[52]

Coming at things from the other direction, Spender still wanted to address the Big Issues, albeit by giving them a human face. In *Trial of a Judge* he attempted to do this by reference to a well-publicised murder in the incipiently Nazi Germany of the early 1930s. Not unexpectedly (according to Louis MacNeice) Christopher Isherwood believed he succeeded and had written 'the greatest play of our time'. John Lehmann too thought the play the 'most imaginative and deeply felt work' in contemporary verse drama. Writing in 1940, he described how it 'is almost entirely in verse, and carefully avoids any of the clowning characteristic of the Auden-Isherwood works'. He even tried to sum up what it was actually about:

> [Its] master-thread is a theme which had for long exercised Spender's mind: the hopelessness of being a 'Liberal' at a time when society's decay is being ruthlessly exploited by Fascism. He takes the notorious Potempa murders in Germany just before the Nazi triumph as his setting, and his chief character is the liberal-minded Judge whose conscience orders him to condemn the Nazi terrorists responsible for the cold-blooded murder of a Jew called Petra, and acquit Communists who are only guilty in his eyes of shooting in self-defence [. . .] but later on, when the Nazis come to power, this does not save him from being tried himself for daring even to have thought that the sentence he gave was wrong.[53]

Liberals, Fascists, Nazis; even a Jew . . . it is no wonder that the story appealed to Spender – nor that when the play was staged (to judge from Humphrey Spender's surviving production photographs) the Expressionist set was dominated by jack-booted Nazi thugs. 'Anyone who has experienced Fascist triumph in any city of Europe will recognise this atmosphere for the genuine article,' Lehmann thought.[54]

Trial of a Judge was eventually produced by Rupert Doone's Group Theatre at the end of March 1938. This was the same company which had produced *The Dog Beneath the Skin* and *The Ascent of F6*, and of which Spender had recently become a director.[55] His appointment was, however, seemingly made out of political correctness rather than any deeply felt commitment to the stage or poetic drama on Spender's part. Indeed, it is difficult now to feel that he had any real interest in either. He lambasted the way in which Auden and Isherwood had trivialised themselves by resorting to poetic drama, and criticised the 'faulty' productions of the Group Theatre in an article in *New Writing* in the autumn of 1938,[56] which must have been written only a matter of weeks after his own production had, for all its contemporary references, conspicuously failed to set the world on fire.

When Virginia Woolf and T.S. Eliot (the ever-faithful editor who published the script of *Trial* that year) went to see the play during its one-week run at the private Unity Theatre Club in Camden Town, north London there were scarcely fifty people in the audience. 'Eye dazzled' and tired, Virginia was at her most elliptical when she got around to summing up her impressions in her diary that night:

> Tom [came] to dinner, & to Stephen's *Judge*. A moving play: genuine; simple; sincere; the mother like Nessa [Bell, Virginia's sister]. Too much poetic eloquence. But I was given the release of poetry: the end, where they murmur Peace freedom [is] an artists's, not an egoist's end. [Spender] gave me a copy, & wants me to write an opinion. I like him always: his large sensitive sincerity better than the contorted nerve drawn brilliancy of the others.[57]

Spender's 'large sensitive sincerity' was, however, beginning to get the better of him. It came down, of course, to little more than the old liberal paralysis of the will. *Fain I would climb* . . .

Even Gabriel Carritt, the self-effacing 'Tristan' of his Oxford days, seemed to have risen to the mood of the times. Having long-since forsaken the Gabriel, as plain, politically correct Bill Carritt he was continuing to make rabble-rousing speeches in favour of the Communists,[58] leaving Spender as a has-been or, at best, a would-be. Yes, Spender had been to Berlin; he had been to Spain. Yes, he had written the poems, struck the postures and made the speeches. Yes, he had even put the Nazis on stage. But now what?

Today, his struggles seemed to be of an increasingly prosaic, domestic kind. He turned in on himself, embarked on a course of psychoanalysis and began trying to paint his dreams.[59] Maybe, between them, science and art could 'cure' him. Maybe he could even become a poet and painter, a Blake rather than a Shelley . . .

He couldn't – for the simple reason that, despite all the best efforts of Coldstream, Victor Pasmore and the other *habitués* of the Euston Road school, he had no artistic talent. He painted the slate-and-brick roofscape he saw from his window at Queen's Mansions in the best rough-brush, pastel-shaded Euston Road tradition. It was, however, art for art's sake. Spender could *see* what he wanted to paint, but was utterly incapable of rendering it on canvas.

He had better success with paper. Indeed, in terms of literary output the period 1938–9 turned out to be something of a blueprint for the rest of his life. There were newspaper articles and reviews written to make quick money. There was a barrage of politico-critical pamphlets – *The New Realism: A Discussion* is the title of one-such – which again and again restated his position. There were pot-boiling collaborations – with Lehmann on the anthology *Poems for Spain*; with Goronwy Rees on an adaptation of Georg Büchner's play *Danton's Death* – and just occasionally there were poems.

The Still Centre, Spender's first collection since the *Poems* of 1933, was published by Faber in May 1939. It contained all the work completed in the intervening six years which he considered worth preserving. Unusually for a book of poems, it also had a prose foreword, an almost ritualistic wringing-of-hands over the lot of the individual and the artist in times of international tension.

Spender retained relatively few of the poems in *The Still Centre* in his 1985 *Collected Poems* – although he had previously recycled 'Darkness and Light', one of the most important, as a preface to *World Within World* – possibly aware that many only raked over old ground. Taken as a whole the collection certainly did little more than reiterate the might-versus-right, public-versus-private debates which he had been rehearsing for the previous five years. Alick West pounced on this when he came to review both *The Still Centre* and *The New Realism* in a single article in the *Daily Worker*. Understandably, Spender was something of a pariah to the Communists and the *Worker* by 1939, but West went deeper than that:

Indeed, [Spender] can persuade himself that his vacillations have historical importance, that the most significant dialectical contradiction is his own mind [. . .] There is more than a hint of this in Spender's new collection of poems, *The Still Centre*. The 'still centre' is a secret retreat where Spender watches Spender's conflicts. Spender is not interested in solving his conflict, but in having one. For he can then feel that his special task is to stand aside and watch it.[60]

Spender's stance in *The Still Centre* and its foreword was, of course, another instance of his personal life mirroring wider issues. In *World Within World* he was uncharacteristically frank about the break-up of his marriage to Inez, the issue which most preoccupied him during the autumn of 1938 and the spring of 1939. He was to blame, he implied; he was too caught up in the Big Issues, too absorbed by politics and the march of events to notice what was happening in his own living room.[61] He loved Inez and was consumed by jealousy when he discovered that she had begun an affair with the poet Charles Madge, who was then setting up the sociological experiment called Mass Observation. But he was also still a member of the Gang, with all that that implied. A diary entry of William Coldstream's from January 1939 graphically depicts the quandary in which he found himself. Professionally he had come a long way in the previous ten years; personally everything was once again beginning to unravel:

In the evening Nancy, [Sharp, then the wife of Coldstream, later Michael Spender's], Wystan, I and a boy Wystan had met at Bryanston went to a party given by Benjamin Britten in Hallam Street. The other guests were Christopher [Isherwood], Stephen and Inez, Christopher's new boyfriend, a German boy friend of Benjamin's and Hedli Anderson. A singer [Peter Pears] who lives with Benjamin was part host. The evening was slightly sticky – probably because Benjamin does not like Stephen and Inez very much because he most likely knows that they don't like his music. Also the presence of two anti-boy

women, Nancy and Inez complicated the atmosphere because
Benjamin likes to be with Wystan & Christopher, all boys
together without disturbing foreign elements such as slightly
hostile ladies and gentlemen hostile to gay music. Stephen thinks
Benjamin's music rather superficial. But then he thinks my
painting very dull and uninspired. He is a natural 'highbrow'. He
really likes the obscure & very serious and as Benjamin's whole
work has been influenced by Wystan's teaching of carefree
lucidity and the non avoidance of banality Stephen does not like
the result. Inez sat looking very self consciously composed –
Nancy said that Stephen took great pains to sit near her at regular
intervals & occasionally touch her as a guarantee of stable
affection when in the camp of the enemy. Stephen sat next to
Nancy and said 'May I hold your hand Nancy?' and giggled.

Hedli Anderson came in very theatrical & assured. 'Queen of
the boys to-night.' [. . .]

She sat on the piano and sang Wystan's songs & Benjamin
played with great gusto [. . .] Then Stephen asked if Benjamin
would play the song which he had made from Stephen's poem. I
can't remember which poem it was but it was a very Stephenish
one full of slightly embarrassing & very strong feelings, very
personal, very big & over life size in emotion but very original and
striking. It had lines like 'I rushed upstairs etc etc' – all rather like
a huge nightmare. People wondered if they might laugh while it
was being sung by Benjamin's singer friend. I giggled a little but
no one laughed.[62]

Spender and Inez separated in the summer of 1939. Inez
wrote to inform her husband that she was going to live with
Madge at the beginning of August[63] and, despite Spender's
frantic requests that she should think again, that everything
would be different if they went away together – to Rome
perhaps, or Paris – they were subsequently divorced.

The failure of this always improbable marriage was a shattering
blow, but worse was to follow. Just as the relationship was
breaking up, it was confirmed that Margaret, the Lolly who meant
so much to Spender, was suffering from an inoperable cancer.

Suddenly, it seemed that there was not even a still centre. Just
as it had in 1914, the inevitability of war was clouding the
horizon – a war with the Germany, the Berlin, which had so

shaped Spender's sensibilities. Closer at hand, he was simultaneously having to cope with the realisation that Inez had left him and the fact that Margaret was dying. Day by day she was growing weaker and weaker, thinner and thinner.

Ironically, it was at exactly this time that Spender began drafting a poem entitled 'The Ambitious Son'.[64] Inez's final departure delayed its completion; and Spender was quick to see a symbolic significance in the fact that, one night in August 1939, the fig tree in the courtyard of the Great House at Lavenham suddenly crashed to the ground.[65]

PART THREE

Being There

EIGHT

War – and Peace of a Sort

Somehow, it should have been raining, or at least dull and overcast. But by a quirk of fate on Sunday 3 September 1939 London enjoyed one of the last days of summer. The sun was out, and those who were there remembered that the sky was almost preternaturally blue. The papers noted that the Duke and Duchess of Kent took their dog for a walk in Belgrave Square.

In Bloomsbury and its purlieus, however, the clouds were distinctly grey after the Prime Minister, Neville Chamberlain, announced on the radio that Britain had declared war on Germany. Virginia Woolf wrote up her diary that evening in the garden at Monks House, her country home at Rodmell in Sussex:

> Its the unreality of force that muffles every thing. Its now about 10.33. Not to attitudinise is one reflection.
> Nice to be entirely genuine & obscure. Then of course I shall have to work to make money. Thats a comfort. Write articles for America. I suppose take on some writing for some society. Keep the [Hogarth] Press going. Of course no beds or heat on at 37 [Mecklenburgh Square, the Woolf's new London home]. So far plenty of petrol. Sugar rationed. So I shall now go in. Nothing in the garden or meadows that strikes me out of the way – & certainly I cant write.[1]

Virginia was not alone in experiencing a feeling of emptiness and complete artistic paralysis. William Coldstream was equally adrift, and unable to paint. George Orwell bleakly acknowledged 'the impossibility of writing books with this nightmare going on'. The war, he thought, would 'practically put an end to my livelihood'. Dylan Thomas agreed, and began frantically casting around for non-literary ways of making a living: 'Does the film-world want an intelligent young man of literary ability, "self-conscious, punch-drunk", who must (for his own sake) keep out of the bloody war, who's willing to do any work – provided of course that it pays enough for a living?'[2]

Inevitably, Stephen Spender too felt himself compelled to abandon all his plans for what would become known as 'the duration'. On the very day that war broke out he once again began keeping a diary (the 1939 'September Journal' now in the Bancroft Library at the University of California at Berkeley) purely because he believed that he too would be unable to write anything else. The always fragile world order had shattered and split open at precisely the same time as his own personal life.[3]

For several days he ruminated at length on the contradictions and irony of it all – of his strong feelings for Germany and his no less strong conviction that fascism was evil wherever and whenever it surfaced. He had German (and German-Jewish) friends about whom he worried. There was Herbert List; there were, for that matter, boys like Lothar and Georg. He loved Germany and he had learned to love its language – he was thinking of the pure *Deutsch* of Goethe, Hölderlin and Schiller rather than the *argot* of Hamburg and Hallesches Tor – but even simple German words like *Heim* and *Ruhe* (home; peace) seemed more loaded with true, poetic meaning than their equivalents in other languages.

And then, of course, there was the personal dimension. He himself had German (and Jewish) blood in his veins: a distant female relative whom had only recently met in London when she gave a piano recital in his grandmother's flat was actually married to a U-Boat commander.[4]

He was worried, too, about his own position, his own attitude to the war. Merely writing seemed futile – *To-day the struggle* – and he appears to have decided that he would even be prepared to fight. In a letter to Isherwood he certainly ruled out doing anything sensational to avoid conscription.[5] He was in any case in no position to follow the example of Auden, Isherwood, the pacifist Benjamin Britten and Peter Pears and flee (as their critics had it) to America. Indeed, it was probably already too late for that; Auden and Isherwood had finally left for New York on the *S.S. Champlain* on 18 January 1939. All he could do now, he told himself, was to go on living, get over the loss of Inez – while still pinning his hopes on the fact that they would discuss things again after six months of separation – and try to work. After all, a writer's job was to record his mistakes in life.[6]

All this persiflage and private agony was nowhere near as effete and selfishly 'intellectual' as it might now appear. Doubts and twinges of conscience were widely felt in Britain as the nation came to terms with the blackout and the crude realities of war. In her Mass Observation diary Naomi Mitchison recorded the thoughts of some Scottish fishermen on the morning of 3 September 1939:

> Young Dick said So it's come. Then he began asking Hank what are *you* going to do? He seemed less enthusiastic than he'd been the night before when he thought 'appeasement' was possible, said he didn't think he'd ever be able to shoot anyone and he would rather do mine-sweeping. He explained his position, that he wouldn't fight, but would do work of national importance – he was too much attached to things and people to be able to be a clear pacifist. They talked about the possibility of dropping leaflets instead of bombs on German towns, and then we talked about these Words people use – National Honour and Justice and all that.[7]

In the event, Spender decided that he would be better employed doing what Naomi Mitchison's fisherman called 'work of national importance' as a translator at the War Office or as a clerk in the newly established Ministry of Information (which was already recruiting writers as disparate as Orwell, Thomas and Graham Greene) rather than letting the side down as a soldier on the front line. Accordingly, he fired off applications to the appropriate quarters, but with little hope of success. At the back of his mind he knew that, since he was still only thirty years of age, he was very likely to be called up for active service.[8] All he could do was wait.

Listless, he spent the final months of 1939 attempting to convince himself that, really, nothing had happened. He wrote a few reviews, forced himself to continue working on a new novel (*The Backward Son*, first published by the Hogarth Press in 1940) and tried to make the best of things. He paid five pounds for a hand-operated printing press and, just as he had done when he was at university, used it to produce pamphlets of his poetry. He saw old friends, notably John Lehmann, Isaiah Berlin and Geoffrey Grigson (with whom he insouciently lunched at the Café Royal on 26 October). He also met his editor T.S. Eliot for lunch at the Garrick Club and poured out his troubles. Just keep on writing, Eliot told him. Poems, reviews, novels, the journal, *anything*; just keep the engine running.[9]

But Spender was still worried about Tony, and could not stop fretting about Inez. More profoundly, he was also concerned about Margaret and he was frankly lonely in the Lansdowne Terrace flat. So, as far as petrol rationing and the sudden exiguity of public transport would allow, he threw himself into a round of frantic socialising. *Anything, anything!* He spent a weekend in Sussex and also went up to Lavenham to be with Humphrey and Margaret.

But it did not fool him, or those who knew him best. Virginia Woolf recalled that, when he burst into the Hogarth Press offices on 11 September, 'His great joints seemed to crack. Eyes stared. Is writing reams about himself [seemingly a reference to the "September Journal"]. Can't settle to poetry.'[10] Less than a fortnight later she found him 'lip sore & addle headed' when he joined her and Leonard for a weekend at Monks House:

Stephen scribbling diary – no, reading Proust in English in the drawing room. [. . .] A loose jointed mind – misty, clouded, suffusive. Nothing has outline. Very sensitive, tremulous, receptive & striding. So we've rambled over Inez: can she forgive herself. She has taken his money. Can she still be generous & large minded? over religion, at breakfast; over justice; & walking the terrace, we plunged & skimmed & hopped – from sodomy & women & writing & anonymity & – I forget. At last I said I must write – tho' my little bowl was clouded & troubled by all this talk – & he must write; & so ordered boiled potatoes for his lunch.[11]

—————

This solipsistic preoccupation was, however, only one side of the story. For – very probably in an attempt to escape the concommitant accidie – at exactly this time Spender was also throwing himself into a project which was ultimately to do more for his reputation than any number of privately printed pamphlets, any amount of self-absorbed scribbling.

Just as the war had started, his friend, the writer and critic Cyril Connolly was finalising plans for the launch of a new literary magazine. Given the mood of the times, it was a mad-cap venture – almost every week, established literary magazines such as T.S. Eliot's *Criterion*, the *Cornhill Magazine*, the *London Mercury*, *Twentieth-Century Verse* and even the original *New Verse* were closing – but it too was born out of a sense of personal insecurity, inner doubt and artistic paralysis.

Cribbed, cabined and confined in the bleak, blacked-out London of 1939, Connolly did his best to fit in with the bureaucratic totalitarianism and blatant sloganeering of the all powerful Ministry of Information – if all else failed, he decided he would even work for them. But he was an Eton-educated high-liver, by nature a gossipy, lazy, continental gourmand. To be told that 'CARELESS TALK COSTS LIVES' and pressed to eat nothing more appetising than wholesome 'Woolton pies' appalled and depressed him. Pent up in Britain when he would rather have been luxuriating in France, he saw nothing but the end of Civilization As He Knew It – and the enduring image of his own helplessness:

As I waddle along in thick black overcoat and dark suit with a leather brief-case under my arm, I smile to think how this costume officially diguises the wild and storm-tossed figure of Palinurus; who knows that a poet is masquerading here as a whey-faced bureaucrat?[12]

Palinurus had been the pilot of Aeneas's ship in Virgil's *Aeneid*. Now – fully aware that Palinurus had fallen into the sea, been washed up on a barbarian shore and finally murdered – Connolly appointed himself the pilot who was going to steer western civilisation through the storms and into calm waters. This was his interpretation of 'To-day the struggle'. But there was no time to be lost. His new magazine was going to enshrine the very best of British and European culture in spite of – no, *because of* – all that was happening across the Channel:

> A magazine should be the reflection of its time, and one that ceases to reflect this should come to an end. The moment we live in is archaistic, conservative and irresponsible, for the war is separating culture from life and driving it back on itself, the impetus given by Left Wing politics is for the time exhausted, and however much we should like to have a paper that was revolutionary in opinions or original in technique, it is impossible to do so when there is a certain suspension of judgement and creative activity. [. . .] Our standards are aesthetic, and our politics are in abeyance.[13]

All Connolly needed to bring this stubborn bastion of culture into existence was the money; and, happily, that soon arrived. In 1937 he had been introduced to Peter Watson (coincidentally, another Old Etonian) whose father was rumoured at his death in 1930 to have been – in that magically Edwardian phrase – one of the richest men in England. Homosexual, cultivated and gentle, Peter was generously provided for in a family trust and was then living in a large flat in Paris, indulging an interest in painting, building up a collection of work by artists including Pablo Picasso, Giorgio de'Chirico, Paul Klee and Joan Miró, and vaguely planning to start his own fine art magazine. Although they did not meet often, in the intervening years he and Connolly had maintained contact and become good friends, not least because of a pronounced snobbish streak in Connolly's make-up.

They met in Paris in late August 1939 to discuss (among other things) Connolly's idea and his bold suggestion that Watson might back the venture. Watson was not keen; but then events intervened. The outbreak of war drove both men back to London where almost immediately they ran into each other at a party given by the novelist Elizabeth Bowen. Connolly patiently outlined his scheme once more and, reluctantly, Watson (who had been forced to forget about running his own paper) agreed to subsidise the new magazine to the extent of £33 a month. It wasn't much – the outbreak of war had put a brake on his high-living – but in those days it was enough to pay for the printing and distribution of the planned 1000 copies. Watson also agreed to act as art editor.

There was just one proviso: Watson had vague doubts that, with no editorial experience and growing personal problems of his own, Connolly might not be able to hold everything together. Tactfully, therefore, he persuaded him that they should invite their mutual friend Stephen to become the third member of a team which would then have 'a complete editorial character'.[14]

Spender was flattered by Watson's invitation. But there was a proviso on his part, too. He was already closely associated with John Lehmann and the ailing *New Writing* and did not want to become personally involved in any future battle of the books. If he joined Connolly and Watson it would be in an *ad hoc* capacity.

They understood his predicament, and agreed; and while Watson kept his distance, Connolly and Spender threw themselves into the planning of the magazine. After a brief disagreement over what they should call it – 'Orion', 'Equinox', 'Sirius', 'Scorpio' and 'Centaur' were all considered[15] – they settled on *Horizon*, and by the end of September they had got down to work.

The first issue was scheduled for mid-December, and Connolly and Spender quickly learnt the realities of independent publishing. They had no office, no subscribers and, most worryingly of all, no writers. Quickly, however, the first two problems were simply and efficiently solved. Despite his initial hands-off stance, Spender volunteered the Lansdowne Terrace flat as a base and, after he and Connolly placed newspaper advertisements, subscription cheques (6/6d for the six issues) began to arrive. Finding writers proved more difficult, though – in no small measure because of Spender's disingenuous belief that he could remain loyal both to *Horizon* and *New Writing*.

Mindful of her obligations to Lehmann (and the Hogarth Press, which published *New Writing*) Virginia Woolf point-blank refused to submit anything. And, after Lehmann told her about a 'deadly feud' which had developed between him and Spender when he discovered Spender's involvement with *Horizon*, she noted in her diary: 'Stephen half lies about *Horizon* & his part in it mostly. Offers to bring it to the Hog[arth Press]. Steals young writers &c. I think its an emotional crux.'[16] T.S. Eliot declined an invitation to contribute – but only, he said, because he had nothing on the stocks. Kenneth (later Lord) Clark backed out of an agreement to be 'guest co-editor' of a future edition devoted entirely to art because of pressure of work . . .

Exacerbating Spender's problems in filling the pages was the fierce editorial rigour of Watson and Connolly. At Watson's invitation, Gertrude Stein had been happy to volunteer a three-page 'poem-opera-play about Lucrezia Borgia', but unfortunately it proved to be 'arrant balderdash' – '*She just wasn't trying*,' Watson wailed[17] – and was returned with a rejection slip. Worse still, at least as far as sales were concerned, was Connolly's decision not to use an essay by the immensely popular novelist Somerset Maugham. The writer Julian Maclaren-Ross read the proofs on one of his work-seeking visits to Lansdowne Terrace.[18] He enjoyed the piece – it was Maugham's subsequently printed essay 'The Decline and Fall of the Detective Story' – and was astounded when Connolly announced, 'I don't think it's a good article.':

'You don't?' I echoed in dismay.
    Benignly smiling, Connolly shook his head. 'In fact I've decided not to print it.'
    'Not print it,' I gasped. 'But it's by Maugham!'
    'I have the greatest respect for Maugham as a novelist,'

Connolly said in his soft bland voice, 'and I don't say this is a *bad* article. It's good enough to be accepted by *Horizon* but not quite good enough for me to publish.'[19]

Eventually, however, Spender managed to badger and cajole enough writers (many of them personal friends) to contribute, and the first issue appeared as planned in mid-December. 'The aim of *Horizon* is to give to writers a place to express themselves, and to readers the best writing we can obtain,' Connolly wrote in his editorial. Among those expressing themselves in the following pages were Auden, Louis MacNeice, John Betjeman, Geoffrey Grigson, J.B. Priestley, Herbert Read and, of course, the editors themselves. There was also a colotype reproduction of Henry Moore's 'Reclining Figures'.

Privately, Watson disliked the 'vague political ramblings' of Priestley and Read, but he was in a small minority. In general, the magazine was well reviewed and widely noticed. Critics and readers alike found it good value for a shilling. At the last moment Connolly had persuaded Watson to increase the print-run from the projected 1000 to 2500 copies. It was a prescient move, for they – and a hurried second printing of a further 1000 –were sold out within days. (The second issue was to do even better, selling some 7000 copies. Circulation peaked in April 1940 at around 8000.)

Virginia Woolf was virtually alone when, on 16 December, she noted bitterly in her diary: '*Horizon* out; small, trivial, dull. So I think from not reading it.'

━━━━━━

Soon, Spender was virtually running the magazine, while Connolly strove mightily to produce his sometimes magisterial, sometimes downright eccentric editorials, and entertained favoured contributors with leisurely and extravagant lunches at the Café Royal. The flat in Lansdowne Terrace rapidly became a national and then – when American subscriptions started to come in – an international cultural redoubt. Soldiers and R.A.F.

officers wrote in to say that *Horizon* represented all that they were fighting for, often enclosing their own poems or short stories. A public school-and-Oxford airman, killed at the age of twenty-three, left a diary in which he had scrawled across one whole page: 'MY STORY ACCEPTED BY HORIZON!' Writers too were beating a path to the door:

> No.6 Selwyn House, Lansdowne Terrace: first one in the row, I'd passed it on the Guilford Street corner and now stood right outside.
> The front door was open, a carpeted hall inside, on the ground floor right another door, with the names Spender and *Horizon*. Cyril Connolly himself answered the bell [. . .]
> We were standing in the front room which overlooked the Terrace and had been Stephen Spender's study: his books were in a glass-fronted case by the cabinet containing the green springback folders among which my stories had been filed in error.[20]

Just when he had expected to be called up, Spender found himself at the centre of things. His black-topped desk had been commandeered by a production secretary and Bill Makins, the business manager who had been taken on when unsolicited manuscripts started arriving by the hundred. Connolly had appropriated a chair by the window in the main office and used one of the smaller rooms as his study. Somewhere else, a succession of typist-secretaries which included Connolly's lover Lys Lubbock and Sonia Brownell (who later married George Orwell) clattered away, battling to keep up with the letters.[21]

As editor *malgré lui*, Spender too had battles to fight, not least when *Horizon*'s printers refused to set Maclaren-Ross's story 'A Bit of a Smash' because of its forthright language. Maclaren-Ross had recalled that they objected

> . . . to several expressions in the text and to the opening sentence in particular, which originally read: 'Absolute fact, I knew fuck-all about it', and was not acceptable even when the offending words were altered to 'Sweet F.A.' Stephen Spender took up the struggle with the printers and sent me a list of the

expressions for which substitutes had to be supplied and which ended, in the form of a short poem:

> 'Pissed-up'
> 'By Christ'
> 'Balls'
> 'Bugger'.[22]

Inevitably, *Horizon* also soon become the principal sounding-board for Spender's own thoughts. The introspective 'September Diary' was serialised in issues two and three, and many more poems and essays were to follow.

But there was still a war going on. Early in 1940 it took all Connolly's post-prandial charm and the relentless lobbying of his friends in high places (notably Harold Nicolson, Parliamentary Secretary to the Minister of Information) even to ensure that the magazine would still be able to obtain the paper on which it was printed. More and more frequently, too, as the Blitz became a way of life, office routine was disrupted by the sound or threat of German aircraft overhead. It distracted Connolly from the perusal of those manuscripts which Spender, Watson, Bill Makins, Lys or Sonia had tentatively judged 'Very Good', 'Good' or merely 'Borderline' – those which had arrived on time, for the post, like all public services, was grievously affected by the nightly bombing.

London in the Blitz was hardly the most conducive setting for Connolly or for the magazine, and in little more than six months Watson had decided that enough was enough. Accordingly, in June 1940, he evacuated the entire *Horizon* operation to Thatched Cottage, a house he had rented at Thurlston, near Salcombe in Devon.

At first everything went well and everyone behaved as though they were at some infinitely prolonged country house party. Spender, in particular, was in his element. He had known Devon since he was a boy, he had been to Salcombe only a few years previously with Inez; now he took a delight in bicycling alone around the country lanes or – again on his own – rowing a boat in the harbour. Within weeks, however, another idyll had come to an end. The Germans began to bomb Plymouth, fifteen miles away, as ruthlessly and almost as regularly as they were attacking London.

Furthermore, Connolly and Watson were predictably bored by the isolation of a house which was five miles away from the nearest village. Everyone realised that there was an unreality, a disengagement, about their position; but it was Spender who summed up it best in a poem describing his long-distance view of the Plymouth raids – 'Air Raid Across the Bay' – which was published in *Horizon* that September.[23]

By August the whole literary caravanserai had fallen apart. Watson and Connolly had moved back to London, concealing personal irritations and professional worries beneath an often mouthed desire to get back to 'the thick of things'. *Horizon* had not benefited from its sojourn in Devon – and now Watson's earlier worries about starting it in wartime seemed to be correct. Its circulation figures were falling from the April 1940 high, so that by the end of the year it was selling only 5000 copies a month. And, as if to highlight its plight, the flat in Lansdowne Terrace – now little more than an office – had been slightly damaged by a bomb on the night of 8 September. (With just one broken window, however, it got off lightly: the same raid virtually destroyed the Woolfs' home in nearby Mecklenburgh Square.) Connolly was forced to resort to what amounted to little short of bullying tactics with his readers: 'If we can go on producing a magazine in these conditions, the least you can do is read it. The money *Horizon* loses would provide you with, if not a Spitfire, at any rate a barrage balloon. If you would rather have that, say so.'[24]

There was a discernible tetchiness in his words, but behind them was his unshakeable belief that *Horizon* and the writers and artists and poets whom it championed had to survive, war or no war. This was made even more explicit the following month when the magazine put out a 'Begging Bowl' in an attempt to persuade its readers to subsidise their favourite writers. A half-page announcement suggested:

If you particularly enjoy anything in *Horizon* send the author
a tip. Not more than One Hundred Pounds: that would be bad
for his character. Not less than Half-a-Crown: that would be
bad for yours.[25]

It is now not possible to discover how much was raised. In
all probability, however, the sums received by its protegés were
very small. Dylan Thomas was, none the less, one of the major
beneficiaries of the scheme. Chronically incapable of handling
money, in the autumn of 1938 he had announced that 'thirty
bloody pounds would settle everything'. Now things were rather
worse; he needed a minimum of seventy pounds. Merely to
survive he was forced to rely on his share of the Begging Bowl
and the rather greater amounts he received as down-payments
for work — his poem 'Deaths and Entrances' first appeared in
that same January 1941 issue of *Horizon* — outright gifts from
Peter Watson and whatever could be raised by an unofficial
support fund set up by Spender, along with Henry Moore and
Herbert Read.

This seems to have come to rather more than £100, but it took
some time to reach him. 'The debtees', Thomas wrote to a friend,
'will have to wait till my Watson comes in' — or even longer, he
might have added. For in another letter he admitted that 'the
Watson money disappeared, quick as a sardine'.[26]

———

Spender too seems to have had his difficulties at this time. For
reasons which are now difficult to ascertain, in the autumn of
1940 he virtually severed his connections with *Horizon* and,
with some trepidation, accepted a job as a teacher at Blundell's
School in Tiverton, Devon. It may have been because there was
simply not enough for him to do and not enough money to pay
him at *Horizon*. It may even have had something to do with the
fact that, in London some months earlier, he had met and fallen
in love with a young pianist called Natasha Litvin.

Whatever, his teaching career was not a success. He remained

at Blundell's for just one term, until Christmas 1940, and hated
every minute of it.[27] He had arrived hoping that he would be
able to do more considered work in his spare time than the
immediate, reactive writing he had produced for *Horizon*. But
down there in Devon, he realised, he too was out of things,
morally, physically and intellectually as well as geographically.
Matters were not helped when Isherwood wrote to say that
England was no place for him. Why didn't Spender join him in
the California he had just discovered?[28]

Depressed, Spender concluded that he might just as well do so.
Devon, California – what was the difference? Both represented a
retreat from immediate events. But, he went on to argue in a
magazine article, those same events had repercussions which one
could not, and should not, escape. The clock could not be put
back; there could be no return to pre-Munich days.[29]

To-day the struggle . . . like a tocsin, the moral imperative of
Being There, Doing Something, rang in his head.

It was at around this time that he wrote 'Air Raid'.[30] The
poem is perhaps his most human and fully engaged war poem, a
compassionate study of the predicament of one family, one
ordinary group of people whose 'delicate squirming life' has
been shattered by 'metallic claws'.

He did not blame Isherwood or Auden (who later served with
the American forces) for leaving Britain; but he knew he could
never do it himself. Accordingly, as soon as he conveniently
could, he left Blundell's and came back to London, firstly to such
space as he could find at Lansdowne Terrace and then to a new
four- roomed attic flat in Maresfield Gardens, Hampstead. He
was Home – in every sense – but Hampstead was Hampstead,
miles away from the City, the docks and the East End, which
were the German bomber's principal targets. Up there on the
Heath, there was still a sense of non-combatant guilt. The film
director Jill Craigie felt it acutely:

Hampstead was comparatively safe, but you really felt you
were in the war because you could hear the enemy aircraft
overhead, and there was this tremendous battery of anti-

aircraft guns. The odd bomb fell in Hampstead, but nothing like in the East End.

You had a tremendous feeling of guilt because you felt thrilled in some ways to be in it, with all that excitement. My little daughter used to say: 'Can I stay up and see the flashes tonight?', and sometimes we'd go up on Parliament Hill, a big hill on Hampstead Heath, and we'd watch the bombing in the East End. We knew people were having a terrible time there, and yet it was fiendishly exciting.[31]

On 9 April 1941, shortly after his divorce from Inez was made absolute, Spender married Natasha Litvin at the St Pancras Register Office. Peter Watson served as his witness and, as he signed the register, Spender unabashedly gave his profession as 'Editor'. (No mention was made on the certificate of the twenty-one-year-old Natasha's occupation.) After the ceremony there were parties – an intimate lunch at l'Etoile, a restaurant in Charlotte Street, Soho, and then a more relaxed gathering at a friend's flat. Among the principal guests were Watson and Connolly, Lys and Sonia, Louis MacNeice and the philosopher A.J. Ayer. Mamaine Paget (subsequently the wife of Arthur Koestler) and Nancy Coldstream were also there. So too was Guy Burgess, the spy who defected to Moscow with the diplomat Donald Maclean almost exactly ten years later. Cecil Beaton took the snaps.

Because the war put foreign travel out of the question, Spender and Natasha spent their honeymoon with friends at Wittersham in Kent. There, and after they returned to London, they attempted to put the marriage on a firmer, more positive footing than Spender had previously managed to do with Inez. Rules were drawn up, understandings arrived at. They were outstandingly successful, for the marriage has endured for more than fifty years.

Only a few weeks after the couple returned from Kent, however, the dreaded buff envelope arrived. No longer teaching and therefore no longer in a reserved occupation, the thirty-two-

year-old Spender was called up for active service. But all his
earlier agonising about what he could or should do were he to be
conscripted was soon to prove superfluous and unnecessary.
After a medical, his still-recurring colitis and other problems led
to his being classified 'C' – incapable of heavy duties and, in
effect, unfit for military service. It took all his powers of
persuasion to get this changed to 'B' so that he could at least do
something for his country. It took a long time, too; and it was
not until later in 1941[32] that he was accepted as a member of the
National Fire Service.

After a period of training during which he was taught basic
fire-fighting techniques, there were lectures about the special
problems caused by bombs, high explosives and the other
hazards confronting a war-time fireman, albeit one serving on
the 'Home Front'. One session, dealing with the likely effects of
poison gas on the civilian population upset him so much that he
had to spend half an hour composing himself in a telephone box.

In a matter of weeks, however, he had completed his training
and been assigned to Cricklewood Fire Station. A temporary
affair, built to last for 'the duration', it was little more than a
huddle of sheds and the four army huts in which the fire-crews
lived, ate and snatched what sleep they could during their tours
of duty. It was also only a short distance from Frognal and,
symbolically at least, the unhappy days of his childhood and
adolescence.

Spender was quick to recognise this, not least because at that
time he and Natasha were lodging with Bertha, Ella and Frank,
the Hampstead postman Ella had married to general incredulity
towards the end of her time at Frognal. The dreaded-but-loved
servants from a vanished era had retired to a house of their own
and offered to accommodate Spender and Natasha while they
looked around for somewhere to live. But, just as they always
had, the devoted sisters still regarded themselves as part of the
family and insisted that Spender and Natasha – together with
Humphrey, Christine and Michael Spender, by then a Flight-
Lieutenant in the R.A.F. – joined them for a proper Christmas
dinner.

Making this interregnum between Lansdowne Terrace and their eventual move to the flat in Maresfield Gardens even more poignant for Spender was the fact that 'Berthella''s house was stuffed with unwanted furniture from Frognal.[33]

The diaries he kept at this time (now seemingly lost, but the basis for one of the final sections of *World Within World*) were full of nervy anticipation. Spender was morbidly aware that, in 'the national interest' he was going to have to immerse himself once again in the hugger-mugger of what was to all intents and purposes a dormitory during his tours of duty at the Cricklewood station. He did not relish the prospect of working forty-eight hour shifts with a predominantly working-class group of strangers who spent their spare time doing little more than sleeping, playing snooker and listening to popular music on the BBC Light Programme.[34]

It promised to be prep school and the rough children of Sheringham all over again – and all the more so because by the time he reported for duty the German blitz on London had ceased, leaving those fire-fighters who had been through it a close-knit team. Spender feared he would be classed as an outsider, a feeling shared by the novelist Henry Green (Henry Yorke) who had been seconded to the Davies Street fire station in Mayfair a little earlier:

> . . . it was noticeable that, whenever a stranger came into the bar, these firemen, who had not been on a blitz for eighteen months, would start talking back to what they had seen of the attack on London in 1940. They were seeking to justify the waiting life they lived at present, without fires.
>
> A stranger did not have to join in, his presence alone was enough to stimulate them who felt they no longer had their lives now that they were living again, if life in a fire station can be called living.[35]

Much to his surprise, however, when he got there Spender found little or none of that at Cricklewood. Instead, the station turned out to be more like Oxford. For all their snooker and boozing, the majority of his fellow-firemen regarded the new

recruit with something akin to the benevolent amusement he had
inspired in the Univ hearties. Most were older than he was, but
when it was discovered that their 'Mr Spender' had had a poem
published in a magazine they all begged him to read it aloud.
That way, they said, they could understand it better.

Inevitably perhaps, he came to be grateful for the way in
which the paramilitary routine at the station, with its 7.30 a.m.
reveille, endless hut-cleaning and daily parades and drills, gave
some sense of structure to his own life.[36] In one sense he was
even sorry to leave when he was later transferred to the less busy
station at Maresfield Gardens. There were compensations,
however. Not only was the new station virtually next door to his
flat, the Maresfield Gardens crew echoed something of the
eclecticism of old Berlin. Spender delightedly discovered that he
was joining a team in which the regular professional fire officers
were augmented by musicians from London orchestras, the
artist Leonard Rosoman and even old friends like the writer
William Sansom (who had arranged his transfer there).[37]

Much later, Rosoman recalled the free-and-easy bohemian-
ism of Maresfield Gardens:

> There were all kinds of people – Stephen Spender was in the
> same fire station as I; so was William Sansom; Henry Green –
> and then you'd be having your lunch with anybody; with a
> greengrocer, with somebody who was previously digging up
> roads. I loved this. I thought it was absolutely marvellous and,
> in a way, I'm very happy that it happened. It's a pity that it
> took a war to do it; but I found those people absolutely
> fascinating, very very interesting indeed.[38]

Spender remained in the fire service, nominally based at the
Maresfield Gardens station, until the autumn of 1944.[39] During
the brief, hectic periods when the fire crew was called out, he saw
the realities of bombing – the ineffectual but frightening fizzing
of the incendiary devices which littered the roads, the smoke and
the all-consuming but still somehow mystical power of flame.[40]
In later, quieter moments he put his observations to good effect
in simple, meditative poems such as 'Rejoice in the Abyss' and

'Epilogue to a Human Drama'.[41] Like 'Air Raid', they succeeded because he had finally begun to engage with the world rather than analyse his own reactions to it. The hurly-burly of life at *Horizon*, the Blitz, its aftermath and, not least, the arrival of Natasha had given a depth and humanity to his work.

Another example of his new-found engagement – so much more convincing than his earlier, formulaic espousal of communism – was his realisation that, for all its diversity, the Cricklewood fire crew had been a real team. He missed the camaraderie and the surprisingly close friendships he formed with the likes of Leading Fireman Abrahams and Alfie, the elderly sub-officer. Even Cooky and Locke who worked in the kitchen and Bill and 'Togger' and the semi-literate Ned were real people with real worries, real lives – and, he might have added, real wives; just like him.

He was grateful to be in such a comparatively 'cushy billet' as Maresfield Gardens, but he was also growing frustrated because there was still very little for him to *do*. Thus he was flattered and delighted when he was asked to become involved in a rather *ad hoc* educational programme devised to broaden the horizons of the Bills and Toggers and Neds of the London fire service. In addition to his exiguous fire-fighting duties, he began visiting other stations to lecture on current affairs, history and art and to lead discussion groups. It made him feel that he was at last 'playing his part'. Ironically, too, it brought him far closer to 'the workers' and all of what he finally came to see as the sordid sentimentality of their lives than any of the artificial fraternising which had gone on during his time in the Communist Party.[42]

Eventually he was appointed director of education for the No.34 Fire Force in north London, a unit which was based at Holland Park fire station. It was a stimulating, interesting job; and whether he was at Holland Park or Maresfield Gardens he still had time to do his own work and even to entertain. But somehow he continued to feel that he had been left on the periphery of things, something of a fraud when compared with his brother Michael who was putting his scientific skills to good effect by developing new methods of photo-interpretation for the R.A.F. As he later noted, he joined the fire service just days after the end of the Blitz and left it only two hours before the first V.2 rockets, the Nazis' *Vergeltungswaffe* reprisal weapons familiarly known as 'buzz bombs,' started raining down on London.[43]

But then, in 1944, a succession of events, unrelated in themselves, abruptly brought him into the centre of the real world.

At the height of the summer Natasha discovered that she was pregnant, and the realisation that, after everything, he was to become a father had its own predictably sobering effect. It also inspired a rush of delicate romantic poems such as 'The Dream' and 'One'.[44]

Then, no more than a few weeks later, the Germans resumed their bombing raids on London. They hardly amounted to a new Blitz; but one night, while Spender and Natasha were huddled with the other residents of the house in Maresfield Gardens in an improvised air-raid shelter, a high-explosive bomb fell nearby. The room shook and, as Spender later discovered, the ceiling of his attic flat was blown in.

Shocked, but also weirdly exhilarated, on impulse he rushed out into the smoke-filled, dust-clogged street. He wanted to see where the bombs had fallen, to be at the centre of things once and for all. He went into the heart of the darkness where flames from a fractured gas pipe made a mockery of the blackout and bricks, broken glass and the sad detritus of other peoples' lives littered the streets.[45]

Purely because his own flat had been rendered temporarily uninhabitable – and his pregnant wife made homeless – there was more to this than Jill Craigie's Parliament Hill voyeurism. In retrospect that night can be seen as a personal epiphany, Spender's final impulsive embracement of the real world. His actions were properly poetic, properly Romantic – in *World Within World* he even cites William Blake in support of them[46] – but even such a nightmarish excursion into the existential depths was no preparation for what was already in train.

Later than most of his coevals – Waugh, Greene, Orwell, Anthony Powell, Terence Rattigan, even Dylan Thomas – in the autumn of 1944 Spender was finally given 'war work' more commensurate with his particular skills. He was seconded to the Political Intelligence branch of the Foreign Office, then based in commandeered offices at Bush House in the Aldwych.

It was routine, even boring work, a desk job which principally involved the preparation of background material on the origins of Italian fascism. But he was not unhappy to have left the National Fire Service and been assigned a role to play in the ultimate struggle. And once again the hours were regular, and his evenings were free. Friends such as E.M. Forster, Elizabeth Bowen and – once he had returned from the United States – Benjamin Britten were soon adding Maresfield Gardens to their lists of conducive London bolt-holes.

As the mention of figures such as Forster and Bowen suggests, throughout this period Spender's intellectual world was still largely that of *Horizon*.[47] He continued to do as much as he could for the magazine and remained at the centre of the close circle which comprised its editors and regular writers. Barbara Skelton (who was to marry Cyril Connolly in 1950) recorded what happened at a typical wartime meeting of this coterie in her diary:

> Lat night Peter [Quennell] and I dined with Cyril Connolly and Augustus [John]. Cyril seemed more human, as he was not being a host at one of his own dinner parties. He was very sweet with Lys, who was being as tiresome as ever, trying to make the apt reply to everything. Augustus became very drunk; he praised Feliks [Topolski]'s talent and described him as being a brilliant draughtsman, but Connolly looked doubtful and said *Horizon* wouldn't print any of his drawings at any price. Augustus swayed a lot and made sweeping gestures with his hands. We ate some very stiff veal which looked as though it had been flattened by a roller, drank whisky, wine, and rum in large quantities . . .[48]

Like his father and uncle before him, Spender had become

bewitched by what Harold had called 'the full glamour of Fleet Street,' and when he came to publish *The Thirties and After* some thirty-five years later, he chose to dedicate it

To Sonia Orwell
remembering those *Horizon* days.

It was a genuine and touching tribute to one of the few survivors of the last truly formative period of his life. (Peter Watson had mysteriously drowned in his bath in 1956; Cyril Connolly had died in 1974.) But, back in the early forties, Spender was also publishing in his own right a series of books whose titles alone testify to his moods and preoccupations at that time. Read in order, they even provide what amounts to a pocket-biography. There was *I Sit by the Window* (1940), then *Ruins and Visions* (1942) and, that same year, *Life and the Poet*. The following year brought the *Spiritual Exercises* and, inevitably perhaps, *Jim Braidy: The Story of Britain's Firemen* (a collaboration with William Sansom).

All of these, however, were essentially minor works. Even the *Spiritual Exercises* were no more than that: exercises. Those reprinted today in the *Collected Poems*[49] are awkward rather than moving, mere jottings when compared to the considered, albeit rather costive, Christian lyrics which Eliot and Auden were beginning to produce. Their strict octave-sestet sonnet form and a self-consciously high-flown vocabulary make them sound hollow and declamatory, a definite regression into self-conscious solipsism.

There was a real poignancy, however, about Spender's first post-war books. *Citizens in War – and After* (1945) and *European Witness* which was published in 1946 were missives from the front line. Indirectly but fittingly, the latter was also one of the last fruits of his association with *Horizon*.

Hearing that, after only a few months at Bush House, Spender had been accepted as a member of the allied Control Commission (then familiarly known as the Civilian Military Force) which was charged with the task of 'de-Nazifying' Germany and rebuilding its political and cultural infrastructure, Connolly had asked him to keep a diary, a personal memoir which *Horizon* would ultimately publish in whole or in part – and which, he stressed, Spender was of course completely at liberty to develop into a book.

Spender was happy to oblige. But his agreement was not motivated solely by Connolly's offer or indeed by the prospect of the eventual book. An element of personal *schadenfreude* also lay behind it; and implicitly the diary developed into a curious, semi-public renunciation of his Berlin years – if for no other reason than that, like some former mistress, the Berlin of the thirties no longer existed. Indeed, the 'Rhineland Journal' which *Horizon* published in 1946 and which was subsequently fleshed out in *European Witness* can now be seen as a literary farewell to the first period of his life.

━━━━━━

'*Nel mezzo del cammin di nostra vita/Mi ritrovai per una selva oscura*', Dante wrote in the first stanza of the *Divina Commedia*, a sentence Longfellow translated as 'Midway upon the journey of our life/I found myself within a forest dark'.

Although he has shown nothing like T.S. Eliot's enthusiasm for the medieval Italian poet, Spender can now be seen as a Dantesque creature. He was thirty-five years of age, at that symbolic mid-point of life, when *European Witness* was published and, as the book describes, he was seeing 'Inferno' for the first time as he visited the sites of concentration camps and interviewed their inmates, as he clambered into bunkers, toured fire-bombed cities and tried to find old friends. Much of his past life had seemed a 'Purgatorio'; but now, at last, with the coming of peace – and Natasha – there was just a chance that a 'Paradiso' of some sort was rising above the horizon.

His initial assignment for the Control Commission was to report on the attitudes of German writers and thinkers in the first weeks and months of defeat. He was flown out to Germany in July 1945 and among the first of the intellectuals and university

professors he contacted was Ernst Robert Curtius, a friend from
pre-war days. It was a sad, salutary reunion in a bombed and
gutted Bonn; the bridges were down, there was a plague of
midges and hardly any food.[50] Hagen too was wrecked when he
got there.

It was a situation he was to encounter again and again. As a
result of R.A.F. Bomber Command's raid on Cologne on the
night of 31 May 1942, there were only three hundred struc-
turally sound houses in the whole city, or so he was told.
Everything had been destroyed. Everywhere he knew or could
remember was in ruins. The bridges kiltered uselessly into the
swirling waters of the Rhine; the stench of putrefying corpses
still buried under tons of uncleared rubble continued to per-
meate the city. Only the spire of the cathedral stood – like the
dome of St Paul's in London – as a beacon of hope.[51]

During the next few months Spender made repeated visits to
Germany – and a four-week trip to Paris – exchanging the
hardships of the London which was emerging from war into
what was called Austerity for the real, bankrupt devastation of
Berlin and the once great cities of the Hanseatic League. Bonn,
Cologne, Hamburg, Düsseldorf, Aachen; they all left their
marks as, awkwardly uniformed, he tried to put together a
picture of the mood of the German intelligentsia. But, against all
the odds, Curtius and his fellow scholars insisted that things
were getting back to normal. Even the *Frankfurter Allgemeine
Zeitung* would recommence publishing by October . . .

However, the tone of Spender's diaries, far more personal and
unaffected than any of his previous writing, indicated just how
much things had changed – and how much he had changed. A lot
that he described would be unpublishable, he realised;[52] but he
wrote on relentlessly, trying to put into some sort of context the
unparalleled chaos, physical and intellectual, which he was
witnessing.

In the late summer he was given a new job. He was deputed to
supervise the re-opening of libraries in Germany, having first
ensured that all Nazi material had been removed. It was a
mammoth task. Not only was there the problem, voiced by one

librarian, of shunting all pro-Nazi works into the basement and restoring to the shelves hitherto-banned Jewish books;[53] the libraries in Düsseldorf had had 60,000 books burnt, those in Bonn had been stripped of no less than 130,000.

Düsseldorf, Aachen, Bonn, Hanover, Dortmund, Bochum, Essen ... during September and the early days of October Spender travelled extensively through cities in the newly established British Zone of West Germany. His official car had broken down and there was, anyway, virtually no petrol. But he kept to a punishing schedule, meeting university professors, civic librarians and on one occasion his Oxford friend Richard Crossman, who had recently been elected a Labour Member of Parliament.[54]

One day in mid-October, his car still off the road, he was reduced to walking – virtually hitch-hiking – down an Autobahn. A car stopped and offered him a lift to Berlin. He got in gratefully, and only then discovered that among its occupants was Natasha. She had come to Germany as a pianist, playing concerts at R.A.F. bases. It was, as Spender himself has acknowledged,[55] an extraordinary coincidence, another epiphany.

Alone with Natasha, he stayed at the Hotel Bristol in the city which only a few months previously been the capital of the Third Reich and which he had once regarded as his second home. Now, although the hotel was only a few streets away from the area in which he and Isherwood had lived, he found it impossible to recognise anything: the hotels, the apartment blocks with their elaborate wrought-iron balcony fronts, the grand Prussian facades of the public offices he had once found so pretentious, not even the Modernist temples of Nazism.

Everything was in ruins. The Kurfürstendamm, the Nollendorfplatz and once familiar streets and buildings had been reduced to rubble or were, at best, charred, scarred and shattered, like the now preserved *Gedächniskirche*. It was as if a

whole chapter of his past life had been wiped out. *Christopher,
Jean Ross, Herbert List, Fritz, Lothar, even Tony — where were
they now?*

Other visitors, too, were horrified by the sheer scale of the
destruction and the enormity of the task facing the allied
reconstruction workers. Malcolm Muggeridge arrived at 'the
non-place where once Berlin had been' at around the same time
as Spender:

> Who that set eyes on this extraordinary spectacle can ever
> forget it? The vast expanse of rubble, with the Brandenburg
> Gate rising up, stark, amidst it; a wasteland of utter
> desolation, like the Mountains of the Moon, which at first
> sight gave an impression of being denuded of all life [. . .] Just
> the grotesque hulks of what had once been buildings — maybe
> the Adlon Hotel, Unter den Linden, the Reichstag, who could
> tell? — and hanging over it all, long after hostilities had ceased,
> a stench of rotting corpses, sickly-sour; the cadaver side of our
> mortality, and stinking at that. Closer inspection revealed that,
> contrary to the first impression, there were actually human
> beings burrowing into this rubble like badgers, constructing
> for themselves little rickety shelters out of it . . .[56]

The day after their arrival, Spender and Natasha were able
to visit the bunker from which Hitler had directed the last weeks
of the war while Berlin burned above his head and where, only
six months previously (on the afternoon of 30 April), he and Eva
Braun had committed suicide. It was an occasion which now
seems almost absurdly symbolic: a Wagnerian version of the
poet Orpheus's descent into the underworld.[57] Together — we
can visualise them hand-in-hand — they toured the burned-out
headquarters of the most evil regime the world had known, even
getting as far as Hitler's bedroom. Spender noticed slightly burnt
books about modern architecture still piled on a bedside table. In
the ruined Chancellery — its ceiling too had collapsed — they
found the charred remains of the Führer's desk, from which
Spender broke off a few pieces as souvenirs.

These fragments I have shored against my ruins, he might

have thought, echoing Eliot.[58] *Da. Dayadhvam. Damyata.* But he did not need them; and when, back in Britain, his sister-in-law Margaret told him that they were evil and that he should get rid of them, he did.

He was no Orpheus, nor was meant to be. He had no intention of looking back.

NINE

Epilogue to a Human Drama

'The second world war (as the first had done at an earlier age) drew a hard line across the story of one's days,' wrote Anthony Powell at the beginning of *The Strangers Are All Gone*, the fourth volume of his autobiography.[1]

It definitely did for Stephen Spender, four years Powell's junior. As he exchanged his army uniform for a demob suit on his return from Germany towards the end of 1945, he might well have reflected that he had stepped into a different world. Certainly, the whole landscape of his life had changed.

A cluster of significant events had conspired to draw that hard line across his days. In the last week of the war his elder brother Michael had been killed in a plane crash. The two had never been particularly close, but although Spender must have experienced some feeling of grief, little or nothing of that was revealed in his published work (except obliquely in 'Seascape', which is subtitled 'In Memoriam M.A.S.').[2] Conversely, he was pitched into a period of intense mourning and equally intense creativity when his sister-in-law Margaret, Humphrey's wife, died on Christmas Day 1945.

Out of it came the extraordinarily moving 'Elegy for Margaret'. In what is a traditional, almost old-fashioned sequence of meditative poems, Spender obsessively re-explored the old *Vienna* scenario of the closeness of love and death (particularly in the lyrics 'Darling of our hearts, drowning' and 'The final act of love'). Memories of the war – the 'world-storm' – also lurk beneath the surface, but the sustained images are bucolic rather than bellicose: they celebrate the trees and butterflies that surround the house at Lavenham in which he had spent so many happy summers with Margaret and the family. Tellingly, the sequence concludes with a beautifully judged consolatory epistle to Humphrey, 'Dearest and nearest brother',[3] in which, although he had died hardly more than six months previously, Michael is not so much as alluded to.

Margaret's, and to a lesser extent Michael's, death had closed off a distinct period of his life. And, as if to finalise the break, in the summer of 1946 Spender and Humphrey sold the house at Lavenham and moved on, determined to create new lives for themselves.

By then Spender and Natasha were anyway already well-established in a roomy early Victorian house of their own in Loudoun Road, Hampstead, a house which was to remain their London base. (Over the years it was also to provide a convenient British *pied-à-terre* for W. H. Auden and other friends from Europe and America.)

It was – in all senses of the word – a crucial move for Spender because, within days of buying the house, he had become a father. His son Matthew was born in March 1945, an experience which quite naturally had a deep effect on him. So too did the protracted but fascinating business of watching him grow up – as he was to describe in poems such as 'Empty House' (dedicated 'To M.F.M.S.') and 'Boy, Cat, Canary'.[4] The birth of his second child, his daughter Elizabeth (Lizzie) a few years later had a similarly profound effect and again inspired him to write.[5] But he was increasingly obliged to spend time away from Natasha and the children: during a spell of lecturing at an American university a few years later he fretted in his diary that he had already missed one sixth of his daughter's life and one fourteenth of his son's.[6]

Unexpectedly perhaps, he was to prove a good, if indulgent father. Lizzie has remembered how, as children, she and Matthew regarded it as quite natural for Auden or Isherwood, Peggy Ashcroft or Henry Moore to be having dinner with their parents. She has recalled too how the ingrained Spender liberalism allowed both her and her brother to develop into the family's fourth generation of writers – she as a playwright and cookery writer; he, more recently, as the author of a book on Tuscany, where he has for many years worked as an artist and sculptor. Lily, one feels, would have been pleased.

Spender's new-found sense of home and family both amused and bemused his predominantly homosexual friends such as Auden and Lehmann. Auden thought that all babies – Matthew included – looked like Winston Churchill, and said as much. For his part, Lehmann wondered quite what Spender was doing. He had built up a carapace of domesticity, but he was not 'at work building poems, a skill which came to occupy less and less of his time'.[7] What was going on?

Lehmann did have a point and Spender, for all the undoubted comfort which Natasha, the children and their life together in a substantial family home undoubtedly brought him, seems at times to have recognised it himself. A late poem, ambiguously entitled 'Lost Days', is printed with the dedication 'For John Lehmann'. Another, dating from the same period, is called 'One More New Botched Beginning'.

But Spender was determined not to 'botch' his second marriage, as he made clear in a third poem, 'Absence' (which, pointedly, he chose to include in the section he called 'Home' in the *Collected Poems*).[8] Seemingly addressed to Natasha, it is part-apologia, part-rededication. Spender acknowledges the existence of a 'blemish' which he has brought into the relationship and which might yet destroy it – unless Natasha is by his side. *Lead us not into temptation . . .*

━━━━━

Professionally, Spender had had what was called 'a good war'. His service record had been by no means orthodox, but he had survived, and – once again by dint of being in the right place at the right time – he had emerged streets ahead of the likes of Lehmann, MacNeice, Isherwood or even Auden, among the top flight of British 'intellectuals', even if he had not quite maintained his early promise as a writer. But, as if to console him for that, he was becoming recognised as more than just a poet, and certainly more than just a 'Thirties poet'.

Almost in symbolic recognition of the fact that in 1945 he had begun work on a new stage-play,[9] he found himself taken on as a bit-part player on the world stage. His very un-British preoccupations with culture *qua* culture, civilisation, old-fashioned liberalism and the life of the mind was pulling him willy-nilly into the centre of a growing pan-European intellectual circus. He was not unhappy about this because 'He was beginning to be more and more dissatisfied with London intellectual life in comparison with what he [had] found abroad,' or so John Lehmann believed. Spender, he remembered, once told him at around this time: 'London is frightful now, it's become like Dublin.'[10]

There were several reasons for his disenchantment. Accustomed to living for several months of every year in Europe, he found it hard to adapt to the comparative provincialism of the literary scene in post-war London where the public looked askance at writers and so-called intellectuals. Abroad, in Paris or Berlin, he had discovered, they were valued, taken seriously and looked up to. At home, too, it was currently almost impossible to make a living as a writer, let alone as a poet – something which Dylan Thomas had discovered rather earlier. At the beginning of the war he had bitterly lamented that he was 'not expecting plums from the war – after all they must go to the kind of chaps who refused to give me anything out of the Royal Literary Fund.'[11]

Basic and obvious though this last point is, it should not be overlooked: by 1945 things were no better, and by then Spender (like Thomas) had a wife and children to support. Occasional royalty cheques and the fees he received for equally occasional articles were not enough to pay the bills. He had to find another source of income.

Better placed than Thomas, and with an altogether more serious reputation, it did not take him long. Soon after his return from Germany, Julian Huxley – whom family connections, as much as anything, had shoe-horned into the front rank of the

intellectual Great and Good – inquired whether he would be
prepared to serve as a member of the commission charged with
setting up the United Nations Educational, Scientific, and
Cultural Organisation (Unesco).

It was to be the first of many such offers, and Spender was
happy to accept, working first in London and then in Paris as a
Counsellor to the Section of Letters. Unexpectedly, however, it
did not prove to be a particularly happy period in his life, and he
resigned when, after a bout of the acrimonious in-fighting to
which Unesco was (and still is) prone, Huxley was removed from
his post as General Secretary.

Ultimately, though, it was good training. Post-war Europe
was rife with good intentions. (In Britain they culminated in the
determinedly optimistic 1951 Festival of Britain.) Conferences
and conventions at which writers and thinkers gathered to shape
or at least to try to influence the new world order were taking
place in every self-respecting city which could rustle up a few
bottles of champagne and a few clean sheets for the beds of *les
délégués* or *die Delegation*. Attending cultural and academic
'junketings' (the word is Spender's) was becoming a way of life
for the very intellectuals among whom Spender was beginning to
move. Auden, a later recruit to the lecturing and teaching circuit,
but never much of a committee man, was to describe this
peripatetic existence to great effect in his poem 'On the Circuit':

> And daily, seven days a week,
> Before a local sense has jelled,
> From talking-site to talking-site
> Am jet-or-prop-propelled.
>
> Though warm my welcome everywhere,
> I shift so frequently, so fast,
> I cannot now say where I was
> The evening before last . . .[12]

Spender's first real experience of all this came in Switzerland in
1946, at the first *'Rencontre de Genève'*. There, attending
debates on, of all things, existentialism, he first got to know

French and German philosophers of the stature of Jean-Paul
Sartre, Maurice Merleau-Ponty and Karl Jaspers. Quite what
Spender was doing at a philosophical *rencontre* remains unclear;
but Sartre and Merleau-Ponty were ever after to remain on the
outer fringe of his rapidly expanding circle of international
friends.

Many more cultural celebrities were to join them there the
following year when he made the first of many trips to America.
Although as we have seen, Isherwood had originally urged him
to come over, even perhaps to emigrate permanently, five years
previously, Spender had always resisted his blandishments. In
the summer of 1947, however, on what seem to have been
predominantly financial grounds, he had no option but to accept
an unexpected invitation to become a member of the English
faculty at Sarah Lawrence College, Bronxville, New York. In the
light of his experiences at Blundell's School at the beginning of the
war, he might have been excused a degree of trepidation at the
prospect of commiting himself to a full year's teaching so far
from home. But in the event teaching, particularly in American
colleges and universities, was to become a mainstay of his life for
the next quarter of a century; and hardly a year went by without
his visiting America during that period.

Not the least of the advantages of working at Sarah Lawrence
was that it brought Spender (and Natasha and Matthew, who
had accompanied him there) into contact with the other
members of the very distinguished academic staff which the
college managed to retain. The novelist and critic Mary
McCarthy and the poets Randall Jarrell and Robert Fitzgerald
could all be found somewhere around the campus, while a
galaxy of other writers, artists and especially musicians were
based not far away in New England. At Westchester, Spender
first met the composers Samuel Barber and Gian Carlo Menotti,
as well as the conductor and composer Leonard Bernstein.

Happily too, until March 1948 W. H. Auden was principally
based at his flat in New York, and therefore easily accessible. It
was probably through Auden that Spender also first met another
composer: at this time Auden and his lover Chester Kallman

were writing the libretto of the opera. *The Rake's Progress*, on which they were collaborating with Igor Stravinsky.

At the end of the academic year, in the early summer of 1948, Spender, Natasha and the three-year-old Matthew left for a coast-to-coast holiday in the United States, visiting Seattle, Los Angeles (where they met up – Natasha for probably the first time – with Christopher Isherwood), San Francisco and New Mexico. There, in Taos, they were introduced to D. H. Lawrence's widow, Frieda (the model for Ursula Brangwyn in *Women in Love* and 'the original Earth-Mother', according to W. H. Auden) and the artist, the Hon. Dorothy Brett, who had been the novelist's closest confidante for some fifteen years until his death in 1930. Brett (as she was always known) was a survivor of old Bloomsbury. She had been very friendly with Virginia Woolf and acted as the 'virgin aunt' of two of the younger members of the group, the painters Mark Gertler and Dora Carrington. She had always been very deaf and was now notably eccentric in her behaviour, as Spender noted with affection in the *Journals*.

Towards the end of the summer, the family returned to New York, and Natasha and Matthew went on back to London. Spender had decided to remain in America and attempt to get down to some serious writing, a decision in part prompted by Frieda Lawrence's unexpected invitation for him to return to Taos and have free use of the ranch in which she and Lawrence had lived during part of the 1920s. It was too good an opportunity to miss. The only problem was how to get there.

That, however, was quickly solved when Leonard Bernstein and his seventeen-year-old brother Bertie invited themselves along. Bernstein was equally desperate to find the peace and solitude he needed to finish his latest work – by coincidence a ballet based on Auden's elaborate 'baroque eclogue' *The Age of Anxiety*. Although he had reservations about how much writing he would be able to do in the company of the voluble, garrulous musician and an excitable teenager, Spender relented when Bernstein offered to drive the three of them to New Mexico in the Buick he had recently acquired.[13]

It was to prove a nightmare journey. Bernstein was intent on completing it in three days, which meant that, since Spender did not drive, he or Bertie would have to be at the wheel for up to fourteen hours a day. They talked incessantly, partly to keep Bernstein awake and alert, partly because Bernstein always did —*Why is Beethoven such a great composer? D'you know, Bruno Walter's earning half a million bucks a year?* — and Bernstein and his brother sang their way through Benjamin Britten's opera *Peter Grimes* which, given Spender's views on Britten's music, cannot have been a wholly enjoyable experience for him.

The Buick's tyres blew with monotonous regularity, at least once a day, necessitating wheel-changes, sometimes in the middle of the desert. (During one of these, Bertie later recalled in an article in *The New Yorker*, he and Bernstein did all the work while Spender merely sat by the roadside thinking about 'Lyric Poetry'.[14]) At Santa Fe, the only beds they could get were in a brothel, but they were at least able to hear a newly released recording of Bernstein's *An American in Paris* in the local record store. In another town Spender and Bernstein decided to hoodwink the roving reporter of the local radio station into believing that they were actually T.S. Eliot and the conductor Serge Koussevitsky; but, fortunately perhaps, the reporter had moved on before they arrived . . .

All in all, it was not the most propitious beginning for the period of rest, writing and contemplation to which Spender had been looking forward, and things did not improve when they finally reached Taos. Almost literally marooned at the ranch-house, which stood in lonely splendour seven thousand feet up the San Cristobal mountain and some fifty miles north of Santa Fe, Spender could find no escape from the boisterousness of 'Lenny' and Bertie. For the first few days he despaired of getting any work done at all. But then, after about a week, the Bernstein brothers suddenly announced that they were bored by the desert solitude and packed their bags and left.

That solitude was exactly what Spender wanted, however — just as Auden and Kallman had when they spent what Auden

called their 'honeymoon' on the same estate in the summer of
1939:

> Here we are ensconced in a log cabin with the most wonderful
> view you can imagine, our horizon is about 300 miles long. It's
> very pioneer and you would laugh to see me rising at six a.m.
> to chop wood and draw water, and this life certainly brings
> home to me my lack of muscular co-ordination. Tell me, do
> you burn yourself much on the stove when you are cooking?[15]

Breathing a sigh of relief at the Bernsteins' departure,
Spender was finally able to settle down to work. And, after six
weeks of isolation, broken only by the occasional visits of Frieda
and her friends, despite having to chop wood, draw water and
generally fend for himself he had completed the first draft of a
book.

It was an autobiography – the book which, heavily revised
and rewritten, would be published three years later under the
title *World Within World*. It was also a considerable achieve-
ment; proof to Spender at least that, despite all that had
happened in the past couple of years, at root he was still a writer.
It was, too, another symbolic tying-off of loose ends.

━━━━━━

Away from New Mexico, his new life continued apace. He was
back in America the following spring (1949) for a month-long
lecture tour of the mid-west – '*I bring my gospel of the Muse/To
fundamentalists, to nuns,/To Gentiles, and to Jews*'.[16] His new
collection, *Poems of Dedication* was also published later that
year. And he made his final, public renunciation of communism.

Appalled by what he had heard about Stalin's purges in the
Soviet Union, he could not accept or understand the 'double
think' of otherwise intelligent men and women who also knew
what was going on but were prepared to turn a blind eye to it and
dismiss it (if they acknowledged it at all) as regrettable but
necessary in the struggle to 'liberate' the proletariat.[17] He
recognised the inherent contradiction in the Communists'

argument – that, as George Orwell put it in *Animal Farm* (1945), 'FREEDOM IS SLAVERY'. Privately, too, he recognised that his own comfortable, bourgeois lifestyle would suffer under a Communist regime.[18]

He agreed to write an essay, a sort of counterblast to his *Daily Worker* piece 'I Join the Communist Party', for a book being edited by Dick Crossman. His was the only contribution by a native British ex-communist to be included in the collection, which was published under the title *The God That Failed*. Crossman explained that he had simply been unable to find any others and was forced to rely on the testimony of distinguished European dissenters such as Arthur Koestler, André Gide and Ignazio Silone, respectively a British-naturalised Hungarian, a Frenchman and an Italian. Their inclusion, however, ensured that the book could not lightly be dismissed; and Spender's very presence among them can now be seen as another important indication of his growing international stature.

So too can his active involvement with P.E.N., the international writers' organisation. This also began at the end of the 1940s, and was to continue for more than a quarter of a century.[19] In September 1949, for example, along with Auden and Cecil Day Lewis, Spender was one of the British delegates at an International P.E.N. Conference in Venice. Nearly half a century on, the conference itself and any business transacted has been long forgotten. Adducing a much reproduced series of photographs taken by Natasha during a free afternoon, however, historians and hagiographers (and the poets themselves) have subsequently recalled it as the first occasion on which the three poets were ever together. In fact, as Humphrey Carpenter has pointed out, it was not; they all spoke in a B.B.C. radio programme about 'The Modern Muse' in October 1938.[20]

Because of all this cultural gallivanting, Spender was the *New York Times Magazine*'s natural choice when they were looking around for a suitably qualified authority to write an extended article on the political stance of European intellectuals as the century reached its mid-point.

He undertook the assignment with relish and travelled

through France and Italy visiting old friends and making new
ones. He had lunch with the connoisseur Bernard Berenson at I
Tatti, his villa outside Florence – and then stayed on for dinner
with Eudora Welty. He met up with the Italian poet Eugenio
Montale and, in Paris, with Arthur Koestler. He had a long
interview with André Malraux at his home – where Picassos and
Dubuffets hung on the walls – and also managed to fit in one of
Nancy Mitford's parties.

His diaries of the two- or three-week trip set the mood for
what was to come. Their pages (or at least the published versions
of them[21]) droop under the weight of famous names and presage
the resolutely public tone of the later *Journals 1939–1983*. For
although Natasha, Matthew and Lizzie fare better in the
Journals than Spender, his mother, brothers and sister had done
in Harold Spender's autobiography *The Fire of Life*, the book is
still primarily an account of Spender's encounters with the
seminal people and places of the post-war world. Thus, quoting
at random from its thirty-page index, there are references to:
'MacInnes, Colin; McKinley, William; McKuen, Rod; Maclean,
Donald; McLeish, Archibald; Macmillan, Harold; MacNeice,
Hedli; MacNeice, Louis; Madge, Charles; Madras; Madrid'[22]
–a bare dozen lines which mention two writers, two poet/
playwrights, two cities, a spy,[23] a pop singer, a (long-dead)
American President and a British Prime Minister.

━━━━━━━

Not the least significant – and at the time, indeed, one of the
more satisfying – fruits of Spender's sudden celebrity was the
invitation which arrived in 1953 for him to co-edit a pan-
Atlantic magazine which was to be published by the Congress
for Cultural Freedom. An anti-communist organisation based in
Paris, the C.C.F. was funded by some forty different American
trusts and charitable foundations. Spender was told that the new
magazine, which was to be called *Encounter*, would be specific-
ally supported by one of these, the Farfield Foundation. *That*, he
was assured, was beyond reproach, having been established by

Julius Fleishmann, a Cincinnati millionaire whom he had himself met during a previous visit to the United States.

Years later, those blithe words were to hurt and haunt him, but at the time there was absolutely no reason to doubt their truth.

Fleishmann was no Peter Watson; however, Spender and his co-editor, the American writer Irving Kristol, were given complete editorial control over *Encounter* – as were the editors of other C.C.F.-funded magazines such as Ignazio Silone, who presided over the Italian *Tempo Presente* – and they rapidly put their own stamp on it. Spender had charge of the arts and literature coverage; Kristol, based in America and by training a social scientist, looked after the political side of things.

In many ways it must have seemed to Spender that *Encounter* would be a phoenix rising out of the ashes of *Horizon*, which had finally tottered to a close in December 1949, ironically defeated by the coming of peace. In its last editorial Cyril Connolly had re-iterated his credo: 'We have always believed that the real vocation of this magazine was to feel its way to what is, in the best sense of the world, contemporary, to print what many years hence will be recognised as alive and original.'[24] Now, nearly four years later, Kristol's editorial in the first issue of *Encounter* announced that the C.C.F. and its new magazine stood for 'Two things: a love of liberty and a respect for that part of human endeavour that goes by the name of culture'.[25]

Spender felt at home in the liberal atmosphere of *Encounter*. It was anti-communist but certainly not McCarthyite – indeed, it drew political contributions from both the Left and the Right – and its arts and literary pages benefited significantly from his extensive and growing European connections.

Its first issue did not, however, meet with the unqualified praise which had greeted the appearance of *Horizon*. John Lehmann, then in the throes of setting up another literary monthly, the *London Magazine*, recalled that 'the reviews in the *Times Literary Supplement*, the *Listener* and the *Spectator* were chastening.' Only *The Economist* had been 'enthusiastic in its praise'.[26] Later, J.R. Ackerley – who was, of course, a *Listener* man – noted that there was 'something very idle or screwy' about it.

Lehmann may well have taken a jaundiced delight in *Encounter*'s lukewarm reception, but at the *London Magazine*'s first editorial lunch some months later, he and the board (Elizabeth Bowen, Veronica Wedgwood, Rex Warne, William Plomer and John Hayward) unwittingly pin-pointed what would prove to be the fatal weakness of their rival:

> There was a good deal of discussion about *Encounter*, and our determination to remain literary without any political bias whatsoever was reinforced by the general dislike or suspicion of the political line to which *Encounter* was committed by its genesis and its backers.[27]

Seemingly unnerved by *Encounter*'s rapidly gained reputation for being 'screwy' or at best high-mindedly dull (an image of which it was never entirely able to rid itself) in the London office Spender worked hard to make it a livelier, less earnest and more eurocentric magazine. With Kristol's support he began casting around to find writers who were prepared to address broad cultural themes; the class system, the role of the intelligentsia, the rich, the poor. He was also prepared to be downright idiosyncratic – as when, for example, he accepted one of Ackerley's first pieces about his dog.[28]

Occasionally – but only occasionally – his diligence paid off. Most notably, he was responsible for commissioning what was perhaps the best feature article that *Encounter* ever published, Nancy Mitford's essay on 'The English Aristocracy'[29] which famously included examples of the 'U and Non-U Usage' of the English language. Adapted from an earlier essay by Professor Alan Ross, this piece of light-hearted class analysis was to be discussed at dinner parties for the next twenty years: *No, honestly, should one say 'wireless' or should one say 'radio', 'table napkin' or 'serviette'? . . .*

On the strength of that one article, the magazine's circulation rose by several thousand; and, although no one was exactly prepared to die for it – as the Spitfire pilots said they were for

Horizon – Encounter gradually established its position on the bookstalls. In Britain, Spender and, to a lesser extent, Kristol became the intellectual arbiters who staffed a somewhat Connollean ivory tower which stood, seemingly impervious, sempiternally impregnable, above the raucous new culture of the streets.

Angry Young Men came and went. In the opening minutes of John Osborne's *Look Back in Anger* (1956) its hero Jimmy Porter and his friend Cliff Lewis had blown open the new hegemony of the Sunday papers (and, incidentally, of Cyril Connolly who, on the closure of *Horizon*, had become literary editor of the *Sunday Times*):

> JIMMY: Why do I do this every Sunday? Even the book reviews seem to be the same as last week's. Different books – same reviews. Have you finished that one yet?
>
> CLIFF: Not yet.
>
> JIMMY: I've just read three whole columns on the English Novel. Half of it's in French. Do the Sunday papers make *you* feel ignorant?
>
> CLIFF: Not 'arf.

Encounter survived, however, aloof and libertarian if only tangentially connected to the mood of the streets. Spender resigned as co-editor at the end of 1965 – his place was taken by Frank Kermode – but he agreed to remain on the letter-head as a 'contributing editor'. It was a fateful decision for, early the following year, *Ramparts*, a hitherto-obscure Californian magazine, managed to prove rumours which had been circulating for some time that *Encounter* and the Congress for Cultural Freedom (although not Julius Fleischmann and the Farfield Foundation) had all along been covertly funded by the American Central Intelligence Agency (C.I.A.).

Spender was stung by what, with some justification, he regarded as the mendacity of the C.C.F. Before the *Ramparts*

story appeared he had specifically asked the Foundation whether
there was any truth in the rumours, and been assured that there
was not. Now, announcing that they had been 'misled', he and
Kermode severed all contacts with *Encounter* and the Congress
for Cultural Freedom. It was the decent thing to do and the only
way out. It was embarrassing too, but only momentarily. The
readers and writers of the magazine and the larger intellectual
community it tried to address took Spender at his word and
believed him – with predictable effects on *Encounter*'s reputa-
tion and influence.

———

Even in the good days when he was a full co-editor of *Encounter*,
Spender was never more than a part-time employee. Conse-
quently, it was from 'the circuit' – the punishing round of
teaching, lecturing, broadcasting and travelling – that he was
making the greater part of his living in the 1950s and 1960s. His
programme for the autumn of 1954 was more than usually busy,
but it remains vividly illustrative of this new peripatetic profes-
sionalism. On behalf of the Congress for Cultural Freedom, he
was then making what amounted to a world lecture tour.

By the end of the first week, in early September, he had visited
Paris, Rome, Athens, Beirut, Karachi, Singapore and reached
Darwin in northern Australia. He met local dignitaries, teachers
and university professors. He lunched with representatives of
the British Council and gave lecture after lecture about T.S.
Eliot, modern poetry, freedom, and freedom and the artist.

> *Since Merit but a dunghill is,*
> *I mount the rostrum unafraid . . .*

By the last week of October he had reached Kandy in Sri Lanka
(Ceylon). Within a couple of days he had made a radio broadcast
and delivered several more lectures at Madras and Chidam-
baram in India (and been forced to listen to a local poet chanting
a Tamil translation of his poem 'Ultima Ratio Regum'). And so it

went on: Bangalore, Bombay and British Council lunches; Poona, protocol and poetry.[30] There was hardly time to register where he was.

> *Another morning comes: I see,*
> *Dwindling below me on the plane,*
> *The roofs of one more audience*
> *I shall not see again.*[31]

Congresses and conferences, lectures and tours; Spender was forging a new literary lifestyle, one as dependant on airline timetables as it was on ink and inspiration. And, for all their previous differences, John Lehmann observed his friend's new role as an international cultural commissar with frank admiration:

> ... he was travelling abroad a great deal, lecturing in America, and involving himself ever deeper in the Committee for Cultural Freedom which had just been formed after the Congress of Writers in Berlin, and which was eventually to be the power behind *Encounter*. In spite of the impression he was apt to make of boyish fluster in public debates, Stephen was really very good at these congresses, showing a strength of will and a political flair that was obviously in his blood. He would sail into a congress like a demolition expert arriving to inspect a row of old cottages that had outlived their usefulness.[32]

The high – or perhaps the low – point of all this cultural junketing came in March 1956 when Spender was one of the three British delegates at a meeting in Venice of intellectuals from both sides of the Iron Curtain – Britain, France and Italy; Russia, Poland and Yugoslavia. It was the first such event to have happened since the fall of Stalin and took place under the auspices of the European Cultural Association. Happily, Spender had his notebook open throughout, and later gleefully immortalised the chaotic, fatuous absurdity of the proceedings in a satirical novella he called *Engaged in Writing*.

Not only was communication difficult – the Russian translator was so inept that the Soviet delegates could reply to questions only after studying the tedious transcripts of a day's deliberations – no one seemed to know which side he was on, which side he was meant to be on, or even if there were any sides at all. Jean-Paul Sartre and Maurice Merleau-Ponty who, along with Vercors (Jean Bruller) comprised the French delegation, became involved in a bitter private argument more suitable, it was suggested, for 'Les Deux Magots or one of the other cafés on the *rive gauche*.' Spender himself managed to upset J.D. Bernal, a scientist who was also representing Britain, when he refused to support Bernal's unreconstructed Stalinist line.

Whole sessions were devoted to discussions about what they should discuss[33] in just the same way that the Cold War was prolonged by infinitely protracted rounds of talks about talks. Was literature political? *Yes! No!* Were they, as writers, necessarily '*engagé*'? *No! Yes!* What was literature anyway? What was politics? What was society? Who were they? Where were they? *Buzz, buzz*[34] . . .

Spender had great fun with the bureaucratic formality and mind-numbingly banal proceedings of the conference in *Engaged in Writing*. The whole paraphernalia of interpreters, travel allowances, hotels, cocktails and communiqués had after all become second nature to him, and the cumbersome but well-meaning organisation he calls 'EUROPLUME' is a satirical representation of the European Cultural Association. But as well as containing a plethora of background detail, the book is undoubtedly a *novella-à-clef*. Indeed, several incidents closely parallel actual events described in his 1956 Journal.[35]

Apparently real-life individuals are similarly thinly disguised. The *chic* existentialists Sartre and Merleau-Ponty are clearly the originals for the book's disputative French philosophers Sarret and Marteau, just as the writer Carlo Levi (best known for *Christ Stopped at Eboli*, 1945) is the model for an epicurian Italian called Leonardo Longhi.[36] J.D. Bernal is lampooned in the character of the stubbornly Stalinist nuclear physicist, Dunstan Curlew; but by contrast the third British delegate, Alan Pryce-Jones, the editor of the *Times Literary Supplement* (and an Oxford contemporary of Spender's) comes through almost unscathed. Perhaps because of this, Alex Merton, as he is called, is the least fully realised character in *Engaged in Writing*.

We certainly get to know a great deal more about the central character, Olim Asphalt – inevitably so, since this is Spender writing about Spender. But although Olim is a writer representing a Paris-based literary body (Spender calls it 'LITUNO') the book presents a complicated, refracted self-portrait. Knowing and self-conscious, Spender is to some extent playing his readers along. Nowhere is this more apparent than at the moment when he announces in *Engaged in Writing* that Olim is writing a novel called *Littérature Engagée*.[37] This is either solipsism of a major kind – author-as-subject-as-author – or a richly baroque parody of the self-absorbed Parisian, existentialist mood of the conference.

Outwardly, Olim is not Spender at all. Like Alex Merton, he is celebrating his fiftieth birthday in the year of the conference (Spender celebrated his forty-seventh in February 1956). More basically, Olim has just come from Paris where his mistress has recently attempted suicide, but he still has no compunctions about attempting to seduce one of the conference's female interpreters.

At a deeper level, however, Olim's thoughts throw a sharp light on Spender's perception of the world and his position in it at this time. All right, the French *philosophes* might in their high seriousness see someone such as Olim as no more than a young novelist of the Anglo-American school, a writer of the *deuxième métier*. But if, in their eyes, that was a category which included such meretricious figures as Truman Capote, William Faulkner, Nancy Mitford and Graham Greene,[38] it was quite good enough for him.

He had earned his spurs and knew that he was in Venice purely because he had been on and around the literary scene for the past twenty-five years.[39] In T.S. Eliot's phrase, he knew 'the dialect of the tribe'; he was one of its chieftains, one of its shamen. Striding along the banks of the Venetian canals in the March of 1956, Stephen Spender acknowledged that, like Olim

Asphalt, he was a cultural power-broker. At *Encounter*, in London, on the campuses of American universities and in the conference-centres of Europe, he had his hand on the strings of power.[40]

═══════

Envoi

Thou hast it now: King, Cawdor, Glamis, all . . .[41] Or so it must have seemed. By 28 February 1979, when he celebrated his seventieth birthday during a brief furlough in London between American teaching engagements, Spender had become what we would now call seriously famous. In America, a friend assured him, everyone recognised him – everyone from dishwashers to executives – even in Gainesville, Texas.[42] In London too, just about everyone – or everyone who was anyone – knew his name.

Around one hundred of the Great and the Good joined members of his family for the grand birthday party which Natasha arranged at the Royal College of Art. Humphrey, Christine, Lizzie, Matthew, Matthew's wife Maro, Michael's widow Nancy (Coldstream) and son, Phillip were all there. Making up the numbers, Isaiah Berlin, Angus Wilson, Lord and Lady Longford and the artists William Coldstream, John Piper and Lucien Freud joined the celebrations, drank champagne and helped consume some fifty bottles of Mouton Cadet claret. Impromptu parties in the following few days involved the novelist Kingsley Amis, William Empson, the philosopher Stuart Hampshire and the pianist Clifford Curzon.[43]

For almost a fortnight glasses were raised to the man who – although he himself had no university degree – had been Professor of English Literature at University College London from 1970 until his retirement in 1977; who had been Consultant in Poetry in English at the Library of Congress in Washington, D.C.; who had been made a Commander of the Order of the British Empire (C.B.E.) in 1962 and a Fellow of the

Royal Society of Literature. It was a spectacular achievement, a triumphant career which was to be capped by Spender's acceptance – much to his son's dismay – of a knighthood in 1983. *Arise, Sir Stephen . . .*

By then, of course, he was a survivor. Following the successive deaths of dear but distant friends such as Louis MacNeice in 1963, Cecil Day-Lewis (1972), W.H. Auden (1973), Cyril Connolly (1974) and Sonia Brownell (Orwell) in 1980, he and, far away in California, Isherwood were all that remained of the Thirties Gang. If he had not quite made it as The Poet, in the same way that Isherwood had not completely lived up to Auden's expectations of The Novelist, he had forged a career which would have been unthinkable to anyone at the Oxford of the late 1920s. More so even than Auden, he had redefined the notion of the English man of letters in a manner which would have been unimaginable to his father or even the censorious J.A.

As is the melancholy duty of all survivors, in his later years Spender has become something of the guardian of the flame. Students, academics and writers contact him several times a week, seeking first-hand information about Auden, *Encounter*, Berlin, Isherwood, *Horizon. What was it like? What was he really like? You were there!* In truth he has already given us the answers. From *World Within World* onwards, much of his work has been memorialising. Indeed, the penultimate section of the *Collected Poems* is rather touchingly entitled 'Remembering' and includes verse tributes to dead friends including MacNeice, Connolly and Stravinsky as well as a stately meditation on 'Auden's Funeral.'

Spender had been there, one of the handful of British mourners who travelled to the Austrian village of Kirchstetten for the interment on 4 October 1973. Charles Osborne, Auden's friend and biographer was another. He recalls how, before the service began, as Auden had requested, a gramophone record of Siegfried's Funeral March from Richard Wagner's *Gotterdammerung* was played: 'I could scarcely see through my tears, but before the watery curtain quite shut out my vision, I glanced across at Stephen, down whose cheeks the tears were also rolling. "Bloody Wagner," I murmured, while the great hero's funeral march proceeded inexorably onward' . . .[44]

———

Back in the summer of 1960, he had bought the ruins of a farmhouse he had discovered above the village of Maussane in Provence, south-west France. For £500 he had acquired little more than a few walls, within which trees were growing, and something like an acre of land.[45]

Gradually, however, local builders made it habitable, and two years later he and Natasha were able to take possession of a long, surprisingly spacious house featuring a large, cool sitting-room whose full-length windows opened on to a terrace and the fierce intensity of the Mediterranean sunlight which had so inspired Van Gogh. There was, naturally, a piano; and, upstairs, the study window looked out across long lines of olive trees to the white ridge of the Alpilles mountains.

Natasha named the house the Mas St Jérôme and, separately or together, she and Spender have continued to occupy it for several months of every year since then. It has become the centre of their life, particularly in the years since they have become grandparents. A late poem 'Grandparents'[46] reflects on how, after thirty years Spender has come to see it as a repository of 'yesterday', of memories of children growing up and of the happy chaos wrought during more recent visits by Matthew's children, Saskia and Cosima.

As in life, so in art. Spender's most recent collection of poetry, *The Generous Days*, appeared in 1971. There have been other books, essays, translations, and, of course, the *Journals* which bring the story of his life up to 1983. But, viewed from the Mas St Jérôme, they seem only to bolster what Spender in another late poem[47] calls 'unsubstantiated fame': by being 'anonymous' and dumping 'that burned-out candle, his name', he suggests, down there in Provence with Natasha, his children and grandchildren, he has at last found happiness, of a sort.

'There's an ancient tree which spreads a broad shadow across one end of the terrace,' says one visitor.[48] 'The whole house seems to radiate light and a vitality of spirit. Down there, of course, one can eat outdoors most of the time. But my most abiding memory is of Natasha pruning the olives in the garden, with Stephen sitting out on the terrace wearing a big straw hat, and reading; always reading.'

APPENDIX

Glossary of the chief pseudonyms used in works by Stephen Spender and Christopher Isherwood, and referred to in the text.

Sally Bowles	(*Goodbye to Berlin*)	Jean Ross
Geoffrey Brand	(*The Backward Son*)	Stephen Spender
William Bradshaw	(*Mr Norris Changes Trains*; *The Temple*)	Christopher Isherwood
Allen Chalmers	(*Lion and Shadows*; *World Within World*)	Edward Upward
Elizabeth	(*World Within World*)	Muriel Gardiner
Miss Fox	(*The Burning Cactus*)	Muriel Gardiner
Dr Jessell	(*World Within World*)	Erich Alport
Bernhard Landauer	(*Goodbye to Berlin*)	Wilfrid Israel
Natalia Landauer	(*Goodbye to Berlin*)	Gisa Soloweitschik
Joachim Lenz	(*World Within World*; *The Temple*)	Herbert List
Arthur Norris	(*Mr Norris Changes Trains*)	Gerald Hamilton
Stephen Savage	(*Lions and Shadows*)	Stephen Spender
Paul Schoner	(*The Temple*)	Stephen Spender
Dr Ernest Stockman	(*The Temple*)	Erich Alport
Tony	(*The Burning Cactus*)	Tony Hyndman
Tristan	(*World Within World*)	Gabriel Carritt
Hugh Weston	(*Lions and Shadows*)	W.H. Auden
Simon Wilmot	(*The Temple*)	W.H. Auden
Jimmy Younger	(*World Within World*; *Christopher and His Kind*)	Tony Hyndman

NOTES AND SOURCES

Wherever possible, references to published work by Stephen Spender (SS) are to readily available current editions. References to lesser and out-of-print works are perforce to their first editions. Principal titles are abbreviated thus:

CP	*Collected Poems, 1928–1985*
Journals	*Journals, 1939–1983*
Letters	*Letters to Christopher*
Son	*The Backward Son*
Temple	*The Temple*
Thirties	*The Thirties and After*
WWW	*World Within World*
Writing	*Engaged in Writing*

Publication details of these volumes will be found in the Bibliography.

Prologue: 'Degree, Priority and Place'

1. J.A. Spender, *Life, Journalism and Politics*, vol, I, p. 4.
2. Harold Spender, *The Fire of Life*, p. 7.
3. J.A. Spender, *op. cit.*, pp. 1–2.
4. W.S. Gilbert, *The Mikado* (1884), Act 1, 1.259.
5. J.A. Spender, *op. cit.*, p. 4.
6. Harold Spender, *op, cit.*, p. 7.
7. J.A. Spender, *op. cit.*, p. 3.
8. *Ibid.*, p. 2.
9. Harold Spender, *op. cit.*, p. 8.
10. J.A. Spender, *op. cit.*, pp. 13–14.
11. *Ibid.*, p. 7.
12. *Ibid.*, p. 9.
13. Harold Spender, *op. cit.*, p. 23.
14. *Ibid.*, p. 17.

15. Sir George Schuster, *Private Work and Public Causes*, p. 1.
16. *Ibid.*
17. *Ibid.*

PART ONE: The Making of a Poet

ONE: A Little Liberal

1. *The Times*, 1 March 1909
2. WWW, p. 4.
3. WWW, pp. 2–3.
4. WWW, p. 3.
5. SS, 'Day Boy', in Graham Greene (ed), *The Old School*, p. 172.
6. Harold Spender, *The Fire of Life*, p. 190.
7. *Ibid.*, pp. 190–1.
8. Son, p. 137.
9. WWW, pp. 323–4.
10. WWW, p. 86; p. 325.
11. SS, *Desert Island Discs*, BBC Radio 4, 10 December 1989.
12. Journals, p. 370.
13. *Desert Island Discs.*
14. Journals, p. 371.
15. *Desert Island Discs.*
16. Harold Spender, *op, cit.*, p. 214.
17. *Ibid.*, p. 196.
18. *Ibid.*, p. 215.
19. *Ibid.*, p. 212.
20. Son, pp. 22–3.
21. *Desert Island Discs.*
22. 'Day Boy', p. 173.
23. Son, p. 160.
24. Son, p. 147; WWW, p. 3.
25. CP, p. 23.
26. WWW, p. 9.
27. *Ibid.*, p. 324.
28. *Ibid.*, p. 326.
29. *Ibid.*
30. *Ibid.*, p. 327.
31. Son, p. 14; p. 16.
32. *Ibid.*, p. 46.
33. W.H. Auden, 'Honour', in Graham Greene, *op, cit.*, p. 9.
34. 'Day Boy', p. 165; WWW, pp. 332–3.
35. 'Day Boy', p. 165; WWW, p. 333.

36. Unattributed; qtd in Humphrey Carpenter, *W.H. Auden*, p. 27.
37. 'Day Boy', p. 166; WWW, pp. 333–4.
38. WWW, p. 332; p. 334.
39. Son, p. 14.
40. WWW, p. 87.
41. Son, p. 219.
42. *Ibid.*, p. 194.
43. *Ibid.*, pp. 191–2.
44. *Ibid.*, p. 46.
45. 'Day Boy', p. 169.
46. *Ibid.*, pp. 167–8.
47. SS, 'A Book That Changed Me', *Independent on Sunday*, 7 April 1991.
48. Son, p. 19.
49. On her death certificate Dr MacFadden certified that Violet ('Wife of Edward Harold Spender, Author and Journalist') had died as a result of '1. Intestinal obstructions due to adhesions [almost certainly the legacy of earlier surgery]. 2. Laparotomy (4 Dec. 1921). Cardiac Syncope'.
50. WWW, p. 6.
51. Although not by any means unusual in the book, this omission is particularly surprising (and indeed indicative of its thorough-going selective nature). *World Within World* was completed on 30 May 1950 (WWW, p. 336) and first published the following year, at a time when The Hall must have been on Spender's mind: he entered his son at the school in 1951.
52. Information provided by The Hall School, Hampstead, April 1991.
53. Letter to the author from R.P. Heazell, Headmaster, The Hall School, (undated), April 1991.
54. WWW, p. 6.
55. 'Day Boy', p. 178.
56. *Ibid* pp. 177–8.
57. *The Gower,* July 1924.
58. *Ibid.*, December 1925.
59. *Ibid.*, December 1926.
60. Derek Scott-Lowe, interview with the author, October 1990.
61. *The Gower*, December 1925.
62. We know, however, that he had continued to write poetry in the years since he penned his ode to Nature. In its 1927 issue *The Hall School Magazine* inexplicably published a poem entitled 'The Poet in Spring: A Triolet' which Spender had written during his time at the school five years previously. (See *One Hundred Years in Hampstead: The Story of The Hall School, 1889–1989*, The Hall School, 1989, p. 247.)
63. 'Day Boy', p. 176.

64. 'The Public Son of a Public Man', CP, p. 99.
65. 'Day Boy', p. 174.
66. WWW, P. 18.
67. *Journals*, p. 24 (5 September 1939); CP, p. 99.
68. WWW, pp. 82–3.
69. *Ibid.*, p. 88.
70. *Ibid.*, pp. 89–90.
71. *Ibid.*, p. 18.
72. *Ibid.*, p. 17.
73. *Ibid.*, p. 19.
74. 'Day Boy', p. 178.
75. WWW, p. 20.
76. *Ibid.*
77. CP, p. 99.
78. *The Gower*, December 1926.
79. *Ibid.*, July 1927.
80. 'Day Boy', p. 169.
81. *The Gower*, March 1927.
82. *Ibid.*, December 1926.
83. *Ibid.*
84. Derek Scott-Lowe, interview with the author, October 1990.
85. *The Gower*, July 1927.

TWO: 'Away from the Women at Last!'

1. Son, p. 16.
2. WWW, p. 4.
3. *Ibid.*
4. See WWW, pp. 280–1, and '1939 Journal' in Letters, p. 199 (entry for 21 October 1939).
5. WWW, pp. 25–6.
6. *Ibid.*, p. 27.
7. *Ibid.*, pp. 15–17.
8. *Ibid.*, p. 10; p. 16.
9. *Ibid.*, p. 21.
10. *Ibid.*, p. 29.
11. See, in particular, the poems 'What I Expected' and 'Not to You', (CP, p. 24 and p. 27 respectively).
12. WWW, pp. 30–31.
13. Harold Acton, *Memoirs of an Aesthete*, Methuen, 1948, p. 122.
14. *Isis*, 17 May 1922.

15. Alan Pryce-Jones, *The Bonus of Laughter*, Hamish Hamilton, 1987, p. 49.
16. Tom Driberg, *Ruling Passions*, Jonathan Cape, 1977, p. 55.
17. Qtd in Humphrey Carpenter, *The Brideshead Generation*, pp. 81–2.
18. WWW, pp. 38–9.
19. Hugh Corbett-Palmer, in a conversation with the author, June 1990.
20. WWW, p. 33.
21. Christoper Isherwood, *Christopher and His Kind*, p. 146.
22. Louis MacNeice, *The Strings Are False*, p. 113.
23. WWW, p. 31.
24. *Ibid.*, p. 35.
25. Hugh Corbett-Palmer, in a conversation with the author, June 1990. This seems to be an almost unerringly accurate hierarchy, for all that it is by a New College man.

    Spender's, though, is seemingly the fullest and most class-conscious account. Carpenter (*op. cit.*, p. 38) merely expands on the conclusions reached by Christopher Hollis in his *Oxford in the Twenties: Recollections of Five Friends* (Heinemann, 1976): 'Christ Church was the smartest, being crammed with Old Etonians; Wykehamists (clever men from Winchester College, the public school with the best academic tradition) generally went to New College; but in other respects intellectual superiority "certainly rested with Balliol".'
26. CP, p. 102.
27. WWW, p. 33.
28. *Ibid.*, p. 34.
29. *The Gower*, December 1928.
30. WWW, p. 39.
31. *Ibid.*, pp. 39–40.
32. SS, Interview with Patchy Wheatley, *Sunday Times Magazine*, 1986.
33. In rather the same way that the 'roughs' did, Lawrence was to hold Spender in thrall for many years. Though Spender never met him (Lawrence died in Venice in 1930) he later became vicariously close to the novelist through his widow, Frieda. It was at the ranch on the mountain above Taos in New Mexico to which the Lawrences had moved in 1922 that, at Frieda's suggestion, Spender wrote the first draft of *World Within World* in the summer of 1948 (*Journals*, p. 94 – Spender's chronology is once again at fault in *World Within World* when he states that this was in the summer of 1947 (p. ix): he had never set foot on North American soil at that time. His first visit began *later* that year when he taught for the academic year 1947–8 at the Sarah Lawrence College, Bronxville, New York. The trip to New Mexico was part of a holiday after that.)

34. WWW, p. 42.
35. WWW, pp. 69–70.
36. WWW, p. 49.
37. Gabriel Carritt, 'A Friend of the Family' in *W.H. Auden: A Tribute*, p. 48.
38. WWW, p. 41.
39. *Ibid.*, p. 49.
40. *Ibid.*, p. 41; my italics.
41. Harold Acton, *Memoirs of an Aesthete*, Methuen, 1948, p. 163.
42. After a glittering career as both student and don at Oxford, Richard ('Dick') Crossman (1907–74) entered Parliament as a 'Bevanite' member of the Labour party. He served as a Minister in the Wilson administrations of the late 1960s and was editor of the *New Statesman* from 1970–72.

    Rex Warner (b.1905) published his first collection, *Poems*, in 1937 and went on to produce a succession of novels, poetry and translation. Most of his work has a strong classical influence.
43. Christopher Isherwood, *Lions and Shadows*, p. 113. Weston/Auden's 'expensive' clothes come as something of a surprise to those of us who remember his later, crumpled demeanour; but Isherwood was not the only one to notice them. Although he does not refer to them in *World Within World* (where they might have detracted from the image?) in the address he gave at Auden's memorial service on 27 October 1973 Spender recalled the Oxford Auden as 'wearing a bow-tie and on occasion wishing one to admire the suit he had on'. (*W.H. Auden: A Tribute*, p. 244.)
44. John Betjeman, 'Oxford' in *W.H. Auden: A Tribute*, p. 44.
45. WWW, p. 49.
46. Isherwood and Day-Lewis were born in 1904; Auden and MacNeice in 1907. Spender, of course, was born in 1909.
47. The phrase is Archie Campbell's. The present author knew him well in the mid-1980s and distinctly remembers his employing it in many similar contexts.
48. Charles Osborne, *op. cit.*, p. 52.
49. *Ibid.*, p. 48.
50. John Betjeman, *op. cit.*
51. WWW, pp. 51–2 and *passim*.
52. 'The Pylons', CP, p. 39.
53. 'Control of the passes was, he saw, the key,' (also known as 'The Secret Agent') W.H. Auden, *Collected Shorter Poems*, p. 22.
54. CP, p. 28.
55. 'Auden's Funeral', III, CP, p. 186.

56. *Ibid.*
57. Christopher Isherwood, *Christopher and His Kind*, p. 11.
58. WWW, p. 70.
59. Corbett-Palmer's poem, 'The Dance of Death' was one of his last. 'I gave up writing poetry the day I was paid for one,' he said – revealing an attitude very much at variance with the ambitions of the Gang. (Interview with the author, June 1990.)
60. *Manchester Guardian*, 28 January 1930.
61. Of the four poems, two have survived in slightly altered form in the *Collected Poems*: 'Marston' (CP, p. 26) and 'Acts passed beyond' (CP, p. 28).
62. *The Gower*, July 1929.
63. SS, *Desert Island Discs*, BBC Radio 4, 10 December 1989.
64. *The Gower*, December 1929.
65. *Ibid.*, March 1930.
66. Letters, p. 31.
67. *Spectator* 3 August 1929.
68. 'Never Being', CP, p. 21.
69. Letters, p. 32.
70. *Ibid.*, p. 33.
71. *Ibid.*, p. 36.
72. More problems with Spender's chronology here. In his Introduction to *The Temple*, he describes it as 'an autobiographical novel in which the author tries to report truthfully on his experiences in the summer of 1929'. (p.*xi*) But he was certainly writing it six (or even nine) months earlier. In a note to Isherwood written in January 1929 he confided: 'I have put the novel aside for the time.' (Letters, p. 31).

  Maybe at that stage he had only written what now appears as the 'English Prelude', but the finished novel, then entitled *Escaped*, was submitted to (and rejected by) Isherwood's publishers Jonathan Cape before Easter 1930.
73. In his remarkably frank comments on *Desert Island Discs* in 1989, Spender actually referred to himself as Auden's (though not Isherwood's) 'disciple'.
74. *The Gower*, July 1930.

THREE: Songs of Innocence and Experience

1. Hugh Corbett-Palmer, in an interview with the author, June 1990.

2. Christopher Isherwood, *Lions and Shadows*, p. 173.

3. *Ibid.*, pp. 172–3

4. SS, in the preface to Letters, p. 9.

5. Temple, p. 7.

6. CP, p. 30.

7. 'Day Boy', p. 177.

8. *Ibid.*, pp. 177–8.

9. Letters, p. 36.

10. WWW, p. 64; p. 66.

11. *Ibid.*, p. 65.

12. Temple, p. 1.

13. WWW, p. 64.

14. Temple, *ibid.*

15. CP. p. 26.

16. Temple, *ibid.*

17. WWW, *ibid.*

18. Letters, p. 34.

19. *Ibid.*, p. 36.

20. WWW (p. 65) suggests that the walk took place in April. Paul, the hero of *The Temple*, sets off with Marston for Ross-on-Wye on 26 March (p. 2). More interestingly, SS's preface to *The Temple* dates the incidents it describes to 1929; i.e. Spender would have known 'Marston' for rather more than a year before it took place – and would have had ample time for the 'many months' of planning (WWW, *ibid.*) he devoted to the trip.

21. WWW, p. 65; Temple, p. 2.

22. Temple, *ibid.*

23. WWW, p. 65.

24. 'The Photograph', CP, p. 29.

25. Temple, p. 3.

26. Wordsworth, 'Tintern Abbey', II.114–119.

27. Temple, p. 8.

28. 'Acts Passed Beyond', CP, p. 28.

29. Letters, p. 33.

30. WWW, p. 66.

31. *Ibid.*

32. Letters, p. 35.

33. *Ibid.*, p. 34.

34. SS, Introduction to *Herbert List: Junger Männer*, Thames and Hudson, 1988, (unpaginated).

35. Temple, p.*xii*.

36. *Ibid*, p.*xiii*.

37. CP, p. 105.

38. Temple, p. 67.

39. WWW, p. 104.

40. Christopher Isherwood, *Christopher and His Kind*, p. 10.

41. Though trivial in itself, deciding on the exact date of his arrival in Hamburg provides a spectacular example of the carelessness and inaccuracy which characterise so much of Spender's autobiographical writing.

   Chapter II of *World Within World* concludes with the opening words of a journal which he began on 22 July 1929 in Hamburg (WWW, p. 104). That reads as though it was written within hours of arriving on German soil. And yet in the Hamburg section of *The Temple* Spender writes that his German hosts expected Paul Schoner to arrive on 20 July. Paul had booked a night passage for 19 July on the Hamburg-Amerika Line ship, the *Bremen*. (p. 15).

   Even more mystifyingly, a few pages later Spender explicitly notes that the boat train from Cuxhaven arrived at Hamburg on 18 July (p. 25). Making matters more confusing still is the complex inter-relationship of the autobiography and the novel which Spender explains in his Introduction to *The Temple*.

42. Temple, p. 25.

43. *Ibid*, pp. 26–7, *passim*.

44. WWW, p. 107.

45. Temple, p. 26; p. 88.

46. WWW, p. 107.

47. SS, Introduction to *Herbert List: Junge Männer*; Temple, p. 46.

48. 'Not good-looking, but interesting; an innocent'; WWW, p. 108.

49. Letters, p. 31.

50. Ibid., pp. 31–2.

51. Temple, p. 43.

52. *Ibid.*, p. 99.

53. *Ibid.*, pp. 100–1; p. 96.

54. *Ibid.*, p. 37.

55. *Ibid.*, p. 64.

56. Spender refers to all this in 'The Port', a poem which was written 'for Herbert List' at the end of August 1929 (Letters, p. 32) and which was included in *Twenty Poems*. In a slightly rewritten form, it survives as 'Hamburg, 1929' (CP, p. 37).

57. Temple, pp. 74–8, *passim*.

58. *Ibid.*, p. 116.

59. *Ibid.*, p. 118.

60. *Ibid.*, p. 119.

61. *Ibid.*, p. 124.

62. *Ibid.*, p. 122.

63. *Ibid.*, p. 127.

64. WWW, p. 116; CP, p. 35.
65. W.H. Auden, *Collected Shorter Poems, 1927–1957*, p. 40.
66. See, for instance, 'Van der Lubbe'; CP, p. 38.
67. Temple, p. 78.
68. 'Hamburg, 1929', CP, p. 37.
69. 'The Sign *Fähre nach Wilm*', *ibid.*, p. 31.
70. CP, p. 40.
71. This is especially marked in 'Us', *ibid.*, p. 32.
72. 'Helmut', *ibid.*, p. 33; 'The Truly Great', *ibid.*, p. 30.
73. Temple, p. 131.
74. WWW. p. 104
75. SS, *Desert Island Discs*, BBC Radio 4, 10 December 1989.
76. Letters, p. 36.
77. *Ibid.*, p.37.
78. Isherwood, *Goodbye to Berlin*, p. 139.
79. *Ibid.*, pp. 139–40.
80. Although there is no Spender-figure in 'The Landauers', it is tempting to hear in a passage of dialogue given to Bernhard Landauer, Natalia's cousin, something of Spender's voice at this time. Certainly, the biographical similarities between the two men are strikingly similar. Not only has his beloved mother died; not only is he preoccupied with his Jewish roots, Bernhard says:

> I was a queer sort of boy, I suppose . . . I never got on well with other boys, although I wished very much to be popular and have friends. Perhaps that was my mistake – I was too eager to be friendly. The boys saw this and it made them cruel to me. Objectively, I can understand that . . . possibly I might even have been capable of cruelty myself, had circumstances been otherwise. It is difficult to say . . . But, being what I was, school was a kind of Chinese torture [. . .] I think that, in my case, there was also something characteristically Semitic in my attitude. Sometimes one is unwilling to make certain admissions to oneself, because they are displeasing to one's self-esteem . . . (*Goodbye to Berlin*, pp. 167–8)

81. WWW, p. 128.
    Spender's reference to having known Gisa for 'seven years' is obviously wrong, and probably no more than a misprint in early editions of *World Within World*. Certainly, in later editions it is amended to 'several years' – although even this sounds rather wide of the mark. 'A year or two' would be more accurate.
82. *Ibid.*, p. 129.

PART TWO: A Man of the World

FOUR: Under den Linden

1. Isherwood, *Christopher and His Kind*, p. 49.
2. Isherwood, *Goodbye to Berlin*, p.7.
3. *Ibid.*, p. 6.
4. *Christopher and His Kind*, pp. 37–8.
5. *Goodbye to Berlin* was orginally conceived as part of 'a huge episodic novel of pre-Hitler Berlin' (*Goodbye to Berlin*. p. 6). The book, which Isherwood planned to call *The Lost*, was never completed – but it is tempting to think that it would have been a sort of Germanic equivalent to John Dos Passos's roughly contemporaneous *U.S.A.* trilogy (first published between 1930 and 1936). The crucial importance of the diaries to this project is brought out in *Christopher and His Kind*:

> As he became aware that he would one day write stories about the people he knew [in Germany], his diary entries got longer. They later supplied him with most of the material which is used to create period atmosphere in *Mr Norris* and *Goodbye to Berlin*. (p. 37)

To the chagrin of historians and biographers alike, the diary itself no longer exists. Tragically, because 'it was full of details about his sex life and he feared that it might somehow fall into the hands of the police or other enemies' (*ibid*) Isherwood burnt it after completing work on *Goodbye to Berlin* – an action he came to rue while writing *Christopher and His Kind*.

6. *Christopher and His Kind*, p. 38; the reference to Otto is taken from *Goodbye to Berlin*, p. 81.
7. *Goodbye to Berlin*, pp. 29–30.
8. *Ibid.*, p. 106.
9. *Christopher and His Kind*, p. 38.
10. *Ibid.*, p. 34.
11. *Ibid.*, p. 29.
12. *Letters*, p. 38.
13. SS, conversation with the author, November 1989.
14. *Christopher and His Kind*, p. 17.
15. WWW, p. 117.
16. *Ibid.*, p. 121.
17. *Christopher and His Kind*, p. 49.
18. WWW, p. 117.
19. *Letters*, p. 37.

20. John Lehmann, *In the Purely Pagan Sense*, p. 44.
21. WWW, pp. 118.
22. *Ibid.*, pp. 117–8.
23. *Ibid.*, p. 123.
24. *Christopher and His Kind*, p. 39.
25. *Goodbye to Berlin*, p. 80.
26. Letters, p. 37.
27. SS, letter to Christopher Isherwood, c. 1972; qtd in *Christopher and His Kind*, p. 47.
28. WWW, p. 126.
29. *Christopher and His Kind*, p. 48.
30. See Hugh David, *The Fitzrovians*, pp. 127–32.
    It is impossible here not to be reminded of Michael Arlen's description of a late-night walk through Soho taken by Virginia Tarlyon, the heroine of his 1922 novel *Piracy*. Not only is Virginia a recognisable portrait of Nancy Cunard, with only minor changes of pronouns and place-names the ironic tone of the passage exactly captures Isherwood's impatience with Spender:

    > Swiftly she would penetrate the black solitudes of Soho in war-time: a rich and fragile figure braving all the dangers of the city by night, an almost fearful figure to arise suddenly in an honest man's homeward path: so tall and golden and proud of carriage, so marvellously indifferent to his astonished stare! Sometimes she would have to walk a long way before she could find a taxi – through Soho to Shaftesbury Avenue, and up that to Piccadilly Circus. Sometimes men would murmur in passing, sometimes they would say the coarsest things, and once or twice a man caught at her arm as she swiftly passed him; and Virginia looked at him straightly, for a swift second, as though secretly understanding his desire and mocking it; and then she went on her way as though her way had been uninterrupted . . . homewards to Belgrave Square.

31. *Christopher and His Kind*, p. 47.
32. WWW, p. 171.
33. Isherwood, *Lions and Shadows*, p. 123.
34. *Christopher and His Kind*, p. 47.
35. WWW, p. 121.
36. *Ibid.*, p. 124.
37. Letters, p. 40.
38. WWW, p. 131; *Christopher and His Kind*, p. 66.
39. *Christopher and His Kind*, p. 9.
40. WWW, p. 46.
41. *Goodbye to Berlin*, pp. 81–5 *passim*.

42. *Christopher and His Kind*, p. 40.
43. John Lehmann, *Christopher Isherwood*, p. 2.
44. *Christopher and His Kind*, p. 67.
45. *Goodbye to Berlin*, p. 100.
46. WWW, pp. 71–2.
47. *Ibid.*, p. 72.
48. Valentine Cunningham, *British Writers of the Thirties*, p. 185.
49. *Christopher and His Kind*, p. 66.
50. Qtd *ibid.*, p. 67.
51. It is reproduced entire as Plate 8 in Humphrey Carpenter's *W.H. Auden* – interestingly from a print which was given to Gabriel Carritt ('Tristan') after it had been signed by all three of its subjects.
52. *Christopher and His Kind*, p. 67.
53. *Ibid.*
54. *Goodbye to Berlin*, p. 195.
55. *Christopher and His Kind*, p. 67.
56. WWW, p. 131.
57. *Goodbye to Berlin*, p. 88.
58. WWW, pp. 129–31 *passim*.
59. See 'Perhaps', CP, p. 43.
60. WWW, p. 132.
61. Isherwood, *Lions and Shadows*, p. 12.
62. W.B. Yeats, 'The Second Coming,' *Michael Robartes and the Dancer*, 1921.
63. Thirties, p. 17.
64. *Ibid*, p. 23.
65. CP, p. 45.
66. *Ibid.*, p. 46.

FIVE: A Charmed Life

1. SS, qtd in Peter Ackroyd, *T.S. Eliot*, Hamish Hamilton, 1984, p. 196.
2. 'I think your idea of a Letter most brilliant – To a Young Poet because I'm seething with immature and ill considered and wild and annoying ideas about prose and poetry.' Letter to John Lehmann, 17 September 1931, qtd in *A Reflection of the Other Person: The Letters of Virginia Woolf, Volume IV – 1929–31* edited by Nigel Nicolson, The Hogarth Press, 1978, p. 381.
3. Virginia Woolf, *A Letter to a Young Poet*, Hogarth Press, 1932, p. 26.
4. Nicolson (ed), *op. cit.*, p. 381.
5. Peter Quennell, *A Letter to Mrs Virginia Woolf*, Hogarth Press, 1932, pp. 15–7.

6. Qtd, Sean Day-Lewis, *C. Day Lewis*, Weidenfeld & Nicolson, 1980, p. 75.
7. Michael Roberts (ed), *New Country*, Hogarth Press, 1933, pp. 223–4.
8. Qtd, Day-Lewis, *op. cit.*, pp. 71–2.
9. John Lehmann, *Christopher Isherwood: A Personal Memoir*, p. 8.
10. Thirties, p. 19.
11. Isherwood, *Lions and Shadows*, p. 123.
12. Auden, *Letter to Lord Byron* IV; *Collected Longer Poems*, p. 75.
13. WWW, p. 142.
14. He wrote to Isherwood in January 1933 announcing that from then on he was going to try and spend at least six months a year in England, (Letters, p. 56) which by and large he did.
15. Letters, p. 55.
16. Lehmann, *op. cit.*, p. 8.
17. WWW, p. 143.
18. *Christopher and His Kind*, p. 86.
19. WWW, p. 174.
20. *Christopher and His Kind*, p. 86.
21. Letter from Hugh Walpole to Virginia Woolf, 31 October 1931. *Berg Collection*.
22. Cunningham, *op. cit.*, p. 111.
23. *The Spectator*, 1 December 1933.
24. SS, Letter to Virginia Woolf, 22 October 1939. *Berg Collection*.
25. Brian Masters, *The Great Hostesses*, Constable, 1982, pp. 189–90.
26. WWW, pp. 161–2 *passim*.
27. Letter to D'Arcy Cresswell, 3 October 1933. Qtd in *Dear Lady Ginger: An Exchange of Letters between Lady Ottoline Morrell and D'Arcy Cresswell*, edited by Helen Shaw, Century, 1984, p. 76.
28. WWW, p. 144.
29. *Ibid.*, p. 167.
30. *Ottoline: The Early Memoirs of Lady Ottoline Morrell*, edited by Robert Gathorne-Hardy, Faber & Faber, 1963, pp. 17–8.
31. Shaw (ed), *op. cit.*, p. 106.
32. WWW, p. 157.
33. Letter to Ottoline Morrell, 31 December 1933. Qtd in *The Sickle Side of the Moon: The Letters of Virginia Woolf, Volume V – 1932–35*, edited by Nigel Nicolson, The Hogarth Press, 1979, p. 266.
34. WWW, p. 153.
35. Letter to SS, 9 October 1931. Qtd in Nicolson (ed), *op. cit.*, p. 109.
36. *The Diary of Virginia Woolf, Volume IV – 1931–35*, edited by Anne Olivier Bell, The Hogarth Press, 1982, p. 128.
37. *Ibid.*, p. 129.
38. WWW, pp. 151–5, *passim*.

39. 24 January 1934. Qtd in Nicolson (ed), *op. cit.*, p. 273.
40. Letter to SS, 10 December 1933, *ibid.*, p. 257.
41. Letter to Quentin Bell, 21 December 1933, *ibid*, pp. 261–2.
42. Letters, p. 54.
43. *Ibid.*, p. 57.
44. *Ibid.*, p. 56.
45. WWW, p. 152.
46. CP, p. 45.
47. Letters, p. 51.
48. SS, Preface, *ibid.*, p. 10.
49. *Ibid.*, p. 55.
50. 1932 Journal, 14 December. *Ibid.*, p. 159.
51. *Ibid.*, p. 51.
52. 1932 Journal, 26 November. *Ibid.*, p. 148.
53. *Ibid.*, p. 50.
54. *Ibid.*, 54.
55. *Ibid.*, p. 57.
56. *Ibid.*, p. 56.
57. *Times Literary Supplement*, 6 July 1933.
58. *Adelphi* 5, February 1933.

SIX: The Ballad of Sexual Confusion

1. Qtd in *Between the Acts: Lives of Homosexual Men, 1885–1967*, edited by Kevin Porter and Jeffrey Weeks, Routledge, 1991, pp. 137–8. It is perhaps of interest to note that the now completely unknown expression 'steamer' was glossed by Eric Partridge in his *Dictionary of the Underworld* (Routledge & Kegan Paul, 1950). Steaming, he noted, meant 'to prepare a "mug" for a fleecing' – and he cited as his authority a book first published in 1936.
2. *Ibid.*, p. 140.
3. Letters, p. 57.
4. *Ibid.*, p. 63.
5. WWW, p. 176.
6. Letters, p. 62.
7. This book, which eventually expanded into *The Destructive Element* (1935), was originally planned to centre on James's 'friendships with Boston lads between the ages of 7–17'. Intriguingly, Spender was also fascinated by the (erroneous) idea that James had been castrated in an accident involving a central heating radiator. (Letters, pp. 62–3; *The Destructive Element*, pp. 36–7.)
8. Letters, p. 58.

9. WWW, p. 175.
10. *Christopher and His Kind*, p. 168.
11. *Ibid*, p. 169.
12. WWW, p. 169.
13. *Ibid*., p. 176.
14. WWW, pp. 175–6.
15. Letters, p. 63.
16. *Christopher and His Kind*, p. 147.
17. WWW, pp. 175–9 *passim*.
18. Letters, p.63.
19. WWW, p. 179.
20. SS, letter to Virginia Woolf, 4 July 1934. *Berg Collection*. Not least because of the reference to 'the James book', the official ascription of this letter to 1939 is plainly wrong.
21. *Christopher and His Kind*, pp. 168–9.
22. The original was unavailable to the present author. However Isherwood quotes extensively from it in *Christopher and His Kind*.
23. *Christopher and His Kind*, p. 172.
24. *Ibid*., p. 176.
25. *Ibid*., p. 170.
26. *Ibid*., p. 169.
27. WWW, p. 185.
28. *Ibid*., p. 182.
29. *Ibid*., p. 193.
30. *Ibid*., p. 194.
31. *Ibid*., p. 193.
32. Letters, p. 66.
33. *Ibid*., p. 65.
34. WWW, p. 196.
35. Much later, in 1982, the American critic Susan Sontag told Spender that she had met Muriel: 'It struck me that she was extremely boring, and made me wonder why it is that people who do good are so boring.' (Journals, pp. 404–5).
36. WWW, p. 195.
37. *Ibid*., p. 197.
38. *Ibid*.
39. Letters, p. 65.
40. SS to Geoffrey Grigson, 6 July [1934]. *Berg Collection*.
41. Letters, p. 72.
42. *Ibid*., pp. 67–8.
43. Letters, p. 74.
44. Letters, pp. 75–6.

Spender's story 'Strange Death' actually appeared in the *London Mercury* in August 1935.

45. BC, p. 265.
46. Letters, p. 43.
47. BC, p. 54.
48. *Ibid.*, p. 47.
49. *Independent Magazine*, 3 November 1990.
50. See 'Solipsist', CP, p. 60.
51. Both poems first appeared in the *London Mercury* in May 1935. They are reprinted in CP; p. 62 and p. 46 respectively.
52. W.H. Auden, 'September 1 1939', *Selected Poems*, p. 88.
    Auden later repudiated this phrase as 'trash which I am ashamed to have written' and changed the line to 'We must love one another *and* die' (my italics).
53. 'Spain', *ibid.*, p. 54.
54. *The Destructive Element*, Jonathan Cape, 1935, pp. 190–1.
55. WWW, p. 198.
56. *Ibid.*, p. 192.
57. T.C. Worsley, *Fellow Travellers*, p. 118.
58. The *Spectator*, 9 November 1934; *The Times Literary Supplement*, 13 December 1934; the *Nation*, 13 March 1935.
59. Letter to SS, 25 June 1935. *The Sickle Side of the Moon*, p. 408.
60. *The Diary of Virginia Woolf*, Vol. 4, p. 288.
61. WWW p. 191.
62. *The Auden Generation*, p. 147.
63. *Fellow Travellers*, p. 9.
    As an indication of the book's authenticity, it is perhaps worth noting that the London Library shelves it among histories of the Spanish Civil War and not in their fiction stacks.
64. WWW, p. 201.
65. Letters, p. 121.
66. *Ibid.*, p. 122.
67. *Ibid.*, p. 81.
68. *Ibid.*, p. 77.
69. WWW, p. 204.
70. Louis MacNeice, *The Strings Are False*, p. 166.
71. *Fellow Travellers*, p. 23.
72. WWW, p. 211.
73. Letters, pp. 108–9 *passim*; SS, letter to W.H. Auden, 6 April 1936, *ibid.*, p. 111.
74. *Ibid.*, p. 123.
75. *Fellow Travellers*. p. 145.
76. *The Daily Worker*, 19 February 1937.
77. Thirties, p. 27.

78. SS, on *Start the Week*, BBC Radio 4, 24 February 1992.
79. WWW, p. 204.
80. *Fellow Travellers*, p. 139.
81. WWW, p. 204.
82. *Fellow Travellers*, p. 143.
83. Letters, pp. 125 *ff*.
84. *Fellow Travellers*, p. 135.
85. Letters, p. 125.
86. WWW, p. 207.
87. *The Diaries of Virginia Woolf*, Volume 5 – 1936–41, pp. 56–7. (Entry for 18 February 1937.)
88. John Lehmann, *In the Purely Pagan Sense*, pp. 131–2.

SEVEN: On the Front Line

1. *Labour Monthly* March 1937; *Left Review*, March 1937.
2. Letters, p. 128.
3. *New Statesman and Nation*, 16 January 1937.
4. Letters, p. 130.
5. *Ibid.*, p. 129.
6. *Ibid.*
   It is unlikely, however, that he kept either engagement. He was writing an article for the *Left Review* in Tangier on 18 January (Thirties, p. 63).
7. WWW, p. 214.
8. 'Tangiers [sic] and Gibraltar *Now*', *Left Review*, February 1937.
9. WWW, pp. 216–7.
10. *Ibid.*, p. 215 *ff*.
11. Letters, p. 129.
12. CP, p. 66; WWW, pp. 218–9.
13. WWW, pp. 213–4.
14. *Fellow Travellers*, pp. 192–6 *passim*.
15. WWW, p. 219.
16. *Fellow Travellers*, p. 212.
17. WWW, p. 221.
18. *Fellow Travellers*, p. 215.
19. *Ibid.*, p. 216.
20. *Ibid.*, p. 217.
21. *Ibid.*, pp. 219–20.
22. WWW, p. 222.
23. *Ibid.*, pp. 222–3.
24. *Fellow Travellers*, p. 213; WWW, p. 223.
25. CP; p. 71, p. 70, p. 69 respectively.
26. *Ibid.*, p. 74; p. 68.

27. *Fellow Travellers*, p. 195; WWW, p. 227.

28. *Fellow Travellers*, p. 223.

29. *Ibid.*, p. 226.

30. WWW, p. 232.

31. *Ibid.*, p. 230.

32. *Fellow Travellers*, pp. 223–4.

33. WWW, p. 238.

34. *Ibid.*, p. 243; *New Writing* 4, Autumn 1937, qtd in Thirties, p. 71.

35. WWW, p. 239.

36. Thirties, p. 73.

37. 'Spain, just *Spain*; that's all we said at the time. Everyone knew what you meant.' Hugh Corbett-Palmer, in a conversation with the author, June 1990.

38. There has been some dispute over Nancy Cunard's authorship of THE QUESTION. However, its style and her answers to questions posed by Professor Hugh Ford in 1961 seem to settle the matter: 'It was indeed, SOLELY my idea. There was no discussion with any of the signatories as to whether or no it would be a good thing to do ...' (Qtd in Anne Chisholm in *Nancy Cunard*, Sidgwick & Jackson, 1979, p. 317.)

39. Chisholm, *op. cit.*, pp. 319–20.

40. A letter to William Coldstream dated 19 August [1937] is headed Church Farm/Mersham/Near Ashford/Kent. *Tate Gallery Archive*. This is presumably the house Spender refers to in WWW (p. 247) as being near the Kent coast – although even Hythe, the nearest seaside town, is some ten miles away from Mersham.

41. WWW, p. 258.

42. *Ibid.*, p. 259.

43. SS to William Coldstream, 19 August [1937]. *Tate Gallery Archive*.

44. *Ibid.*, Coldstream drafted his reply on the reverse of Spender's letter.

45. SS to William Coldstream, 26 August 1937. *Tate Gallery Archive*.

46. Letters, p. 130.

47. WWW, p. 248.

48. SS to William Coldstream, 26 August 1937. (*Tate Gallery Archive*)

49. WWW, p. 248.

50. SS to William Coldstream, 26 August 1937. (*Tate Gallery Archive*)

51. In each case the dates relate to publication of the text and then the year of first performance. It is clear from the fact that both *The Dog Beneath the Skin* (known to all involved as 'Dogskin') and *F6* were both published *before* being staged that Auden and Isherwood regarded them as literary rather than theatrical works.

52. Qtd in George Orwell, *Collected Essays, Journalism and Letters*, Secker & Warburg, 1968, vol I, p. 311.

53. John Lehmann, *New Writing in Europe*, Penguin, 1940, pp. 72–3.

54. *Ibid*, p. 74.

55. WWW, p. 249.
    When and why Spender was appointed a director remains unclear. Along with Auden, Eliot, Grigson, John Masefield, Harold Nicolson, Hugh Walpole, Antonia White and twenty others – he is listed as one of the company's writers in the programme for *The Dog Beneath the Skin* (which opened on 12 January 1936). He was not, however, then a member of its nine-strong board of 'Producers and Directors', an august body which included Harley Granville Barker, Nevill Coghill and Tyrone Guthrie.

56. 'The Poetic Dramas of W.H. Auden and Christopher Isherwood', *New Writing*, Autumn 1938; Thirties, p. 54.

57. *The Diary of Virginia Woolf*, vol. 5, p. 131. (Entry for 22 March 1938.)

58. WWW, pp. 253–4.

59. *Ibid.*, p. 255.

60. *Daily Worker*, 10 May 1939.

61. WWW, pp. 257–60.

62. Diary of William Coldstream, 17 January 1939. *Tate Gallery Archive*. Hedli Anderson probably sang 'Our Hunting Fathers', Britten's setting of some of Auden's lyrics (Op.8.; 1936). No Britten setting of a poem by Spender is, however, mentioned in the current lists of the composer's work.

63. Letters, p. 131–3.

64. New Writing, December 1939.

65. WWW, p. 260.

PART THREE: Being There

EIGHT: War – and Peace of a Sort

1. *The Diary of Virginia Woolf*, Vol. 5 1936–41, p. 234.

2. Dylan Thomas to John Davenport, 14 September 1939. *Dylan Thomas: The Collected Letters*, p. 410.

3. 'September Journal,' 3 September 1939, qtd in Letters, p. 161.

4. *Ibid.*, pp. 163–73 passim.

5. Letters, p. 132 (3 August 1939).

6. *Ibid.*, p. 133.

7. *Among You Taking Notes . . .: The Wartime Diary of Naomi Mitchison*, edited by Dorothy Sheridan, Victor Gollancz, 1985, pp. 35–6.

8. Journals, pp. 34–5.

9. *Ibid*, p. 45.

10. *The Diary of Virginia Woolf*, vol. 5, p. 236.

11. *Ibid.*, p. 238 (24 September 1939).

12. Cyril Connolly, *The Unquiet Grave*, Hamish Hamilton (second, revised ed.), 1951, p. 29.

13. *Horizon*, January 1940, p. 5.

14. Connolly, qtd, in Michael Shelden, *Friends of Promise*, p. 31.

15. WWW, pp. 295–6; Journals, p. 41.

16. *The Diary of Virginia Woolf*, vol. 5, p. 247.

17. Letter from Peter Watson to Cecil Beaton, 12 December 1939.

18. These visits were ultimately successful: 'A Bit of a Smash', one of Maclaren-Ross's best short stories appeared in the June 1940 issue of *Horizon*. By an irony of fate and the inattention of a proof-reader, however, the story is there credited to one 'J. Maclaryn-Ross'.

19. Julian Maclaren-Ross, *Memoirs of the Forties*, p. 78. (Spender seemingly refers to this episode in WWW, p. 295.)

20. *Ibid.*, p. 61; pp. 62–3.

21. WWW, p. 295.

22. Maclaren-Ross, *op, cit.*, p. 59.
When 'A Bit of a Smash' appeared in the magazine its first sentence read: 'Absolute fact, I knew damn all about it . . .'

23. 'The Air Raid Across the Bay', *Horizon*, September 1940; reprinted as 'Air Raid Across the Bay at Plymouth', CP, p. 121.

24. *Horizon*, December 1940.

25. *Horizon*, January 1941.

26. Letter to John Davenport, 8 January 1941. *Dylan Thomas: The Collected Letters*, p. 471.

27. Journals, p. 57.

28. Qtd in Shelden, *op. cit.*, p. 66. I have been unable to discover the full text of this letter.

29. *New Statesman*, 16 November 1940.

30. *Horizon*, February 1941.

31. Jill Craigie, interviewed in *Blitz*, Thames Television, 3 September 1990.

32. The dates are uncertain. In the *Journals*, Spender implies that this was in early 1941 (p. 57); in *World Within World* he specifically states that it was during the autumn of 1942 (p. 266). I have plumped for the former – as, quite recently, did Michael Shelden in *Friends of Promise*, his study of Cyril Connolly and *Horizon* magazine (p. 5).

33. WWW, p. 280.

34. *Ibid.*, p. 269.

35. Henry Green, 'The Lull', *New Writing and Daylight*, Summer 1943; reprinted in *Surviving: The Uncollected Writings of Henry Green*, edited by Matthew Yorke, Chatto & Windus, 1992, p. 104.

36. WWW, pp. 269–70.

37. *Ibid.*, p. 279.

38. Leonard Rosoman, O.B.E., interviewed in *Blitz*, Thames Television, 3 September 1990.
39. Journals, p. 58.
40. WWW, pp. 318–22.
41. CP. p. 124; p. 128 respectively.
42. WWW, pp. 306–7.
43. *Ibid.*, p. 281.
44. CP, p. 131; p. 132 respectively.
45. WWW, p. 308.
46. *Ibid.*, p. 309.
47. Journals, p. 58.
48. Barbara Skelton, *Tears Before Bedtime*, Hamish Hamilton, 1987, p. 40.
49. CP. p. 113 *ff.*
50. Journals, pp. 62–5 *passim.*
    Curtius, however, was not pleased by Spender's account of their meeting (*ibid*, pp. 59–60).
51. Thirties, pp. 133–5.
52. Journals, p. 59.
53. Thirties, p. 100; Journals, p. 73.
54. Journals, p. 89.
55. *Ibid.*, p. 60.
56. Malcolm Muggeridge, *The Infernal Grove*, William Collins, 1973, pp. 283–4.
57. Inevitably perhaps, the myth of Orpheus, the poet who travels to the underworld to rescue Euridice, was on Spender's mind at around this time: see 'Elegy for Margaret', VI, stanza 4 (CP, p. 96).
58. T.S. Eliot, *The Waste Land*, 1.430.

NINE: Epilogue to a Human Drama

1. Qtd in Anthony Powell, *To Keep the Ball Rolling*, Penguin, 1983, p. 325.
2. CP, p. 146.
   We have already seen that Michael is a distant presence in *World Within World*. In the *Journals*, Spender merely reports his death in his Commentary to the years 1940–45 (p. 57).
3. CP, p. 89; p. 94; p .95 respectively.
4. *Ibid.*, CP, p. 136; p. 141 respectively.
5. See specifically 'To My Daughter' and 'Nocturne', CP, pp. 137, 138.
6. Journals, p. 118 (entry for 15 February 1953).
7. John Lehmann, *The Ample Proposition*, p. 119.
8. CP, p. 133.
9. The now forgotten *To the Island*, which was eventually produced as a

Festival of Britain event at the Oxford Playhouse in 1951. There are no references to the production in the *Journals*.

10. Lehmann, *op. cit.*
11. Dylan Thomas, letter to John Davenport, 14 September 1939.
12. 'On the Circuit', *W.H. Auden: Selected Poems*, p. 248.
13. Journals, p. 94; SS, 'On the Road with Lenny', *Times Saturday Review*, 3 November 1990.
14. Qtd in 'On the Road with Lenny'. I have been unable to trace the original *New Yorker* article.
15. W.H. Auden, letter to Mrs A.E. Dodds, 11 July 1939.
16. Auden, 'On the Circuit'.
17. In *Engaged in Writing* the scientist Dunston Curlew expresses exactly this view (p. 127).
18. Thirties, pp. 157–9.
19. Spender's continuing involvement with P.E.N. would later take him to conferences in India (1957), Japan (1958) and Korea (1977).
   He was appointed President of the organisation's English branch in 1975.
20. Humphrey Carpenter, *W.H. Auden*, p. 366.
21. *London Magazine*, June/July 1976; Thirties, p. 167 *ff*.
22. Journals, p. 500.
23. Maclean receives seven mentions in the *Journals*, but Spender and Natasha were closer to Maclean's fellow-defector Guy Burgess (who is also mentioned seven times). He had after all been a guest at their wedding reception.
   Indeed, although they knew nothing about his espionage activities, the Spenders unwittingly played a part in Burgess's defection; for, alerted that the authorities were closing in on Maclean, Burgess panicked. He had been instructed to escort Maclean to the continent and – although there was not at that time (May 1951) any conclusive evidence against him – he feared for his own safety. He decided that, while Maclean made his own way to Moscow, he should also stay abroad until the heat died down.
   He hoped to stay in Auden's villa at Ischia and phoned the Spenders' house in Loudoun Road, where Auden was then staying, to try to arrange this. Unfortunately, Auden was out. He left messages first with Natasha, then with Spender; but neither reached Auden in time (Journals, pp. 95–6; Carpenter, *W.H. Auden*, pp 368–70) and Burgess was left with no alternative but to accompany Maclean to Moscow. A sideshow in the ensuing furore was the controversy about how much Spender knew about Burgess's espionage work. The *Daily Express* illicitly reproduced a letter he had received from John Lehmann saying that he must have known all about it. It was embarrassing for Spender,

and provoked another row with Lehmann. Several years later the newspaper's editor made a full apology (Journals, p. 173).

24. *Horizon*, December 1949.
25. *Encounter*, October 1953.
26. Lehmann, *The Ample Proposition*, p. 245.
27. *Ibid.*, p. 254.
28. 'My Dog, Tulip', *Encounter*, March 1954.
29. *Encounter*, September 1955.
30. Journals, pp. 133–44.
31. Auden, 'On the Circuit'.
32. Lehmann, *op, cit.*, p. 118.
33. Writing, p. 42.
34. *Ibid.*, pp. 48–9; Thirties, pp. 177–8.
35. See, for instance the accounts of a boat trip to Torcello (Thirties, pp. 181–2; Writing p. 115 *ff*) and a visit to the cinema (Thirties, p. 180; Writing, pp. 130–1).
36. Writing, pp. 68–9; Thirties, p. 179.
37. Writing, p. 85.
38. *Ibid.*, p. 20.
39. *Ibid.*, p. 34.
40. *Ibid.*, p. 121.
41. *Macbeth* III.i.1.
42. Journals, p. 340.
43. *Ibid.*, pp. 342–3.
44. Charles Osborne, W.H. Auden p. 310.
45. Journals, p. 221.
46. 'Grandparents', *London Magazine* April/May 1992. p. 33.
47. 'The Palatine Anthology', *ibid.*, p. 34.
48. Information privately supplied to the author, April 1992.

BIBLIOGRAPHY

This is little more than a check-list of those volumes to which I have had most frequent recourse. Publication details relate to first editions, except where these have been supplanted by more recent, generally available impressions. The place of publication is London unless otherwise stated.

Just as this book makes no claim to be a full critical biography, the following list of the works of Stephen Spender is selective —although perhaps exhaustive enough for the general reader. The serious student will in any case be aware of H.B. Kulkarni's meticulous *Stephen Spender: Works and Criticism, an Annotated Bibliography* (Garland Publishing, New York, 1976) and A.T. Tolley's *The Early Published Poems of Stephen Spender: A Chronology* (Carleton University, Ottawa, 1967). No less thorough, the unnecessarily self-deprecating 'Working Bibliography' appended to Valentine Cunningham's *British Writers of the Thirties* catalogues virtually all the available material on that period.

1. Books by Stephen Spender

The Backward Son, The Hogarth Press, 1940.
The Burning Cactus, Faber & Faber, 1941.
Collected Poems, 1928–1985, Faber & Faber, 1985.
Engaged in Writing and *The Fool and the Princess*, Hamish Hamilton, 1958.
European Witness, Hamish Hamilton, 1946.
Forward from Liberalism, Left Book Club; Victor Gollancz, 1937.
Journals 1939–1983, Faber & Faber, 1985.
Letters to Christopher: Stephen Spender's Letters to Christopher Isherwood, 1929–1939, (edited by Lee Bartlett), Black Sparrow Press, Santa Barbara, 1980.
Selected Poems Faber & Faber, 1965.
The Temple Faber & Faber, 1988.
The Thirties and After: Poetry, Politics, People (1933–1975), Fontana, 1978.
Twenty-five Poems, Eurographia, Helsinki, 1988.
World Within World, Faber & Faber, 1951; 1977.

2. Other Books Consulted

Auden, W.H., *Collected Longer Poems*, Faber & Faber, 1968.
  Collected Shorter Poems, 1927–1957, Faber & Faber, 1966.
  Selected Poems (edited by Edward Mendelson), Faber & Faber, 1979.
Carpenter, Humphrey, *The Brideshead Generation*, Weidenfeld & Nicolson, 1989.
  W.H. Auden: A Biography, George Allen & Unwin, 1981.
Connolly, Cyril, *Enemies of Promise*, 1938; rev. ed., Routledge & Kegan Paul, 1949.
Cunningham, Valentine, *British Writers of the Thirties*, Oxford University Press, 1988.
David, Hugh, *The Fitzrovians*, Michael Joseph, 1988.
Day-Lewis, Cecil, *The Buried Day*, Chatto & Windus, 1960.
Day-Lewis, Sean, *C. Day-Lewis: An English Literary Life*, Weidenfeld & Nicolson, 1980.
Driberg, Tom, *Ruling Passions*, Jonathan Cape, 1977.
Ferris, Paul, *Dylan Thomas*, Hodder & Stoughton, 1977.
Ferris, Paul (ed), *Dylan Thomas: The Collected Letters*, J.M. Dent, 1985.
Gowing, Laurence and Sylvester, David (eds), *The Paintings of William Coldstream, 1908–1987*, Tate Gallery Publications, 1990.
Harris, H. Wilson, *J.A. Spender*, Cassell and Company, 1946.
Hewison, Robert, *Under Siege: Literary Life in London, 1939–45*, Weidenfeld & Nicolson, 1977.
Holroyd, Michael, *Lytton Strachey: A Biography*, Penguin, 1971.
Hynes, Samuel, *The Auden Generation*, Faber & Faber, 1976.
Isherwood, Christopher, *Christopher and His Kind*, Eyre Methuen, 1977.
  Goodbye to Berlin, Chatto & Windus, 1939; Penguin, 1945.
  Lions and Shadows, Hogarth Press, 1938; New English Library/Signet, 1968.
  Mr Norris Changes Trains, Chatto & Windus, 1935; Penguin, 1942.
Lehmann, John, *The Ample Proposition*, Eyre & Spottiswoode, 1966.
  Christopher Isherwood: A Personal Memoir, Weidenfeld & Nicolson, 1987.
  I Am My Brother, Longman, 1960.
  In the Purely Pagan Sense, Blond & Briggs, 1976; GMP, 1985.
  New Writing in Europe, Penguin, 1940.
  Thrown to the Woolfs, Weidenfeld & Nicolson, 1978.
List, Herbert, *Herbert List: Junge Männer* (introduction by Stephen Spender), Thames and Hudson, 1988.
Maclaren-Ross, Julian, *Memoirs of the Forties*, Alan Ross Ltd, 1965; Penguin, 1984.
MacNeice, Louis, *The Strings Are False: An Unfinished Autobiography*, (ed. E.R. Dodds), Faber & Faber 1965.

Osborne, Charles, *W.H. Auden: The Life of a Poet*, Eyre Methuen, 1980.

Peukert, Detlev J.K., *Inside Nazi Germany*, Batsford, 1987; Penguin, 1989.

Prochaska, Alice (ed), *Young Writers of the Thirties*, National Portrait Gallery, 1976.

Schuster, Sir George, *Private Work and Public Causes*, D. Brown and Sons, Cowbridge, 1979.

Shelden, Michael, *Friends of Promise: Cyril Connolly and the World of Horizon*, Hamish Hamilton, 1989.

Stanford, Derek, *Inside the Forties*, Sidgwick & Jackson, 1977.

Spender, Harold, *The Fire of Life*, Hodder & Stoughton, 1926.

Spender, J.A., *Life, Journalism and Politics*, Cassell and Company, (two vols), 1927.

Spender, Stephen (ed), *W.H. Auden: A Tribute*, Weidenfeld & Nicolson, 1975.

Usher, H.J.K., Black-Hawkins, C.D. and Carrick, G.J., *An Angel Without Wings: The History of University College School, 1830–1980*, University College School, 1981.

Woolf, Virginia, *The Diary of Virginia Woolf*, Volume 4: 1931–35 (edited by Anne Olivier Bell), The Hogarth Press, 1982.

The Diary of Virginia Woolf, Volume 5: 1936–41 (edited by Anne Olivier Bell), The Hogarth Press, 1984.

The Sickle Side of the Moon, The Letters of Virginia Woolf, Volume V: 1932–1935 (edited by Nigel Nicolson), The Hogarth Press, 1979.

Worsley, T.C., *Fellow Travellers: A Memoir of the Thirties*, London Magazine Editions, 1971.

INDEX